The
Berimbau

The
Berimbau

Soul of Brazilian Music

Eric A. Galm

University Press of Mississippi
Jackson

www.upress.state.ms.us

The University Press of Mississippi is a member of the Association of
American University Presses.

Musical transcriptions by Eric A. Galm unless otherwise noted
Artwork courtesy of Raquel Coelho, originally part of her book *Berimbau*
published in Brazil by Atica Editora in 1992

First printing 2010
∞
Library of Congress Cataloging-in-Publication Data

Galm, Eric A.
  The berimbau : soul of Brazilian music / Eric A. Galm.
    p. cm.
  Includes bibliographical references and index.
  ISBN 978-1-60473-405-8 (cloth : alk. paper) 1. Berimbau—History. 2.
Music—Brazil—History and criticism. 3. Music—Brazil—African influ-
ences. I. Title.
  ML1015.B4G35 2010
  787.9'2—dc22   2009031475

British Library Cataloging-in-Publication Data available

Contents

Acknowledgments

I dedicate this work to my grandfather, Kenneth J. Galm, and my father, John K. Galm. My father brought my family to Brazil in 1972, and again in 1977, and this planted the seeds for my continued interest in Brazilian music and culture. My grandfather's support of my studies in Brazil in the late 1980s and early 1990s enabled me to explore and build upon my knowledge of Brazilian percussion music and culture so that I could eventually return as a Fulbright scholar. I sincerely thank both of them for encouraging my personal and professional career.

Through the process of researching, writing, and revising this work I have depended upon the generous assistance of many individuals and organizations. It is clear that this project would not have been possible without the motivation and support I have received along the way. My research received financial assistance from the United States Fulbright Program and the Comissão Fulbright in Brazil, as well as a Dissertation Write-Up Award from Wesleyan University upon my return from Brazil.

I would like to express my sincere thanks to Eric Charry, Mark Slobin, Samuel Araújo, and Claudia Tatinge Nascimento, all of whom have provided clear insight and vision in helping shape this work. I would like to give a big thanks to Su Zheng for her continued support over the years. It is with great regret that I must thank Lise Waxer posthumously for her personal, academic, and professional support. She eagerly solicited drafts, and helped me produce material during the early stages in the writing process. Also thanks to K. David Jackson, Lynn Frederiksen, Sarah Malinoski, Bryan McCann, Nick Zebb, Evanira Mendes Birdman, and John Galm for reading drafts and offering valuable suggestions that helped me clarify my overall narrative. I also owe a debt of gratitude to many of my colleagues at Trinity College in Hartford, Connecticut, including Douglas Johnson, Gail Hilson Woldu, John Platoff, Gerald Moshell, Milla Riggio, Anne Lambright, Leslie Desmangles, Luis Figueroa, Tom Harrington, and many others. Pablo Delano has taken countless outstanding photographs of my work at Trinity, and has donated photographs for use in this volume, for which I am grateful. David Tatem was generous with his time and expertise, helping to create the map of Brazil. My colleagues and friends have gone through several drafts and have offered insightful comments, suggestions, and direction, throughout this entire process. I thank all of them for helping provide a supportive and creative environment!

In Brazil, I thank the Comissão Fulbright Brasil staff: Marco Antônio da Rocha, Anderson Lima, Jeferson Gonçalves in Brasília, and Nilza Waldeck, Rita Moriconi, Marisa Leal, and Charles Souza in Rio de Janeiro. Thanks to all of the U.S. Fulbright scholars who provided a week of exciting academic interdisciplinary exchange in Brasília, and especially Rhonda Collier for her help in São Paulo and Brendan Flannery for his help in Salvador. Extra special thanks to Rita and Luca Moriconi and their daughter, Maria Rita, as well as Rosa and Pedro Zanker and their family for helping my family feel at home in Rio.

Thanks to Samuel Araújo, who sponsored my Fulbright research and assisted with my appointment as visiting scholar at the University Federal do Rio de Janeiro. And thanks to his wife, Ligia Bahia, who helped my family locate excellent medical resources. Also at UFRJ I thank graduate studies director Fátima Tacuchian, professor Leonardo Fuks, graduate students Vincenzo Cambria, Francisca Marques, and all of the ethnomusicology students for their lively exchanges, Portuguese translation assistance, and feedback about my research. I also thank Elizabeth Travassos, professor at UniRio, for her support, Marisa Colnago Coelho of the Instituto do Patrimônio Historico E Artistico Nacional, and the entire staff at the Biblioteca Amadeu Amaral, especially Luciana de Noronha Versiani, who allowed me to work at her computer for weeks on end. Thanks to Marcelo Rodolfo, Antônio Adolfo, Livio Sansone, Carlos Sandroni, José Jorge de Carvalho, Raimundo Batista, Isaura de Asis, Kelly Sabini, Phil Malinoski, Mark Overmyer-Velazquez, Zinho Brown, David Locke, Guthrie P. Ramsey, Jr., Mark DeVoto, Alfred Frederick, Emily Ferrigno, Kai Fikentscher, and many others, including John Wyre, who encouraged me to listen closely to the berimbau, and it would tell me what I would need to know.

I send another big thank you to all of my colleagues in Brazil, including Luiz D'Anunciação, Carlos Negreiros, Tim Rescala, Nelson Macêdo, Ramiro Musotto, Marcos Suzano, Tandi Gebara, Dinho Nascimento, Manoel Vanni, Franco Júnior, Mestre Negoativo, Adriano George, John Boudler, Carlos Stasi, Eduardo Gianasera, Frederico Abreu, Cícero Antônio, Ivanzinho, Ricardo Souza, and Angela Lühning. I also thank the many capoeira practitioners who shared their insights with me, including Mestres João Grande, Deraldo Ferreira, Efraim Silva, Nenel, and countless others who have engaged in energetic conversations about the berimbau's connection to capoeira. Thanks also to percussionist Di Lutgardes for helping locate some key information about art music in Rio de Janeiro.

I am especially grateful to Luiz D'Anunciação for his mentorship of Brazilian percussion performance techniques, and his patience and continued encouragement over the years, which has led to my understanding of many aspects of Brazilian music and culture. Also thanks to his family for inviting me into their home for an extended stay during my research trip in 1990–91.

Primary fieldwork for this project was conducted at multi-sited research points in Brazil between August 2000 and July 2001, supported by a Fulbright fellowship. Initial study and research took place in Brazil during 1989 (five weeks) and 1990–91 (six months). In 2000–2001 I conducted formal interviews with Brazilian musicians and composers in Rio de Janeiro, Salvador, and São Paulo.

Library and archival research was conducted principally in Rio de Janeiro at the Biblioteca Amadeu Amaral at the Museu do Folclore, and the Biblioteca Nacional, the Museu da Imágem e do Som (as well as in São Paulo), the UFRJ music library, and the library at the Centro dos Estudos Afro-Asiáticos at the Universidade do Cândido Mendes. I also obtained valuable information from the archives of the Fundação Pierre Verger and the Instituto Mauá, both in Salvador, and a broad range of important materials were loaned to me from private collections. Additional research was conducted through full-text archival resources on the Brazilian newspaper websites of *A Tarde* (Salvador), *O Globo* (Rio de Janeiro), *Jornal do Brasil* (Rio de Janeiro), *Fôlha de São Paulo* (São Paulo), and *O Estado de São Paulo* (São Paulo).

Finally, this project would not have come to fruition without the support of my immediate family. Extra special thanks to my wife Amy, my

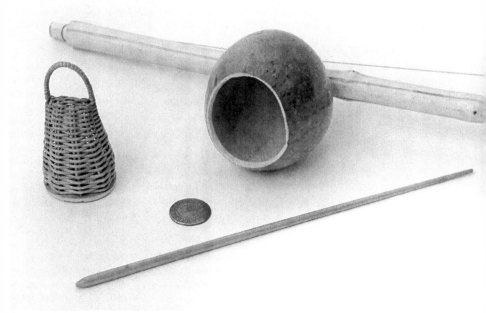

Figure x.1: The berimbau (Photo by Pablo Delano 2008). Courtesy of Pablo Delano.

children Kenneth, Isabella, and Simone, as well as the entire Galm and Yarbrough families, all of whom have made personal sacrifices to accommodate the research and writing process of this work. Thank you all for your motivation and support!

A Note Regarding Musical Transcriptions

The *berimbau* (musical bow) presents a complex combination of sounds comprised of pitched sounds and timbres (non-pitched sounds).[1] The graphic representation of these musical sounds has posed a challenge to musicians and scholars for decades. In the 1950s, ethnomusicologist Charles Seeger[2] distinguished between "prescriptive" and "descriptive" musical notation schemes. In this sense, a musical transcription could function either as a prescription for accurately reproducing all of the sounds, or as a description of the overall effect. While many notation options exist for the berimbau, Luiz D'Anunciação introduced one of the most comprehensive berimbau notation systems for performers and composers.[3] This is the first scheme that rhythmically notates the gourd movement against and away from the body, and it is unique in its approach to incorporating timbre into its structure, instead of creating new symbols for each sound. Although D'Anunciação's notation provides a means to comprehensively and systematically depict all of the sounds produced by the berimbau, it requires the ability to simultaneously read three separate staff systems. Since my goal for the musical notation in this study is to provide a brief snapshot for easy comprehension, I have modified D'Anunciação's notational scheme in order to capture fundamental aspects of the berimbau's music, similar in concept to a piano reduction of a complete orchestral score. My modification omits the separate functions of the left and right hands, and provides a basic schematic outline of the berimbau music.

In this study, the berimbau notation is depicted on a one-line staff. The note below the line represents the freely vibrating string, or unaltered fundamental pitch of the berimbau. The note above the line represents a distinct altered fundamental pitch produced by pressing the coin firmly against the string. The note that appears on the line represents an indeterminate buzz sound. In special cases, I include a second line that depicts overtly exaggerated sounds produced by the gourd movement against and away from the body (see T x.1).[4]

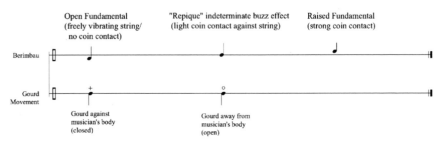

Transcription x.1: Key to musical notation

I have made special accommodations for new techniques, such as in the case of Dinho Nascimento's music, where I depict the berimbau on a conventional five-line staff, with a separate one-line staff for the *caxixi* (small basket rattle). I have maintained a separate single-line caxixi staff for Ramiro Musotto's solo of "La Danza del Tezcatlipoca Rojo." In this case, the caxixi has been moved to the electronic sequencer and functions as a modified audible click track.

When timing marks appear in transcriptions (e.g. 1:45), they correspond with the specific location in the original sound recording.

The
Berimbau

Introduction

A young woman was on her way to her first trip to Brazil. She had developed a fascination for Brazilian music and culture in her hometown in the United States, and wanted to learn more. It started when she was in a city park, and saw two dancers engaged in a conversation of free-flowing movement. She later learned that this was called *capoeira*, and it was set to the sounds of singing, hand clapping, and musical instruments, including something that looked like a bow, called a *berimbau*. Perhaps many years ago, this may have been associated with a hunter's bow, although this one had a metal string, a coin, stick, rattle, and calabash gourd that produced a myriad of sounds and timbres. The circular movements and their supporting sounds created a gravitational pull that caught the attention of everyone in the vicinity. As this ritual progressed, the level of engagement increased for all involved, with onlookers wondering how the drama would finally play out. Suddenly, the berimbau started playing a different rhythm, and without breaking stride, the dancers abruptly changed to a non-confrontational samba dance exposition. Within moments, two police officers arrived at the dancing space, asking to see their performance permit. Possessing none, the performers abruptly dispersed, leaving the curious onlookers disappointed.

What was it that drew her to this myriad of musical sounds and windmill of movement? It was certainly more exciting and interactive than the usual aerobics or spinning classes. She soon began attending regular capoeira classes at a neighborhood academy, where she trained in the fundamentals of capoeira movement, but she also learned how to sing songs in Portuguese and play some basic melodic-rhythmic patterns on the berimbau. As she became transfixed with Brazilian culture, she only listened to the music of Brazilians like Caetano Veloso, Milton

3

Nascimento, and Gilberto Gil, experimented with various Brazilian culinary dishes, and learned as much as she could about all things Brazilian. She was already familiar with Brazil's most prominent calling cards like soccer and the famous carnival celebrations, but this trip was driven by her desire to learn more specifically how capoeira related to Brazilian society. She was not prepared for the multiple layers that she found permeating the social spectrum.

Her first stop was in Salvador da Bahia, largely credited as the birthplace of Brazilian capoeira. As she walked through the historic Pelourinho neighborhood, images of berimbaus adorned signs above storefronts, and when she arrived at the city's central marketplace, she saw thousands of berimbaus being sold as souvenirs to tourists, as well as their images on t-shirts, necklace pendants, and a plethora of other merchandise as symbolic representations of Brazil's largest community of African descent. She also encountered several games of capoeira that featured two opponents sparring in a flurry of near-contact spins and kicks, accompanied by the sounds of singing, dancing, hand clapping, and the berimbau. After making her way through the city, she stops at a telephone booth to make a call, and notices that the booth is also made in the shape of a berimbau. Returning to Pelourinho for an evening concert, she encounters a concert that features 1960s bossa nova music combined with contemporary samba/reggae/pop fusions. All of these musical styles are peppered with references to the berimbau and capoeira, including new musical genres that have fused the sounds of North American Motown with the circles of capoeira.

Her second stop in Brazil is Rio de Janeiro, where she heads to the Biblioteca Nacional (National Library), and discovers a children's book that relates the story of a young mischievous boy who encounters a mystical Afro-Brazilian man in the forest holding a berimbau. The boy is entranced by the mysterious music that floated from the berimbau, symbolizing a history entwined with Africa. Leaving the library, our protagonist crosses the street and enters the Theatro Municipal for a matinee performance of the symphonic choral epic *Ganguzama*, a work about the creation of Brazilian society. In the middle of this performance, an old *quilombola* (man of African descent, from *quilombo*—Can encampment for people who had escaped from slavery) conveys the final moments in the life of Zumbi, the notorious quilombo leader. The spaces between the phrases within this man's story are filled with the sounds of a berimbau. At the nearby corner newsstand, she reads an article in the *Jornal do Brasil* about a corruption scandal that has led a Bahian senator to resign. Above this article is an editorial cartoon showing the senator thrown in the trash outside of the Brazilian congress building, along with his berimbau. As she glances at other publications, she discovers a copy of the children's animated series, *Luana*, about a young Afro-Brazilian girl who can be transported through time and correct historical inaccuracies with the power of her magic berimbau.

Her final stop in Brazil is the nation's capital, Brasília, where she encounters a large sculpture of a berimbau prominently displayed as a marker of national Brazilian identity. When she returns to her hotel, she notices that the twenty-foot wooden sculpture in the lobby is a modernist portrayal of a berimbau musician whose body encompasses the twists and turns of the capoeira dance.[1]

Although these examples demonstrate how the berimbau's deeply imbedded historical strands have helped define a national experience within the fabric of Brazilian society, this has not always been the case. In a 1936 article about the berimbau, writer and folklorist Edison Carneiro provided a description and photo of the instrument, since he believed this musical bow was virtually unknown beyond the northeastern city of Salvador, Bahia. In the ensuing four decades, the berimbau became so pervasive in Brazilian society, that Carneiro exclaimed, "who, in this country, at this point of the century, has still not seen a berimbau?"[2] Such an impressive shift in status raises questions concerning how this musical instrument moved from near extinction in the 1930s to omnipresence in the 1970s. Perhaps one of the most poignant examples of the berimbau's breadth within Brazilian culture can be observed through the comments of Antônio Natalino Manta Dantas, at the time coordinator of medicine at the Universidade Federal da Bahia, in response to low student test scores. In April 2008 he "justified" an assumption of low intellectual aptitude by declaring: "the Bahian plays the berimbau because it only has one string. If it had any more, he couldn't play it."[3] Of course, many individuals, institutions, and politicians publicly repudiated this derogatory comment, resulting in his resignation.

This book is the first in-depth study to view Brazilian music and culture through the lens of the berimbau, and that is its principal

Figure 0.1: Capoeira (Photo by Pablo Delano 2008). Courtesy of Pablo Delano.

contribution to the field. I demonstrate how this critical icon traverses a broad range of social, class, and racial boundaries in both national and global contexts. Although some aspects of the berimbau's historical presence in colonial Brazil and its performance practices within the context of capoeira have received scholarly attention, the use of the berimbau in Brazilian popular and art music has not been extensively studied.[4]

In addition to its inherent musical richness, the berimbau has become a metaphor for constructed notions of tradition, blackness, and Brazilian nationalism. These elements coexist in multiple planes, in proximity to each other, and can appeal to people of different social classes and ethnic backgrounds. The berimbau's identity embodies a connection with its African roots. It is also inextricably linked with the African-descended dance, capoeira (see Fig. 0.1).

A martial art/dance/game that exalts grace and beauty through its swift attacks and defenses between the sparring dancers, capoeira is situated on the edge of a precipice—this dance can turn into a combative encounter within a fraction of a second. Both the berimbau and capoeira are believed to have originated in the Northeastern region of Bahia, but there is also evidence of these traditions in colonial Brazilian Rio de Janeiro and Recife (see Fig. 0.2).[5]

Figure 0.2: Map of Brazil (David Tatem and Eric A. Galm 2008)

Capoeira is supported by vocal and instrumental musical accompaniment that energizes the dancers to ensure that they will perform at their peak levels. The berimbau directs these proceedings through a variety of melodic-rhythmic musical patterns called *toques*. These nonverbal musical codes can warn the dancers and other participants of mischievous trickery within the dancing space, and alert participants of approaching dangers from beyond. Some practitioners believe this musical bow

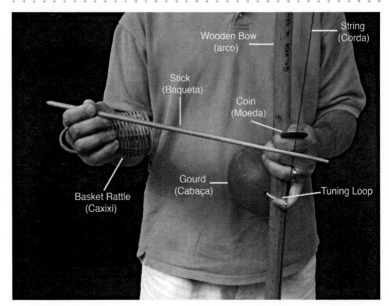

Figure 0.3: Components of the berimbau (Photo by Amy M. Yarbrough, graphic by Eric A. Galm 2008)

connects the past with the present and the future, is interconnected with Afro-Brazilian spiritual belief systems, and has the power to make a dancer invincible.

The berimbau has repeatedly been framed by scholars within historical contexts as a folkloric instrument that remains in the past. The first comprehensive study of the berimbau and its relation to capoeira in Bahia was published in 1958.[6] Waldeloir Rego's[7] 1968 detailed anthropological survey of Bahian capoeira laid the groundwork for Kay Shaffer's[8] 1976 investigation of the berimbau within the discipline. Most capoeira and berimbau studies from the 1970s to the present have built upon these principal works, and have confined their focus within this limited scope.[9]

I propose that scholars look beyond the berimbau as a static object, fixed within the context of capoeira, and examine its distinct historical origins and development within multiple overlapping cultural contexts. I explore the berimbau's movement across diverse genres and social strata, and I pursue how its meaning and significance has changed over time. From this new vantage point, the berimbau can help highlight broader sociological and cultural aspects of the Brazilian experience.

One contemporary theme among music scholars and anthropologists is the analysis of globally popular phenomena that are reinterpreted in local contexts. By pursuing changes in the berimbau's musical aesthetics as it moves beyond the capoeira tradition, I address issues of race, class, and Brazilian nationalism and how they relate to commoditization and commercialization in the musical genres of Brazilian popular and art music. These points of identity are part of a complex structure of interlaced meanings that are subtly transformed from culture producers to their receivers. For example, as a musical instrument moves away from its ritual context, some individuals or groups use it to create forms of perseverance and resistance; others use it to reinforce concepts of nationalism, both of which may alter the initial meaning and significance. The berimbau therefore represents a diverse range of locally constructed identities that change over space and time.

The Berimbau

The *berimbau de barriga*[10] (lit., "belly bow") is an African-derived (predominantly from West, Central, and South African cultures) gourd-resonated musical bow, with the gourd held against the musician's stomach (see Fig. 0.3). This musical bow is distinct from other types of musical bows such as the *berimbau de boca* (mouth bow) and the *berimbau de bacia* (similar to a washtub bass).

The berimbau consists of an *arco* (wooden bow) with a *corda* (taut steel string) attached in various ways at each end. A hollowed-out *cabaça* (calabash resonance gourd) is secured by a small cotton twine-tuning loop that passes through two holes in the gourd and encircles the wood and metal string at the lower-end of the bow (see Figs. x.1, 0.4, and 0.5).

This tuning loop creates a fixed point of tension that establishes a fundamental tone.[11] The bow is held by placing the little finger of the left hand under the tuning loop between the bow and the wire, and the ring and middle fingers of the same hand are wrapped around the wood of the bow (see Fig. 0.3). The thumb and index finger secure an object that can raise or alter the timbre of the fundamental pitch. This nondescript object can be a large *dobrão* or *moeda* (metal coin) or *pedra* (stone)[12] (see Figs. 0.6 and 0.7).

Figure 0.4: Cabaça (Photo by Eric A. Galm 2008)

Figure 0.6: Example of a possible coin dobrão, front (Photo by Eric A. Galm 2008)

Figure 0.5: Lower end of berimbau (Photo by Eric A. Galm 2008)

In the right hand, a long, thin *baqueta* (wooden stick) is held between the thumb, index, and middle fingers, and a *caxixi* (basket rattle), often filled with seeds or beans, is placed around the middle and ring (or ring and little) fingers of the right hand (see Figs. 0.8 and 0.9).

Enslaved Africans in Brazil re-created songs, dances, and musical instruments from their collective memories, including the berimbau. Although there was significant musical production and creation of musical instruments by indigenous South American populations, there is no evidence of indigenous musical bows in Brazil. As a result, musical bows in Brazil have become iconic representations of African-descended culture throughout the country.

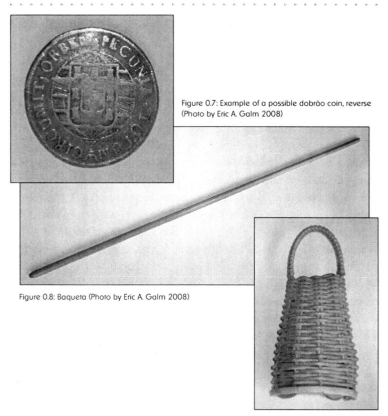

Figure 0.7: Example of a possible dobrão coin, reverse (Photo by Eric A. Galm 2008)

Figure 0.8: Baqueta (Photo by Eric A. Galm 2008)

Figure 0.9: Caxixi (Photo by Eric A. Galm 2008)

In nineteenth-century colonial-era Brazil, African bows existed under an array of names, the most common of which included *urucungo* and *gunga*. Perhaps it is due to the variety of names for musical bows that the term berimbau became used as a generic label.[13] Similar to the process of terminology distillation, the resulting musical bow now known as the Brazilian berimbau has roots that stem from many types of African-derived musical bows. Many instruments of African origin have also disappeared from use in Brazil, and the berimbau itself was on the verge of extinction by the early to mid-twentieth century, when it again experienced a transformational process that led to its emergence as a national symbol.

Music and *Brasilidade* (Development of a National Character)

Although Portuguese explorers arrived in Brazil in 1500, the country did not begin to develop a centralized cultural-intellectual infrastructure until the arrival of the Portuguese royal family in 1808. Fleeing from the impending invasion of the Iberian Peninsula by Napoleon Bonaparte, the royal family transferred their empire to Brazil. At this moment, Brazil gained the distinction of becoming the only colony in the Americas that was the head of a European empire, as opposed to a jewel within a crown. In the ensuing decade, institutions were established to support an enlightened intellectual environment, including a royal library, museum, botanical garden, and press in Rio de Janeiro alone.[14] Brazilian nationalistic ideals were formally set into motion when Dom Pedro I declared independence from Portugal in 1822, establishing an imperial monarchy that lasted until 1889. As a result of the academic environment, some Brazilian intellectuals undertook scientific cultural studies within the framework of social evolutionism (Darwinism) inspired by French positivism (positive associations as they deal with natural phenomena).[15]

Literary and artistic works that incorporated themes of the development of the Brazilian "race" include José de Alencar's *O Guarani*, authored in 1857, and Carlos Gomes's operatic adaptation under the same title that premiered in Milan in 1890.[16] *O Guarani* portrays the story of a Portuguese maiden who falls in love with the Guarani Indian chief, and their interracial union symbolically produces the first Brazilian child, and thus the Brazilian nation.[17]

One of the defining moments in Brazilian cultural nationalism was the broad-based *modernismo* (modernist) movement, which included expressions in literature, fine arts, and art music, launched at the *Semana da Arte Moderna* (Week of Modern Art) that transpired in São Paulo in February 1922. During this event, Brazilian artists were inspired to break with conventional practices and ideology of the time and radically forge a unique Brazilian cultural expression, instead of merely imitating established European masters. This was achieved by incorporating European fine art techniques with Brazil's diverse range of folkloric expression. Spearheaded by notable young literary figures Oswald de Andrade and

Mário de Andrade, this event was designed to coincide with the centenary of Brazil's independence, with the intent to expand the notion of independence beyond the political realm to include moral and "cognitive" aspects.[18] In his subsequent writings on the subject, Oswald de Andrade developed various manifestos that suggested if Brazilian culture producers were to compete with European fine and literary arts, they should incorporate elements of Brazil's regional forms of expression to develop their own national voices. His "Manifesto Antropofágo" (Cannibal Manifesto) outlined principles based on *antropofagia* (cultural cannibalism), where European composition and literary techniques would be "consumed" by Brazilian cultural producers and, through a process of incorporating unique Brazilian cultural elements, new forms of expression would emerge.[19]

By the 1930s social scientists had begun articulating detailed hypotheses of racial integration as a means to define a Brazilian "race" and culture. This is a central theme that is addressed in contrasting musical genres featured throughout this book. These ideologies were incorporated into Brazilian national policy, and fueled international myths of Brazil as a racial paradise. One of the most internationally well-known works regarding Brazilian racial ideologies is Gilberto Freyre's *Casa Grande & Senzala*,[20] which promoted supposedly beneficial aspects of the *mestiçagem* process of "whitening" in Brazil.[21]

Much of Freyre's work was adopted by the authoritarian government of Getúlio Vargas, who ruled as president and dictator from 1930 to 1954.[22] Vargas built his Liberal Alliance coalition comprised of prominent military officials and leaders from geographically dispersed non-coffee-producing states ranging from the northeast to the far south of the country.[23] Recognizing regional and cultural differences, the Liberal Alliance identified the need for the development of a national ideology to help unify the diverse cultures of these regions. In 1937 Vargas manipulated aspects of Freyre's ethnic integration concepts, and incorporated them as "an official euphemism for race mixing, which became formal policy for the authoritarian *Estado Novo*" (New State).[24]

Many cultural management projects of the Vargas regime are attributed to Gustavo Capanema, the Minister of Education and Health between 1934 and 1945. Historian Daryl Williams documents how the state managed cultural production in a multifaceted reflexive manner.[25]

Williams's analysis unveils how this process highlights the development of a distinct Brazilian national and aesthetic identity that crystallized by the mid-1930s. In this instance, popular cultural production was directed to promote interests of the state through official regulation of governmental entities, as well as through businesses, professional associations, and the press. As a result, a national aesthetic emerged that enabled both the public and the state to embrace Brazilian cultural production above all other works of art.[26] The final law that was enacted omitted most of Andrade's proposals concerning popular culture, and became an official entity for the enshrinement of Brazilian artifacts with a Eurocentric emphasis, including erudite arts and Catholic churches.[27] In the span of just seven years, Vargas's administration created a comprehensive historical, religious, economically prosperous, militaristic, and independent Brazilian identity.[28]

Popular and Art Music in Brazil

Cultural artifacts on display in national Brazilian museums developed during the Vargas era privilege material aspects of the elite over the middle and lower classes. Similar indicators of social hierarchy have driven distinctions in Brazil between "popular" versus "art" music and culture. Popular music in Brazil is considered to be an expression that is produced by and for the masses.[29] Terms such as *música folclórica* (folkloric music), *música popular* (popular music), and *música erudita* or *música de escola* (art music) are among a host of generally accepted terms used to identify musical expression that signifies class distinction and social function.[30] The rise of the radio industry in the 1930s helped promote popular music into the national psyche through prominent Rio de Janeiro stations that broadcast nationally.[31] As a result of this prominence, nationally espoused ideals have been channeled through Rio de Janeiro–emergent popular musical traditions. For example, Brazilian anthropologist Hermano Vianna demonstrates how the Vargas regime promoted samba music that adopted the mulatto as an ideal symbol of progress. The mulatto then became a symbol of industrial progress, since samba was centered in the context of an urban setting. As a result, samba as a national symbol has been developed as a central focal point of this process, while musical styles from other regions of Brazil are portrayed as secondary tiers representing geographical distinction.[32] Although emphasis was placed on cultural mixing within the country's literary ideologies, urban popular musics (such as tangos, waltzes, polkas, and *maxixes*) and their composers were excluded from being considered representative of a national music until the early twentieth century. Composers such as Chiquinha Gonzaga and Ernesto Nazareth pioneered musical syntheses between urban public and elite spaces in the late eighteenth and early nineteenth centuries. It was this process of mixing within popular musical expression that helped define Brazilian music and culture in an international arena. Only a few decades later, Brazil's most internationally celebrated composer, Heitor Villa-Lobos, was hailed for his incorporation of urban popular music into his art music compositions, which was seen as a fundamental component for the development of Brazilian nationalistic music.[33]

Resistance through Music
The Bahian Blocos Afro

The *blocos afro* (Bahian carnival parading associations) in Salvador, Bahia, demonstrate how political processes have been redirected by Afro-Brazilians as a means to create and reclaim symbols. Following decades of polarizing debate about definition and status of people of African heritage in Brazil, the term *afro descendente* (African descendant) emerged as a means to de-emphasize bipolar white/nonwhite relationships, and has been expanded to include cultural activities such as the affirmation of black culture communities.[34] Osmundo de Araújo Pinho suggests that a series of "transnational connections" affected young Afro-Brazilians, such as political struggles related to African decolonization, North American soul music, and the Black Power movement.[35]

In the 1970s and 1980s, the bloco afro carnival groups emerged from the predominantly lower-class neighborhoods of Salvador da Bahia in northeastern Brazil, promoting positive images of black identity. Based on the model of the Rio de Janeiro *escolas de samba* (samba schools), the blocos afro are officially organized as community cultural groups, committed to struggles against marginalization and racial discrimination.[36]

Some have become nationally and internationally prominent voices in Brazil's music industry, such as Olodum, a bloco afro that gained international popularity in collaborative projects with Paul Simon and Michael Jackson in the late 1980s and early 1990s.[37] Olodum and other organizations have expanded their scope to become profitable black enterprises providing jobs, shelter, education, and other community-based activities on a year-round basis.

The blocos afro have challenged other aspects of national culture—such as the Brazilian recording industry, which is principally based in Rio de Janeiro and São Paulo; the blocos have helped establish a regional center of musical production in Bahia, by constructing and recording at studios in northeastern Brazil. This process has reduced their dependence on traditional centers of power in the Brazilian music industry. These musical ensembles present an extraordinary opportunity to observe and analyze globally popular phenomena that can become reinterpreted in local contexts. In the blocos afro, elements have been borrowed from various Brazilian, North American, and Jamaican musical genres.[38]

Symbols of African culture are an important part of this reinterpretive process, and the berimbau offers multiple sites of meaning within a single iconic entity that can simultaneously symbolize Africa and/or Brazilian nationalism. The berimbau has long represented African culture in Brazil, as it is a musical instrument that has been used by Africans and their descendants in public marketplaces, and its use and meaning has transformed over generations, particularly during the past several decades. One of the important markers in defining *brasilidade* (a nationalistic sense of Brazilianness) is the ability to undergo a transformative process, and emerge as a uniquely Brazilian entity. This is how the berimbau has been able to not only survive, but also emerge and thrive as a national Brazilian icon. The berimbau that exists today is the synthesized result of standardized physical characteristics from several types of African musical bows; it has been reinvented as the Brazilian national instrument with a higher social status than other musical instruments that maintained distinctly African identities.[39] More recently the berimbau has been reinterpreted to become an icon of contemporary black cultural expression and a symbol of resistance. Through this process, musicians have used it to advocate an alternative understanding of race with rhetoric of challenge and contestation that directly confronts the accepted notions of harmony and integration. As a result, the underlying processes of musical integration are complicated by this discourse, which is justified ambiguously as evidence.

Book Overview

Within these popular and art musical genres, I address notions of assumed traditions and explore the introduction and transformational development of berimbau and capoeira thematic material spanning from the late 1950s to recent years. In chapter 1 I present a historical introduction to the berimbau and capoeira. Chapter 2 focuses on the early 1960s, when bossa nova composer Baden Powell adapted the berimbau's melodic rhythms to the guitar, resulting in the internationally successful composition, "Berimbau." I analyze Powell's composition within the context of capoeira-related musical performance practices, and view how the musical trope that emerged from this composition continues to be used in Brazilian popular music today. I demonstrate how this motif has changed from the 1960s to the 1990s. Continuing my chronological study of the berimbau's transformation in Brazilian popular music in chapter 3, I focus on the fusion of musical genres, and how the berimbau as a metaphor has transformed from a symbol of capoeira to one of blackness, resistance, and change.

The emergence of the berimbau virtuoso is marked by the development of novel performance techniques and innovations by musicians that have moved this musical instrument into genres beyond capoeira. This process began in the late 1960s but has become more prominent in the last two decades. In chapter 4 I present three individuals within Brazilian popular music who demonstrate this process: Naná Vasconcelos, Dinho Nascimento, and Ramiro Musotto. Vasconcelos brought the berimbau from Brazil into a global jazz marketplace and, through his recordings, inspired the Bahian Nascimento and the Argentinean Musotto to follow his ideas for developing new concepts. Through this framework, I address issues of globalization, tradition, and transformation.

In chapter 5 I contrast the popular music discussion with an analysis of the berimbau in Brazilian art music. In 1958 the berimbau was introduced into the symphony orchestra in a composition by Mário Tavares titled *Ganguzama*. This work is a nationalistic epic about the "birth" of the Brazilian national character (following the concept of Gomes's *O Guarani*) in which the union of a Portuguese and indigenous couple creates the "first" Brazilian child. In this work, the African presence is constructed through the notion that Africans "helped" build Brazilian society, and the berimbau is used as a symbol to authenticate this creation myth.[40] This work has inspired some scholars to develop musical notation for the berimbau as a means to elevate the berimbau's status in the world of art music. As a result, capoeira scholars have incorporated this specific musical notation to help further their own studies within the oral tradition.

Chapter 6 follows with a survey of visual and literary images that were referenced in the tourist's journey at the beginning of this introduction. The conclusion connects several strands of history, cultural studies, music, and the multiple diasporic presences within the black Atlantic, analyzing the threads of a rich tapestry of Brazilian music and culture, to demonstrate how the berimbau has become a symbol of Brazilian identity and an icon of brasilidade throughout the world. I present a comprehensive portrait of the use and meaning of the berimbau in Brazilian music and culture by investigating how its position has been constructed, modified, and adapted by Eurocentric and Afro-Brazilian, marginalized and elite culture producers to construct opposing notions of Brazilianness. Today, the berimbau retains its prominent significance within capoeira, but also serves as a metaphor for a nationalistic "traditional" Brazilian musical element that is prominently featured in many Brazilian music genres and in art forms throughout Brazilian society. The berimbau is a symbol of blackness, tradition, nationalism, and authenticity in Brazilian music and culture. These icons then become important foundations upon which new musical and cultural expressions are created.

Chapter 1

Historical Connections and the Emergence of a National Symbol

Descriptions of the *berimbau de barriga* in colonial Brazilian life were a favorite subject of foreign travelers to Brazil, beginning in the early 1800s.[1] Musical bows appeared in marketplaces and were played exclusively by black street vendors and beggars until the 1888 abolition of slavery. Unique African-derived musical instruments were employed with the intention to increase sales; instruments such as musical bows functioned as novelties and had an exotic appeal at a relatively early stage in Brazilian history.

European chroniclers who traveled to Brazil were frequently enchanted by the sounds that emerged from the berimbau. They captured its various physical components and performance techniques in paintings and travel journals. One such account attempted to equate the berimbau with a violin and Orpheus's lyre. Peppered with romantic Classical analogies, French chronicler Ferdinand Denis's account reported that he was impressed by how a black servant constructed a "violin" using a turtle shell and a string made from part of a whale. Combined with vocal accompaniment, the musician produced some "singular low sounds" that were "monotonous."[2]

Nineteenth-century colonial attitudes towards berimbau musicians can be observed in the following example cited by Alfredo Brandão, who researched Afro-Brazilian culture in Alagoas in the early 1930s.[3] Although Carneiro[4] believes that the type of berimbau referenced in this passage is a mouth bow, Brandão describes this instrument as "a bowl, which the musician places against his chest," a performance technique directly associated with the berimbau de barriga.[5] Describing the context in which the berimbau was used, Brandão reports that it produced "melancholical and sad" music in the middle of the night that permeated the quiet nights on slave plantations. He continues: "when the 'saudades' [bittersweet recollections] of the distant homeland caused grief within the soul, they chased these feelings away with the vibrations of musical instruments."[6] This passage also highlights public perception of the berimbau within the colonial and early republic eras, as well as how it was used to demarcate class and racial distinction among Afro-Brazilians. Brandão notes that people of lighter complexions ("*mestiços* and mulattoes") looked down upon people of darker complexion ("Africans"), and that the latter were the only ones who played the berimbau, resulting in the following taunting refrain:

Sua mãe é uma coruja	Your mother is an owl
Que mora no oco de um pau;	Who lives in the hole of a tree stump
Seu pai negro da Angola	Your father is a black man from Angola
Tocador de berimbau	A berimbau player[7]

The allusion to an owl in the first line of the verse draws upon a strong Brazilian association between owls and bad luck. Moreover, this phrase is one of many derogatory references of this nature. It is a play on the popular Brazilian expression *é feia como uma coruja* (you are as ugly as an owl), thus reflecting poorly upon the subject's mother. This reference could also signify that the mother is a witch, since many superstitions are associated with owls. The comment regarding the father might draw upon imagery of the vendor, storyteller, or beggar playing the musical bow in the Brazilian marketplace, thus suggesting that this man is a lower-class skilled laborer. Nonetheless, the allusions to mother and father are both strongly connected with notions of blackness and a close inter-relationship to the earth.

Although there is an abundance of information regarding the separate traditions of the berimbau and capoeira, capoeira scholars have concluded that there are no direct references to the berimbau in conjunction with capoeira prior to the 1900s. Oral tradition and many capoeira practitioners suggest that, during the colonial era, capoeira training survived within the confines of slavery. Capoeira practitioners would train for combat, including the use of *navalhas* (razors) held between the toes, and when a field hand or slave owner approached the activity, it instantaneously transformed into a recreational dance.[8] Gerhard Kubik suggests that the berimbau was not incorporated into capoeira until after the abolition of slavery in 1888, when capoeira slowly began to change from a combative fight into a non-contact game. According to this theory (adopted by several scholars),[9] the berimbau came to be integrated into capoeira around 1900 as part of a migration of non-Yoruba Afro-Brazilians from southern Brazil to Bahia, which created conditions for the blending and reinterpretation of several similar African traditions. Capoeira tradition bearers resisted external cultural influences in order to preserve an Angolan identity.[10] As a compromise, additional musical instruments were brought into the practice of capoeira, but they also incorporated a musical bow of Angolan origin.[11] The following examples offer a brief glimpse into alternative perspectives of the berimbau in Afro-Brazilian life prior to Kubik's discussion.

Descriptions provided by nineteenth-century chroniclers demonstrate how the berimbau was used as musical accompaniment for dance long before the late 1880s as Kubik suggests. In French chronicler Ferdinand Denis's diary written between 1816 and 1819, he reveals a moment in which the musical bow is used to accompany dance during an impromptu interaction between a berimbau musician and a passing pedestrian. This meeting takes place in a marketplace, and the berimbau musician is described as playing the string in "diverse manners." As one person passes by a berimbau musician, he is drawn to the music, and places the bundle that he is carrying on the ground, and begins to dance. The musician and dancer then interact with improvised music and lyrics, and corresponding expression through the dance. After a short while, the passerby picks up his bundle and resumes his errand without speaking to the musician or other onlookers.[12] This interaction could have easily taken place with a drum or other musical instrument, but there is evidence in this passage to demonstrate that the berimbau was indeed used in association with dance, whether formal or informal, in the early nineteenth century.

In 1858, forty years later, Charles Ribeyrolles separately documented the berimbau and capoeira, the latter accompanied only by a drum. In his observation of the *batuque* (a central African dance of Bantu origin), he not only observed that the berimbau provided musical accompaniment, but it also controlled the speed of the dance, a prominent characteristic of the berimbau within contemporary capoeira practice.[13] There is also mention of a possible reference to capoeira being accompanied by a musical bow as early as the 1880s, and perhaps earlier. João da Silva Campos describes a Bahian popular celebration surrounding a religious procession. Although Campos's work was published posthumously, he provides a timeline for the development of the celebration and procession for the Senhor dos Navegantes (Lord of the Navigators) in Bahia prior to the 1890s.[14] "The excited dark crowd performed *Batuques*. *Samba*. Capoeira circles. One heard *pandeiros* [Brazilian tambourines], *cavaquinhos* [four-string guitars similar to ukuleles], *violas* [ten- or twelve-string guitars] . . . , berimbau and cadential hand clapping. It was a pandemonium."[15] It is plausible that Campos divulges the musical genres and associated musical instruments in sequential order. In this respect, *"Batuques"* and *"Samba"* would be accompanied by pandeiros, cavaquinhos, and violas, many of which continue to be used in samba today. The music that Campos identifies with capoeira would therefore include the berimbau and cadential hand clapping, two fundamental aspects that exist today within capoeira musical practice. If accurate, this account provides clear evidence that the berimbau was used in conjunction with capoeira prior to the arrival of the twentieth century.

Capoeira
From Public Menace to National Icon

Capoeira is an African-derived art form with qualities of dance, acrobatics, and play incorporated into its movement style. The *jogo* (game) of capoeira takes place in a circle, formed by *capoeiristas* (capoeira practitioners). Within the *roda* (circle), two capoeiristas launch into an array of attacks and corresponding defenses. One of capoeira's advantages over other hand-to-hand styles of combat is that practitioners possess a much larger range of motion, allowing them to be farther away from their opponents. The master of the game controls various facets of the dance with a berimbau, by dictating the tempo and duration of each game. The capoeiristas surrounding the dancers provide musical accompaniment, playing instruments, hand clapping, and singing in a call-and-response manner alternating between leader and chorus.

The capoeira musical ensemble generally consists of one or more berimbaus, pandeiro, *agogô* (double bell), *reco-reco* (scraper), and *atabaque* (single-head, conical drum similar to a conga). If there is an ensemble of three berimbaus, each instrument is distinguished by the size of the resonating gourd. The largest and lowest-pitched is the *gunga*, and the smallest and highest-pitched is the *viola*. The remaining berimbau is called the *médio* (middle); when there is only one present in the musical ensemble, it is simply called the berimbau. These instruments also have separate musical functions in which the gunga plays a basic motif with little or no variation. The médio plays a combination of the basic motif with more variations than the gunga, although the médio rarely plays any extended variations. The viola is free to either improvise or reinforce the melodic rhythms established by the other two berimbaus.[16]

The name capoeira is believed to have many origins. One of the most popular is related to new secondary growth that appears after a virgin forest has been clear-cut. The word capoeira is believed to have derived from the South American indigenous Tupi language *caá* (forest) and *puêra* (extinct). Others believe that the name is derived from the Portuguese *capão* (castrated male chicken) and refers to a chicken coop, perhaps in an allusion to cockfighting.[17]

The history of capoeira in Brazil can be viewed in four major phases: (1) the rise of the colonial and imperial era (1500s to 1888, during slavery); (2) the early republic following the abolition of slavery (1889 to 1930s); (3) the rise of Getúlio Vargas, followed by his Estado Novo (beginning in the 1930s); and (4) the globalization of capoeira (from the 1970s to the present). The third stage features the establishment of formal training academies.[18] Oral traditions assert that capoeira was a fight utilized by enslaved Africans to overtake their masters and escape from slavery. Identified by authorities as a threat to society, capoeira was outlawed during these first two phases and its practitioners suffered severe repression by police, and were sometimes punished by death.[19] Negative associations and the marginalization of capoeiristas were so pervasive in Brazilian society that the word capoeira "became a synonym for bum, bandit and thief."[20] Beginning in the 1930s the practice of capoeira was legalized and allowed to operate behind the closed doors of academies, and through this structure it has developed into a dance that features moves without contact between opponents. This transformation was promoted in large part by the Brazilian government, and is discussed later in this chapter.

The most recent phase of capoeira has spawned two distinct ideological disciplines representing traditional (capoeira Angola) and modern (capoeira regional). Capoeira Angola, promoted by mestre Pastinha (Vicente Ferreira Pastinha, 1889–1982), is seen by many capoeira practitioners as the preservation of a traditional art form that has been passed along from generation to generation, and is envisioned primarily as a game. Although capoeira is an artistic expression developed in Brazil from various African martial dances, the name *capoeira Angola* suggests that it has come from a specific location on the continent of Africa.[21] Capoeira regional, philosophically viewed as a fight, was developed by mestre Bimba (Manoel dos Reis Machado, 1899–1974), who incorporated external movements from the *batuque* (a central African dance of Bantu origin) and structural modifications such as the graduated belt advancement system from Asian-based martial arts. It appears that the term *regional* was principally developed in reaction to a sports-oriented Brazilian gymnastics based in capoeira movements by Anibal Burlamaqui in 1928.[22]

Differences between capoeira Angola and capoeira regional are evident in both dance movements and musical instrumentation. Capoeira Angola is characterized as a slower game, played low to the ground, and closer to a dance, whereas capoeira regional tends to be faster, higher, and closer to a fight.[23] Moreover, capoeira regional has developed as a dance for public display; this style of capoeira is almost exclusively featured in folkloric shows. Capoeira regional tends to have an unspecified number of berimbaus, whereas capoeira Angola maintains a fixed number of three, somewhat similar to the three atabaques in the sacred drumming associated with *candomblé* (an African-derived religion based on a pantheon of spirits that represent elements of nature).[24] Capoeira regional also tends to have a broader variety of berimbau melodic-rhythmic toques performed within the roda.[25]

The incorporation of capoeira academies began a process that introduced capoeira into the Brazilian mainstream in the late 1960s and early 1970s. As a result of this process, the social stigma and marginalization associated with capoeira and its practitioners was de-emphasized as it was transformed from an African-derived fight into a national Brazilian sport. Today, capoeira has become a hallmark of Bahian culture that has maintained its identity after having been absorbed into a national context. Ethnomusicologist Elizabeth Travassos calls this a form of "social rehabilitation" that can simultaneously represent a national Brazilian sport and be a reinforcing agent of Afro-Brazilian identity, which most likely has helped support philosophies of capoeira Angola as a natural component of an African-descended cultural heritage. [26] In recent years, capoeira Angola has become internationally recognized as an expression of "authentic" Brazilian capoeira, as represented by its assumed direct link to an African heritage.[27]

Transformations
The Berimbau's Survival and Formal Association with Capoeira

Other African-derived musical instruments, such as the *marimba* (ten- or twelve-key portable xylophone with gourd resonators), have disappeared from use in Brazilian musical practice.[28] In a comparative study between these two musical instruments, Travassos suggests that the berimbau benefited from a process of urbanization, and thus successfully moved from a marginalized universe to one of prestige within and beyond Brazil's borders. In contrast, the marimba remained in rural communities and became disassociated from processes of modernization, and therefore became extinct in Brazil. It is also possible that the berimbau's compact size and ease of construction may have also played an active role in the perseverance of this musical bow in comparison to the cumbersome marimba. Perhaps the performance technique of holding the berimbau's resonating gourd against the body may have enabled a more intimate connection between musician and instrument. With the transformation of traditional forms over time, boundaries become blurred, but all of the elements do not necessarily disappear. While they may lose their direct association within the context of a ritual, they may diffuse into other realms, and become symbols that are representative of national or ethnic identity; or they may become active agents in the preservation of an idealized folkloric past.[29] In these terms, the berimbau's symbolism has come to represent a broad range of locally constructed identities as well as national folklore.

As the berimbau has become inseparably intertwined within the capoeira ritual, both have served to reinforce capoeira as a public spectacle. Moreover, it is a central focal point of both Angola (traditional) and regional (modern) schools of capoeira, thus affirming its identity as an integral component of all capoeira forms, regardless of philosophical orientation. Kay Shaffer suggests that the union between the berimbau and capoeira worked in tandem to ensure each other's survival, the music preserving the dance-game, and the movement exhibition keeping the berimbau from fading away.[30]

Musician Dinho Nascimento, who was born and raised in Bahia—where he learned how to play capoeira on the street, as opposed to within the structure of academies—believes that the berimbau was incorporated into capoeira as an agent to instill a sense of order into the tradition. After the abolition of slavery, capoeira was essentially a street fight with no established rules. As capoeiristas encountered each other on the street, order was established through the development of mutual respect for the berimbau. Participants were obligated to follow rules that were dictated by an object—the berimbau—rather than the person who was responsible for directing a particular game.

> I think the berimbau came to give the rules. Who gave the rules to capoeira? It wasn't either Bimba or Pastinha. It was the berimbau. Because when you play the time [i.e., establish the rhythm], you go there together with me, because this guy's playing [the berimbau]. So I say that the berimbau is the mestre . . . And this resolves whatever fight, whatever thing, because it has to be respected, . . . and the dance goes with the music. You dance the part of the music. So the game is supported by the music, and the berimbau gives it [order].[31]

Within the capoeira academy of mestre Nenel, mestre Bimba's son, the berimbau's music dictates the pace and style of dance movements, yet the berimbau also embodies historical, symbolic, and emotional qualities that form the basis for deeper, more complex expression. The berimbau retains its importance within capoeira because all of the practitioners follow its melodic rhythms as an unquestioned basic element of the discipline. The berimbau is relevant for any practitioner who observes these rules, listens to its music, and can therefore be emotionally affected by its stimulating soundwaves.[32]

Oral tradition suggests that the berimbau toque *cavalaria* was used in the 1920s to warn capoeira practitioners of mounted police who approached on horseback.[33] Nestor Capoeira recalls mestre Pastinha's description of how sharp objects were attached to each end of the berimbau, thus converting it into a weapon: "In the moment of truth it would cease to be a musical instrument and would turn into a hand sickle."[34] Capoeira scholar Letícia Vidor de Sousa Reis believes that this use of the berimbau as a defensive instrument against police repression is an invention of Bahian capoeira tradition that is maintained within the collective memory of black resistance in the region. She hypothesizes that the berimbau's connection to capoeira serves as a powerful symbol of distinction from white Brazilians. As a result of the berimbau's strong representations of African culture, themes of capoeira's African origins have been reinforced through this association. In this context, the berimbau presents a dual nature that is "simultaneously sacred and profane, weapon and musical instrument," and as a result of these ambiguities has become "an ethnic symbol of the black Brazilian."[35]

For capoeira practitioners and some Afro-Brazilians, the berimbau and capoeira also represent active agents against racially motivated oppression, perhaps derived from oral traditions that cite capoeira as an effective means to escape from slavery.[36] If the berimbau is considered a symbol of black resistance, its portability, shape, and pitch range should be considered significant factors in this equation. A single berimbau can be symbolically equated to the vocal range of an individual person. When this is combined with others of varying sizes and ranges, and played in contrasting ways, a broader range of sound and stronger group unity can be conveyed.

Berimbau and Capoeira
Emergence of the National

In the 1930s the Vargas regime targeted symbols of black culture as a means to incorporate symbols of resistance into a national scheme. Certain forms of African-derived cultural expression such as capoeira, candomblé, and neighborhood carnival parading groups had been repressed by the authorities in the early decades of the twentieth century and deemed a public menace, or a public threat. The Vargas government legalized the practice of capoeira with the restriction that it was confined to indoor "academies," which were then registered with authorities. In conformation with his nationalist agenda, Vargas supported the concept that "physical education could be used to instill a sense of discipline in children if taught at an early age."[37] In 1953, he declared capoeira "the only truly national [Brazilian] sport."[38]

In the 1950s and 1960s, Bahian capoeira masters began to move southward through Brazil and to establish academies in large urban areas such as Rio de Janeiro and São Paulo. Capoeira began to expand to areas outside of Brazil, such as Europe and the United States, in the 1970s. Promoted principally as a sport, capoeira was able to shed some of its social stigma within Brazil. Elizabeth Travassos comments that capoeira captured the attention of the middle classes in urban settings, who adopted it as a musical sport or a national pastime, devoid of connections with Afro-Brazilian culture.[39] The prominent status of the berimbau has been maintained as capoeira has spread throughout the Brazilian nation and the world, and as a result, the musical bow has been exposed to other cultures that have expanded its musical presence in genres beyond the context of capoeira. In this sense, capoeira has undergone a transition, moving from an impoverished Afro-Brazilian lower class to a more economically and racially diverse middle-class population, where it is casually practiced as a sport. In recent decades capoeira has continued to be incorporated into the country's nationalist agenda, as variants of capoeira regional are currently taught at military police training academies in Brazil.[40] Moreover, capoeira apprenticeship is increasingly being utilized in Brazil as a social service program to work with homeless and at-risk youth populations.[41]

Clearly, both the berimbau and capoeira have assisted with each other's survival through transformation into prominent icons. As a result, the berimbau has gained an international presence and has been incorporated into a broad range of musical contexts. Following a process of cultural appropriation, the berimbau and capoeira have been transformed into national symbols of folkloric expression.

Although capoeira has emerged as a national sport, it is not necessarily accepted in the Brazilian mainstream as a cultural expression that is distinguished from African-descended tradition. As it has transformed toward a recreational exercise activity, its identification has been distanced from its African heritage and has become a "Brazilian" art form.[42] This is due in part to a complex interrelationship between definitions of race and class in Brazil. Political scientist Michael Hanchard discusses how contradictory and confusing racial categories and terminology have developed in Brazil, explaining that once a common framework of racial identity has been constructed, it can then be reinterpreted and redefined by all participants, thereby thwarting unified political organization along racial lines.

The Berimbau and African-derived Religious Beliefs

There is a strong connection between African-derived religious beliefs, capoeira, and the berimbau. Capoeira embodies many African-derived religious practices and concepts, as evidenced in the songs and rituals of the discipline. In the introductory portion of a game of capoeira, the symbolism of the berimbau can be seen in both physical and spiritual realms. Many capoeira practitioners believe that the berimbau is the solitary element that directs the pace and style of each game, and functions as a referee; the berimbau that is held by the oldest mestre must be obeyed and respected by all participants. This respect moves to a deeper level when the berimbau is perceived as a musical instrument that brings spiritual forces of the past and future together in the present.[43]

The berimbau is played during funeral ceremonies of some capoeira practitioners, and its sound is believed to help the spirit move to another realm. Examples of supernatural beliefs in conjunction with musical bows can be seen in African and African diasporic cultures. Capoeira mestre Nestor Capoeira cites an example from oral tradition: "It is said that in certain parts of Africa it was forbidden for the young who cared for the livestock to play this instrument; it was thought that the sound would take the soul of the youth—which was still inexperienced—to the land of no return."[44]

This concept may have broader pan-African implications, as Fernando Ortiz notes that Cuban musical bows such as the *burumbumba* (similar to the Angolan styles of musical bows found in Brazil) are believed to be instruments that "speak with the dead." Ortiz gives the etymology of the term *burumbumba* as coming from *buro* (to speak or converse) and *mumbumba*, related to *nganga* (a cauldron that contains spiritual powers—and is used in the Afro-Cuban religious practice of *Palo Monte*), which captivates the familiar spirit and keeps it near.[45]

Moreover, some capoeira practitioners believe that through the process of paying proper respect to the berimbau—by kneeling at the foot of the berimbau musician(s) before entering into a game—they will attain a *corpo fechado* (closed body) and will not be susceptible to cuts or injuries.[46] Carneiro notes that at this moment, a *ladainha* (litany, an introductory solo) is being sung by the mestre, and the participants are *esperando o santo* (waiting for the saint).[47] This concept is borrowed from candomblé practice when an initiate is preparing for spirit possession. Mestre Negoativo[48] suggests that many of the spiritual belief practices associated with the berimbau have emerged from various forms of African-derived religious systems, including *umbanda* (a mixture of various Afro-Brazilian and indigenous religious practices and Catholicism) and candomblé.

> After slavery was abolished, [Afro-Brazilians] didn't have anything to do. They ran away to the *morros* [hills], they created the *favelas* [impoverished urban neighborhoods], and the religion that they had was African religion, which is candomblé. And capoeira was [one of their] manifestations—it was their art, their manner to defend, to rob, to attack, to celebrate, to train, so it mixed all of this through the African cults, like candomblé. [Capoeira also] had chants, percussive instruments and handclapping. So the connection is very strong.[49]

Reis suggests that both the game of capoeira and the berimbau exist in an ambiguous space that encompasses the sacred and profane. The capoeira circle simultaneously represents the world and "a different world," where practitioners must receive permission to enter and exit at the foot of the berimbau. Moreover, the berimbau is simultaneously a "musical instrument and a spiritual authority" whose melodic rhythms feature names of Catholic saints, other people, and regions of Africa and Brazil.⁵⁰ Reis also conducted an interview with Seu Tomás, a berimbau artisan based in São Paulo, who related that the colors of his painted berimbaus possessed fundamental relationships with some divinities within the Afro-Brazilian religious practices of umbanda and candomblé.⁵¹ He noted that the blue berimbau represented *Yemanjá* (the goddess of the sea), and two other berimbaus represented *Oxumaré* (*orixá* of the rainbow) and the *Preto Velho* (Old Black Spirit).⁵²

Three recent examples demonstrate how symbolic associations of the berimbau are utilized to incorporate elements of Afro-Brazilian culture into Bahian Catholic and evangelical religious services. In Rio de Janeiro in 1990, a black Pentecostal church began formally practicing an "inculturated" or "Afro-Mass," developed from ideological models in preceding decades.⁵³ This movement later spread to some of Brazil's other large cities, and in 1997 the Archbishop of Salvador, Dom Lucas Moreira, announced that an Afro-Brazilian Pastoral would be composed as a part of Brazil's 500th anniversary celebration, with the aim of introducing Afro-Brazilian cultural traits into the Catholic Mass. He states, "The berimbau and other Afro-Brazilian cultural instruments can be incorporated into a diocese that embodies this type of influence, such as in Bahia."⁵⁴ In the year 2000, during the commemorative celebration, an individual Catholic church held a mass to ask forgiveness for its association with colonial Brazilian oppression. The African component of this mass included a berimbau, which was played in the church as a part of the service.⁵⁵ During the March 2001 inauguration of the evangelical sanctuary of *Mãe Rainha e Vencedora* (Victorious Queen Mother), a group of adolescents brought altar offerings of berimbaus, Bahian fruits, and flowers, which complemented the traditional offering of bread and wine.⁵⁶

Capoeira and Gender

Capoeira is a male-dominated sphere, although women have greatly increased their presence in recent decades, leading to new demographics that challenge established practices and assumptions within the discipline. Metaphorically, notions of gender have been intertwined with a metaphysical berimbau that appears in legends and stories. For instance, Oliveira recounts a legend about a girl who fell by the side of a stream, died, and upon her death, various parts of her body transformed into components of a berimbau.[57] Mestre Nô made similar associations, by comparing the wood of the bow to his skeleton, the resonating gourd to his head, the wire to his hair, and the rattle as the same one that he played with as an infant.[58]

Prominent women capoeiristas have occasionally been mentioned in capoeira literature, but they have been exceptions, often viewed as "tough" women who were not considered to be authentic capoeira practitioners.[59] It is widely believed that mestre Bimba trained his daughters how to play capoeira, and there is photographic evidence from "approximately the 1930s . . . that shows various black women training capoeira in a yard, under the command of mestre Bimba."[60] As of the early 1990s, informal estimates suggested that less than one percent of women played capoeira in Salvador, and possibly five to ten percent participated in Rio de Janeiro and São Paulo academies. Lewis observed that women generally participate at dance studios and academies, as "capoeira is generally considered more socially acceptable by middle- and upper-middle-class people."[61] North American women trained with Bira Almeida's capoeira group in California and won formal competitions against Brazilian women capoeiristas.[62] Although Lewis never encountered a female *maestra* during his fieldwork in Brazil,[63] capoeira maestra Edna Lima established a successful academy in New York City.[64]

Gender-based insults are frequently used in capoeira songs to challenge the masculinity of male participants. Lewis believes that this follows patterns of machismo found throughout Latin America and the United States. Women are often cited as promiscuous in capoeira song texts, which suggests one of the reasons why the sport has encountered limited female participation. In general, references to women are designed as insults to challenge male masculinity and they are used as an incentive for more aggressive play. For example, the common phrase *quem bate palmas é uma mulhé* (who claps their hands is a woman) implies that if someone only provides the musical accompaniment, they always remain at the periphery and are afraid to enter into combat. These types of challenges extend to equating women with children, thus suggesting that inexperienced practitioners do not possess the physical or emotional capabilities to survive within the ring. Of course, the presence of women practitioners within the ring inverts these meanings in practice. As capoeira masters are attempting to attract more students, they are faced with changing potentially offensive song texts and stereotypical attitudes. Lewis believes that the "conscious change in image is one of the factors influencing the creation of new songs in the capoeira repertoire."[65]

Capoeira practitioner and musician Dinho Nascimento observed the practice of capoeira on the streets of Salvador, Bahia during his youth, and recalls that he had heard about a few women involved with capoeira in the 1930s. He occasionally saw women informally playing capoeira on the beach in the 1950s, and many women began to play capoeira by the 1970s. Nascimento recalls that capoeira masters carefully guarded the berimbau from all inexperienced students regardless of gender, so access to the berimbau within capoeira was limited for all lower-level students. He remembers that "a student couldn't pick up the berimbau, because the berimbau wasn't for a kid. It was a special instrument that principally the mestre picked up . . . [because he] had to know how to play a good berimbau to be a good capoeirista. . . . And today, this has changed in the contrary. The mestres want to have students playing berimbau, and the more students playing the berimbau, the better."[66]

Nascimento is aware of the changing attitudes about women's participation in capoeira, observing that today, "there are women playing berimbau. And the masters are accepting it. This is a great evolution in capoeira."[67]

Chapter 2

Theme and Variations
Tracing a Musical Motif from Bossa Nova to the 1990s

━ ━

Berimbau me confirmou	Berimbau confirmed to me
vai ter briga de amor,	that there will be a fight for love,
Tristeza camará.	Sadness, friend

—lyrics from "Berimbau"[1]

Brazilian popular music composers began to search for a national voice drawing from traditional genres during two distinct periods. (See related discussion in chapter 5 regarding the search for a national voice prior to the 1950s.) The first phase took place with the rise of bossa nova music in the late 1950s and early 1960s, when composers started incorporating elements of Brazilian folklore into their jazz-influenced works. The second phase can be seen in public popular song festivals that were initially designed to promote tourism and that were sponsored by the military dictatorship from October 1966 until the early 1970s, when strict censorship limited artistic expression. Beginning with the Festival Internacional da Canção (International Song Festival), popular music festivals expanded the notion of MPB (popular Brazilian music) beyond the context of bossa nova. Works at these festivals often featured contemporary fusions of musical styles from disparate sources. Some of these compositions encountered negative public reaction, which was often framed as a type of cultural protectionism, whether in defense of a folkloric tradition or of a national ideal.

The song "Berimbau," composed by Baden Powell and Vinícius de Moraes, is an example of the first phase. One of the hallmarks of this song is Powell's adaptation of the berimbau's melodic rhythms for the guitar. This work served to nationally popularize the musical bow beyond the folkloric context of capoeira and propel it into the Brazilian musical mainstream. This guitar motif has since become an iconic trope that symbolizes the berimbau, capoeira, Bahia, and northeastern music in many genres of popular Brazilian music.

Four subsequent songs expand upon and amplify themes raised in "Berimbau." In the late 1960s, "Lapinha,"[2] by Baden Powell and lyricist Paulo Cesar Pinheiro, raises questions about authorship and the use of traditional material in popular music contexts.[3] Around the same time, Gilberto Gil's "Domingo no Parque" (Sunday in the Park) draws upon the berimbau's status as a publicly legitimized national folkloric instrument.[4] His local status enabled Gil to incorporate non-Brazilian musical elements and instruments into his composition—an aspect that was vigorously contested by radical audience members. By the late 1980s, the berimbau's image in Brazilian popular music suggested more than a physical instrument, as demonstrated in Carlinhos Brown's "Meia-Lua Inteira" (Full Half-Moon), recorded by Caetano Veloso, and another composition entitled "Berimbau" produced by the musical ensemble Olodum.

Bossa Nova and a Modernizing Brazil

Although bossa nova is celebrated today as a Brazilian musical treasure, the genre was not always received with open arms, due to its prominent influences from North American jazz music. Brazilian music critics and cultural nationalists like José Ramos Tinhorão launched scathing attacks in the mid-1960s on bossa nova composers as musicians who did not properly know how to feel the subtleties and swing of Afro-Brazilian rhythmic syncopation.[5] He suggested that these composers could not be true carriers of Brazilian national musical traditions. In an extreme example, he portrayed bossa nova composers as culturally bastardized children from Rio de Janeiro's wealthy southern beach neighborhoods that were influenced by North American music and culture. He believed that, because these composers did not know their own roots, bossa nova betrayed its Brazilian musical traditions.[6]

Issues and debates surrounding bossa nova and cultural authenticity mirrored Brazil's struggles as a nation.[7] The government of president

Juscelino Kubitschek (1956–60) undertook an ambitious modernization policy, in which the goal was to achieve the progress of fifty years in only five.[8] Kubitschek's largest project included the design and construction of a new capital, Brasília, located in the state of Goiás in Brazil's heartland. This architecturally planned modernist Federal District was conceived as a means to draw the overpopulated coastal populations towards the center of the country. As a result of this rapid industrialization, financed in large part with foreign loans and investment, Brazil's inflation rate increased dramatically. Kubitschek encouraged the importation of foreign products, which began to affect trade imbalances, and highlighted inequities between Brazil and industrialized countries. Brazil imported finished products, such as industrial machinery and consumer items, and exported raw materials, including agricultural and mineral resources.[9]

Accompanying this wave of ideological optimism of a modernizing Brazilian society was an ideologically leftist national cultural organization, the Centro Popular de Cultura (CPC, the People's Center for Culture). The CPC was developed as an arts-based revolutionary organization that strove to effect social change while attempting to reduce Brazil's dependency on foreign economic influences. The CPC was founded under the auspices of the National Student Union (MNU), and was modeled after a literacy movement in the impoverished northeastern state of Pernambuco. Enhanced with participation from prominent poets, filmmakers, dramaturges, and musicians, the two principal ideological goals of this movement evolved into culturally contested national debates of Brazilianness versus foreign influences. The CPC did not appeal to the masses, in large part due to its paternalistic and condescending attitudes of "enlightenment" toward its intended audience.[10]

Brazil's modernist aspirations can be seen in the rise of bossa nova music in the late 1950s and early 1960s. Bossa nova musicians were interested in creating a new style of music that represented their interpretation of Brazil's changing society. Composers wanted to distance this new style from the singing traditions established by the samba canção recording artists in the early 1950s. The samba singers modeled their vocal production after the Italian bel canto singing style, which featured a loud volume and a wide vibrato. In contrast, the bossa nova singing style presented a softly delivered melody with little or no vibrato. Aesthetically, bossa nova musicians were not interested in creating authentic reproductions of samba music, as North American jazz musicians such as Frank Sinatra, Sarah Vaughan, Stan Getz, and Miles Davis influenced them. As a result, bossa nova became a product representative of this emerging modern Brazilian national culture.[11]

In 1964 a repressive military government took power in a coup, and ruled until 1985. The regime implemented economic reforms that led to a six-year boom, with annual growth averaging greater than ten percent, which was dubbed Brazil's "economic miracle."[12] Through consolidation of various communications and cultural entities, the government established EMBRATEL (Empresa Brasileira de Telecomunicações [National Telecommunications Company]), EMBRATUR (Empresa Brasileira de Turismo [National Tourism Company]), and the Campanha de Defesa do Folclore Brasileiro (Campaign in Defense of Brazilian Folklore), all in the mid-1960s, which enabled military leaders to assert their influence beyond public view. A combination of government pressure and fragmented ideological disputes effectively disbanded the CPC's and the MNU's progressive organizational base.

In the mid-1960s the rise of television and the continued presence of radio ensured that popular music would become the most accessible cultural vehicle for reaching Brazil's masses. This is one of the primary reasons why Brazilian popular music drew heavy attention from government censors. While bossa nova represented a sophisticated modern music, popular protest songs began to emerge in the mid-1960s that projected working-class musical resistance by drawing on regional musical traditions, such as samba, *samba de roda* (ring samba), and the berimbau, which musically represented capoeira's origins in resistance to slavery, as well as being an organic Brazilian product that had been cultivated from national soil. The incorporation of these raw musical traditions into this newer musical framework was designed to restore a "national-popular authenticity to the song of political protest, against the imported, 'Americanized' culture which bossa nova and increasingly rock, were held to represent."[13]

Although the CPC had been officially disbanded, ideological themes were set in motion that moved beyond an official political structure, and became a core component in constructing and manipulating definitions of brasilidade within popular artistic expression. Musical experiments like bossa nova featured musical hybrids that synthesized visible

Brazilian musical influences and superimposed them on other Brazilian as well as non-Brazilian musical structures.

Brazilian Popular Music Festivals

The rise of televised music festivals offered another venue for themes of the berimbau and capoeira to be incorporated into mainstream Brazilian culture. Beginning on São Paulo television stations in 1964, popular music festivals became nationally broadcast events that redefined boundaries of Brazilian music and culture. In 1966 the first Festival Internacional de Canção (FIC) (International Song Festival), held in Rio de Janeiro, was designed to internationally promote Brazilian music and Rio as the "world capital of popular music."[14] These festivals soon became a cultural competition between Rio and São Paulo. The military regime that took power in 1964 viewed the FIC as an opportunity to promote Brazil's potential to use popular music as a refined export commodity. Moreover, the festival was used by the military regime as a means to portray Brazil as a politically stable tropical paradise—while, at the same time, student opposition groups used this medium as a way to promote political ideals to a commercial audience.

The Brazilian song festival format structure was modeled on the Italian San Remo song festival. The FIC was divided into two categories (international and national), as a means to draw established international singers. Public reaction was often most pronounced when popular opinion contradicted the official results, leading the III Festival de MPB to become frequently referred to in the press as the *festivaia* (festival of boos).[15] This formula was successful until 1968, when the government heavily censored participating entries at the festival. Abuses of the censorship resulted in many artists being exiled from Brazil.

The popularity of Brazilian music festivals reflected the synthesis of a developing televised media distribution network in tandem with a greater understanding of youth culture. By receiving instant feedback, the culture producers (artists) and the culture moderators (audience members and government-sponsored judges) produced a system in which traditional elements like capoeira and the berimbau could be incorporated into debates about contested national space and identity.

Baden Powell, *Afro Sambas*, and "Berimbau"

Baden Powell de Aquino, the composer of the bossa nova tune "Berim-bau," was born in 1937, and was one of the preeminent Brazilian guitar-ists and popular music composers of the 1960s. Baden's father was the director of the Brazilian Boy Scouts (*Escoteiros de Varre-Sai*), and named him after Lord Robert Baden Powell (an Englishman who founded the Boy Scouts).[16] The young Powell's father was also a classically trained vio-linist, and their Rio de Janeiro home was often a meeting place for *choro* musicians, including the legendary artists Donga and Pixinguinha.[17] At thirteen years of age, Powell worked at Rádio Nacional as a guitar ac-companist to various artists, and was a regular participant at informal samba de roda celebrations on the hill of Mangueira, the location of Rio's oldest and most famous samba school.

Powell became a prominent bossa nova composer whose compositions are now part of the standard repertoire, but he achieved only moderate success in Brazil; he gained broader international recognition in Europe, where he lived for many years. His most successful collaborations were with Vinícius de Moraes, beginning in the early 1960s, and with Paulo César Pinheiro in the late 1960s. As an instrumentalist, his performance style combines aspects from many traditions. Music critic Tárik de Souza described Powell as a musician who "combined the energy of a flamenco guitarist, who possessed the technical aptitude of a choro musician, and who had the rhythmic feel of someone who attended a lot of *samba de roda* celebrations."[18] His compositions blended aspects of early samba traditions with more complex harmonies of modern-sounding bossa nova, without becoming formulaic representations.

Between 1962 and 1966, Powell and de Moraes jointly composed a series of songs called *Afro sambas*, most of which were released in a 1966 recording entitled *Os Afro Sambas*. Speaking about the inspira-tion for the Afro sambas, Powell suggested: "Afro is all of Brazil. It's within the people."[19] Thematic material was derived from Afro-Brazil-ian cultural and religious practices and made use of descriptive titles such as "Samba da Benção" (Blessing Samba),[20] "Canto pra Ossanha" (Song for Ossanha, a spirit of medicinal plants within candomblé), and "Berimbau." The composition of "Berimbau" was a decisive point in the "history of popular Brazilian music, [regarding] the adoption of the beat and song of capoeira. 'Berimbau' was and continues to be a success, recorded and rerecorded by famous interpreters and this was the stimulus for new compositions within this theme."[21] Powell believes that his compositions were "stigmatized" by the descriptive label "Afro sambas," imposed by the media, that in his opinion did not constitute an entirely new musical genre.[22] He clarifies that the Afro sambas are a type of samba, like the *samba lento* (slow samba), *samba canção* (song samba), *samba carnaval, samba choro*, and the *samba lamento* (lamenting samba), and he considers Afro sambas to be most closely aligned with the *samba lamento*.

The Afro sambas emerged from a combination of Powell's compositional studies in Rio de Janeiro; a research trip to Bahia; and his increased interest in Afro-Brazilian music and culture. Vinícius de Moraes believes that Powell increased the "Afro" element in the Afro samba compositions by drawing from the rhythmic roots of popular Brazilian music. This effectively provided a regional Rio de Janeiro–based influence of Afro-Brazilian musical expression that was partially based in Bahian culture because he turned his compositional antennas "to recent Bahia and to ancestral Africa."[23]

Around 1962 Powell met Bahian sculptor Mário Cravo Jr., who introduced him to the berimbau and demonstrated a few toques representative of the capoeira tradition. Powell soon began accumulating life experience in Afro-Brazilian culture, resulting in the composition "Berimbau."[24] Powell's interest in Afro-Brazilian culture led him to the well-known Bahian capoeira master Canjiquinha, who initially rebuffed him by suggesting that he instead attend a capoeira presentation at a downtown Salvador nightclub to learn about his craft. Powell responded that he would prefer the confines of Canjiquinha's house, as the setting would be more authentic.[25] Later in this discussion, someone produced a guitar, leading Canjiquinha to have a change of heart. Biographer Dominique Dreyfus states that at this moment, "Canjiquinha brought the gold. [He] began to sing and tell everything to Powell. He told him the history of the berimbau, that later inspired [Powell] to compose 'Berimbau,' the music that turned this into the most well known instrument in Brazil. . . . [In this song] Powell translates to perfection the harmonies of capoeira songs and the sound of the berimbau."[26] Canjiquinha also exposed Powell to ceremonies at candomblé temples and various capoeira exhibitions. Powell later confided to Rego that he had no direct contact with any capoeiristas prior to his meeting with Canjiquinha.[27]

Journalist and biographer Ruy Castro suggests that Powell might have composed "Berimbau" prior to visiting Bahia.[28] He posits that all of Powell's material came from recordings instead of firsthand experience, raising questions whether or not this material had been composed from a distance. Perhaps Castro developed this concept from de Moraes's comments in the *Afro Sambas* recording liner notes, which referenced a folkloric recording of sambas de roda, candomblé songs, and capoeira music that served as a basis for many of their musical ideas.[29] A late 1990s interview with Powell sheds light on many elements that came together that inspired what he saw, heard and felt when he was motivated to compose "Berimbau."

> When I heard the berimbau, I was emotional. I thought that it was a marvelous thing, because I heard the berimbau on the *praia de Amaralina* (Amaralina Beach), 9:00 at night, almost in complete darkness—an extremely important capoeira fight. I think it was two people fighting for valor . . . , and I was [thinking about] that . . . the feel of a ballet, the noise from the sea, nocturnal. . . . And I took a toque of the berimbau that goes "don don dein, don don dih." I took and assimilated the sound of the berimbau on the guitar and wrote a beautiful melody remembering that nocturnal seaside, thus very much representative of Bahia.[30]

In a related article, Powell describes the feeling and historical significance of what he perceives as the essence of Bahia: "When I go there, I stay very still. . . . I sit down in a plaza at night . . . and it feels as if I'm sitting within history. . . . I begin to live all of the history. This for a composer is a beautiful thing! It's not what I see, it's what I feel, you know? The Afro sambas are my strongest side as a composer [and] instrumentalist. . . . When the guitar is tuned really low, it remembers Bahia."[31] It is clear that Powell's use of berimbau melodic rhythms on his guitar are intended to evoke the spirit of capoeira. What also becomes clear is that "Berimbau" represents Powell's personal vision of Afro-Brazilian history and how it connects with Bahia as a sacred space. By tuning his guitar lower, it creates a buzzing timbre, a musical aesthetic that is a characteristic component of musical instruments from several African cultures.

This is yet another way in which Powell invokes essences of Africa within the musical structure.

Also in the early 1960s, Powell studied compositional techniques in Rio de Janeiro with Moacyr Santos, one of the premier arrangers in Brazil, and César Guerra-Peixe, a composer, arranger, conductor, and musicologist.[32] As a component of Powell's training, he was given composition exercises based on the seven Greek modes, the liturgical modes of the Gregorian chants. During these studies, he perceived a similarity between the Afro-Brazilian and Gregorian chants. "I began to work on a type of samba that was more black, which had a lament close to the African chants and which appeared [similar to] the Gregorian chants. The same ones that even the Jesuits taught the indigenous people in [northeastern Brazil]. Because of this, northeastern music has a scale with a lowered fifth, as do the Gregorian Chants."[33]

Powell developed thematic material for the Afro sambas from his Bahian research trips, as well as "a live folkloric recording of sambas de roda and songs from candomblé, with various exhibitions of berimbau in its diverse rhythmic modalities."[34] "Berimbau" was the first Afro samba composition; released in 1963, its theme centered on capoeira and the musical bow. The principal contribution of "Berimbau" to Brazilian popular music has been derived from Powell's adaptation for guitar of a capoeira-related berimbau melodic-rhythmic theme.[35] This musical trope has been a major component of Brazilian popular music for several decades. On the surface, it appears that Powell's goal was merely to imitate the sound of the berimbau's melodic rhythms, but a deeper analysis of his compositional process reveals structural characteristics of Powell's compositional motif in relation to berimbau performance practice within the capoeira tradition and its adaptation to the bossa nova genre. This analysis suggests that Powell drew his material directly from a single berimbau playing the capoeira toque (melodic-rhythmic motif) commonly known as Angola.[36]

Powell transformed the berimbau's melodies and rhythms into a theme that could be performed on the guitar, by creating a low E pedal tone, supported by an E minor 7/11 chord alternating with an F# minor 11 chord. This passage features a jump from the E to the F# minor chord twice in the first two measures, but does not return to the final F# chord until a syncopated rhythmic interaction is introduced in the

third measure and first half of the fourth measure. This is supported by a
melodic line repeating the word "berimbau" (see T 2.1).[37]

Transcription 2.1: Baden Powell's adaptation of the berimbau for the guitar (Powell 1963-disc)

. This musical example has become a standard trope of the berimbau
in Brazilian popular music, and has been extended to the entire musical
ensemble, with the instruments of the lower register playing an E pedal,
and the instruments of the higher registers playing either the higher guitar or vocal lines. Powell's recordings begin with the above theme and
immediately depart to a series of variations, rarely returning to the basic
motif. Two general characteristics of his improvisations on this theme
feature the removal of the tied notes at the end of the first and second
measure, as well as a displacement of the bass line by one eighth note in
the second and third measures (see T 2.2).[38]

Transcription 2.2: Variation of berimbau motif (Various artists 2001-disc)

It is highly probable that Powell encountered capoeira musical ensembles that featured multiple berimbaus during his research trip to Bahia. If
this is the case, a comparison of Powell's material with a fragment of the
Angola capoeira toque played by three berimbaus may demonstrate how
Powell conceived this theme for use on the guitar (see T 2.3). Although
it is possible for other composers to have witnessed capoeira firsthand
and created their own compositions based on a similar theme, the international success of bossa nova and of Powell's "Berimbau" certainly must
have factored significantly into this process.

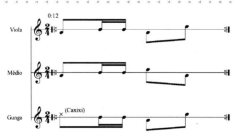

Transcription 2.3: "Angola for Three Berimbaus" (Grupo de Capoeira Angola Pelourinho 1996-disc)

Transcription 2.4: Analysis of the Toque de Capoeira Angola (D'Anunciação 1990a)

Using Luiz D'Anunciação's analysis of berimbau toques within capoeira, Powell's theme has been constructed from a combination of the "Motif with the Addition of the Repique" (see T 2.4 measure 1 and "Motif with Addition of Repique") and a "Classic Variation" (see T 2.4 measures three and four and "Classic Variation").[39] The basic motif consists of the theme reduced to its minimal structure (as in T 2.4).

In general, this motif is elaborated upon, and these ornaments all support and reinforce the rhythmic ostinato without breaking its flow. These elaborations of the motif include the addition of the repique (buzz stroke) and the basic variation. A combination of the motif with the repique and basic variation establishes the *toque de centro* (central beat). A "classic variation" tends to temporarily interrupt the smooth flow of the ostinato, without interrupting the continuity of the overall time cycle. Analysis of Powell's adoption of berimbau melodic-rhythmic material reveals that he has drawn on two specific berimbau compositional elements from the capoeira tradition: a "motif with repique" which is repeated, followed by a "classic variation."

By drawing upon the berimbau's melodic rhythms on his guitar, Powell evokes the spirit of capoeira. He views capoeira as a means to settle a dispute of valor, which then explains why he approaches the opening passage to "Berimbau" as an active dance between two chords.

"Lapinha"

Powell experienced a different reaction to some of his compositions in the late 1960s. Although he followed compositional processes similar to those he developed for his Afro-Sambas and "Berimbau," the song "Lapinha" created controversy that circulated in the Brazilian press. "Lapinha" presents a case study for examining issues of authorship and authenticity, as well as the role of popular song festivals in affecting public perception in the late 1960s. It bears repeating that these festivals provided a space in which brasilidade was defined and interpreted among three principal groups: composers, the audience, and official festival judges. Since "Lapinha" won first place in a national music festival, it appears that Powell's participation in this festival may have sparked most of the controversy surrounding the song. "Lapinha" is set to a fast samba rhythm, and is comprised of newly composed verses, with a chorus that has been directly taken from the capoeira song genre. This instability of the acceptance and/or rejection of capoeira thematic material possibly can also be attributed to tensions among capoeira practitioners from different regions in Brazil.

In 1968 the first and only Primeira Bienal do Samba (First Samba Biennial) was an invitation-only music festival sponsored by *TV Record* in São Paulo. When festival organizers invited Powell, they assumed that he would bring his longtime collaborator Vinícius de Moraes. Instead, he brought a young unknown lyricist, Paulo César Pinheiro. The festival jury initially rejected Powell's partnership with Pinheiro, but finally allowed the duo to participate, due in large part to Powell's potential box-office draw as a prestigious guitarist and composer. After his appearance, charges of plagiarism appeared in São Paulo newspapers, accusing Powell of stealing from the capoeira tradition. Powell publicly responded in another newspaper article by claiming that the song merely cited a refrain of Bahian folklore.[40] These public exchanges raised questions about

Powell's use of capoeira thematic material, specifically whether or not he was correctly attributing authorship, and more pointedly, stealing and profiting from the tradition. A February 1968 interview with Powell notes that "'Lapinha' is a song which is simple, harmonious, has good lyrics, is nice to sing and has something that the people like: a strong refrain."[41] In this interview, months before the music festival, there is no mention of this "strong refrain" coming directly from the capoeira tradition.

"Lapinha" is based on the legend of Besouro Mangangá (Sorcerer Beetle), believed to be one of the greatest capoeiristas of all time. He was a valiant man, defender of women and the persecuted, and according to legend, he confronted entire troops of mounted police by himself.[42] Besouro was betrayed by a lover, and upon his death, his spirit began to roam and invade the minds of capoeiristas who became possessed by the sound of his war cry, "zum-zum-zum," a command that directed them to do things that they could not later remember.[43] The only way they could break this curse was to sing a song. A São Paulo newspaper article cited the lyrics of this song, suggesting that "by coincidence," it had a beginning exactly like Baden Powell's "Lapinha":

E quando eu morrê	When I die
Oi, me enterre na Lapinha	Bury me in Lapinha
Chapéu de Panamá,	'Panama hat,
Paletó almofadinha	Soft, fancy clothes[44]

Powell's principal responses to charges of plagiarism suggested that he continued the same compositional path established in Brazil by Heiter Villa-Lobos, and that folkloric themes belonged to the public domain. He also asserted that "if a composer wants to use a folkloric theme, it would be better for folklore, since . . . it gains a new force and ends up being well known in a different region from which it was born and lived."[45]

In a counterattack directed at São Paulo–based capoeira practitioners, as opposed to supposedly more knowledgeable ones from Bahia, he added that "only the São Paulo capoeiristas think that this is plagiarism."[46] Drawing upon his previous compositional successes, Powell continued: "when I composed a theme based on the beat and sound of the berimbau, up to then, no one had remembered this musical instrument, whose sound is the most authentic Brazilian sound, if and only if we could say that Brazilian sound existed."[47] Powell acknowledged the sound of the berimbau as a culturally authentic sonority that has become a national icon while simultaneously challenging the possibility that a sound could be associated with a national ideology. He defends his use of traditional material to make his work particularly Brazilian while he dismisses notions of an "authentic Brazilian sound."

Powell's final rebuttal to his critics in the São Paulo press cited a definition of the term *folclore* from the Aurélio Buarque de Hollanda dictionary (the most comprehensive dictionary of the Brazilian Portuguese language), and a quote from North American composer Leonard Bernstein.[48] Powell suggested that uninformed music critics should educate themselves about folklore, and advised them of an upcoming course offered by César Guerra-Peixe in Rio de Janeiro. Attacks on Powell also came from Canjiquinha, his Bahian capoeira informant, who recalled that Powell was particularly interested in the song about Lapinha, and he repeatedly inquired about obtaining rights to the song. He states that Powell "asked me how much the songs cost, saying that he could pay, but only a little, since he didn't have any money. I said that they didn't cost anything, because they weren't mine. I only asked that he note that these are the songs that Canjiquinha sung to him, to say that they were from folklore. He then promised me that if he were to ever use them, he would put on the record that I had related the music to him."[49]

Canjiquinha claimed that he did not want to personally profit from the song, but he did want the proper origin of the song to be credited. He continued that, due to the brevity of capoeira songs, they are sung one after another, and that "the song of Besouro has nothing to do with the Largo da Lapinha" in Salvador, since Besouro was from Santo Amaro da Purificação,[50] and "almost never came to Salvador."[51] Canjiquinha's comments appeared in the press throughout the next few years, publicly claiming that he was fighting for the rights of Bahian folklore, although clearly advocating for his own importance as well as the process of transmission from within the capoeira tradition.

What Are the Roots of "Lapinha"?

"Lapinha" simultaneously draws from the capoeira song tradition and from popular urban musical styles from Rio de Janeiro, where Powell was located. Powell's "Lapinha" is divided into three principal sections that correspond with alternate versions. The first section begins with an initial chorus that is comprised of the first two stanzas, each repeated (see T 2.5A). It then presents a through-composed verse, which is not included in the musical transcription. The second section bids farewell to Besouro and Bahia (see T 2.5B), and the third section consists of a tag line added at the end (see T 2.5C). Powell's version of "Lapinha" features syncopated rhythms that accentuate the first or second beat of each measure. This is a commonly employed compositional technique within the genre of samba. The first chorus and verse of Powell's "Lapinha" are sung by a solo voice, and upon return to the chorus, a group of voices joins the refrain. In general, the tempo gradually increases, and dramatically speeds up in the last two sections.

Transcription 2.5: "Lapinha" by Powell and Pinheiro (Various artists 1968-disc)[52]

The three principal sections outlined above appear in the following version of "Lapinha" by mestre Pastinha and his academy.[53] Since this recording was produced after the success of Baden Powell's "Lapinha," it is possible that Pastinha's arrangement is the result of consumer expectations due to the popularity of Powell's recording. Nevertheless, it provides a contrast between Powell's version and how this song would be performed within a capoeira context (see T 2.6).

This song features less syncopation than Powell's version. The entire form is sung by a lead solo voice, and the choral response only appears in the final section. This demonstrates how Powell's version was designed to evoke the solo and group call-and-response, although this occurs over the span of an entire chorus. In contrast, capoeira call-and-response sections alternating between the leader and group, tend to feature interaction in much smaller sections.

Transcription 2.6: Mestre Pastinha's version of "Lapinha" (Pastinha 1969-disc)

Other capoeira songs that are similar to "Lapinha" include a recording by mestre Traíra in the late 1950s, and a closely related version by mestre Suassuna.[54] The version presented by mestre Traíra demonstrates a likely source that inspired Powell's interest in the legend of Besouro during his research trip to Bahia.

Quando eu morrer	When I die
Não quero gritar nem mistério	I don't want crying or secret rites
Quero o berimbau tocando	I want a berimbau playing
Na porta do cemetério	At the gate of the cemetery

Uma fita amarela	A yellow ribbon
Gravada com o nome dela	Engraved with her name
Que ainda depois da morte e o homem	And still after death is the man
Chamou cordão de ouro	Called the golden belt
O melhor nome	The best name
Besouro, Cordão de ouro	Besouro, the golden belt
O melhor nome	The best name
Cordão de ouro	*Cordão de ouro*[55]

Although this song is about Besouro and a funeral, it is quite different from the song presented in the previous two examples. Here a berimbau plays at the gate of the cemetery, perhaps in a nod to the tradition in which the berimbau is played at the funeral for some capoeira practitioners. A similar version of this song appears on a recording by mestre Suassuna (see T 2.7):

Quando eu morrer, disse Besouro	When I die, said Besouro
Quando eu morrer, disse Besouro	When I die, said Besouro
Não quero choro nem vela	I don't want crying or a candle
tambem não quero barulho	I also don't want a lot of noise
na porta do cemitério.	At the gate of the cemetery
Eu quero meu berimbau	I want my berimbau
eu quero meu berimbau	I want my berimbau
com uma fita amarela	With a yellow ribbon
gravado com o nome dela	Engraved with her name
E o meu nome	And my name
é Besouro	**It's Besouro**
E como é meu nome?	What is my name?
é Besouro	**It's Besouro**[56]

This song is similar to the previous ones in that it features the same ascending melodic line at the beginning, as well as the same group response at the end. The middle section is somewhat different, although the general theme about Besouro and death is still prominent.

In the 1990s capoeira scholar Greg Downey became particularly interested in this song about Besouro within a capoeira context, since it

Transcription 2.7: "Quando eu Morrer Disse Besouro" (Suassuna and Dirceu 1975-disc)

was one of the most popular songs among novice capoeiristas.[57] What perplexed him was that this song did not conform to commonly practiced song structures exhibited within the Grupo Capoeira Angola do Pelourinho (GCAP), a capoeira association that has taken a leading role in shaping capoeira performance practice in Brazil and the United States.[58] In many traditional *ladainhas* (introductory songs), the dance is stopped while the mestre sings an extended solo verse, followed by a *chula* (an extensive salutatory call-and-response section), which leads into a succession of *corridos* (short call-and-response songs) that accompany the dance. Downey considers the capoeira song "E Besouro" to be a *quadra* (a type of ladainha that features an extended verse), in which the dance continues without interruption. Moreover, this song moves directly to a call-and-response section that closely resembles the corridos, thus bypassing the chula section. As a result, Downey believes that "E Besouro" is a quadra text, modified and sung by members of GCAP with the melodic inflection and rhythmic structure of a ladainha, but still retaining the call-and-response ending not associated with ladainhas." He cites examples of this anomaly, ranging from individual preference in that it is "shorter and simpler than other ladainhas," to contemporary practitioners' imitation of mestre Traíra's recording of this song (cited above). He concludes that "E Besouro" provides "evidence that the solemnity and pacing that many *angoleiros* [capoeira Angola practitioners] consider traditional orthopraxy may not have been pervasive formerly in the rodas of capoeira."[59]

I believe that there may be another reason for this structural departure from capoeira performance practice. The song represented by the three previous examples (Pastinha, Traíra, and Suassuna) exhibits strong connections to another song not derived from the capoeira tradition: Noel Rosa's "Fita Amarela," a nationally popular samba piece that was composed in Rio de Janeiro in 1932.[60]

"Fita Amarela" was one of more than thirty of Noel Rosa's compositions recorded for the 1933 carnival season (see T 2.8).[61] It was the eleventh most popular song of 1933, in terms of national record sales and radio airplay.[62]

Transcription 2.8: "Fita Amarela" by Noel Rosa (Reis 1932-disc)

This song features the same ascending introductory motif presented in the capoeira songs cited above.

Quando eu morrer	When I die
Não quero choro nem vela	I don't want crying or candles
Quero uma fita amarela	I want a yellow ribbon
Gravada com nome dela	Engraved with her name[63]

These lyrics have been derived from a collective compositional process where samba songs were developed by groups of samba musicians.[64] The notion of music freely passing between individuals and groups was a common practice in Rio's informal samba gatherings in the early twentieth century. It is likely that Rosa's "Fita Amarela" was nationally disseminated through the airwaves of Rio's Rádio Nacional, a station that emerged as a national cultural voice in the 1930s. Although the first registered composition of the samba genre, "Pelo Telefone" (On the Phone), was credited to a single composer in 1917, evidence demonstrates that there were several versions of this song circulating throughout Rio prior to the published recording. Ethnomusicologist Carlos Sandroni demonstrates how authorship from the collective tradition was a common practice in early sambas from Rio. These songs consisted of a refrain, which was acknowledged as the formal composition, supplemented with improvised verses during informal musical encounters. This established a framework that created a vibrant environment for musical challenge competitions.[65] This type of musical interaction can also be seen in North American jazz music, where the basic musical structure enables musicians to play together without prior negotiation or arrangement. A component of this experience included "cutting" contests, where musicians who were able to perform to the highest level were allowed to remain on stage. Therefore, "Fita Amarela" follows a standard practice of early-twentieth-century samba circles, in which a traditional chorus formed the basis of the composition, supplemented by a new verse. As a result, "Fita Amarela" could have easily entered Bahian musical culture through national radio, and subsequently filtered into the capoeira genre as a result of this process.

Additional evidence of interplay between Bahian capoeira song texts and popular culture emerging from Rio de Janeiro highlights an artistic connection between these two regions. Mestre Bola Sete cites the following capoeira song, whose authorship is attributed to the public domain as "folklore."

A melhor coisa do mundo	The best thing in the world
É tocar berimbau	Is to play berimbau
Lá no Rio de Janeiro	There in Rio de Janeiro
Na Rádio Nacional	On *Rádio Nacional*[66]

This song perhaps ironically demonstrates the impact of commercially produced popular culture emerging from Rio de Janeiro and spreading throughout Brazil. The notion of playing the berimbau on *Rádio Nacional* highlights the commercial appeal of certain aspects of Brazilian folklore, therefore enabling berimbau musicians to access a narrowly defined window for national exhibition of their music.[67]

"Lapinha" and "Fita Amarela" are representative of how music has circulated and transformed within formal and informal Brazilian popular musical practices. Although capoeira is a distinct tradition, with instilled codes that govern its boundaries, the carriers of this tradition have not been isolated from Brazilian popular culture. Capoeiristas also performed samba and other genres that were all historically related to African-derived musical expression in Brazil. The uncertain and perhaps circuitous history of the roots of the song that Powell incorporated into "Lapinha" would certainly make an exciting case study in today's debates of legally contested intellectual property rights in the twenty-first century.

The issues surrounding "Lapinha" demonstrate how contrasting cultural and political pressures helped create the controversy. On one hand, Baden Powell was fulfilling the mandates of CPC and Brazilian nationalistic ideologies, by incorporating the country's folkloric expression into modern contexts. On the other hand, because this composition became commercially successful—including public television exposure and an official cultural stamp of approval in the form of festival award—it provoked criticism that Powell was inappropriately co-opting the tradition. Powell's use of folkloric materials was a continuation of compositional processes that were well established at that time. This process followed the ideological mission of the Brazilian modernist movement founded in 1922, as well as subsequent composers like Luiz Gonzaga's 1950s popular music compositions that drew from northeastern folkloric musical genres, such as the *baião*.

Although Baden Powell and Paulo César Pinheiro followed conventional practices of the 1960s, it appears that Powell's accusers had politically motivated reasons, by claiming that he had been stealing from the capoeira tradition. From a legal perspective, this is a baseless claim, since there was no individual copyright holder for the capoeira domain in Bahia. Although Canjiquinha was one of Powell's public accusers, Powell's 1999 biography briefly discusses, and quickly dismisses the controversy sparked by "Lapinha" as a smear campaign instigated by the organizers of the São Paulo festival as a way to discredit Paulo César Pinheiro.[68]

In the mid-1990s, near the end of his life, Powell converted to evangelism and refused to perform certain Afro sambas, such as "Canto de Iemanjá" (Song of Iemanjá)[69] and "Samba de Bênção," due to their identification with candomblé. In 1999 Powell revisited Gregorian chant studies for a series of evangelical compositions[70]—another striking example of re-combining and reusing musical compositions. Baden Powell died in September 2000; at his funeral his oldest son picked up Powell's guitar and played "Lapinha," a song that celebrates a capoeirista's passing.[71]

Gilberto Gil and "Domingo no Parque"

"Domingo no Parque" (Sunday in the Park), composed by Gilberto Gil in 1967, drew heavily on the berimbau's status as an iconic Brazilian instrument to create a collage of international and regional musical expressions. Since "Domingo no Parque" was composed a few years after the national popularity of Baden Powell's "Berimbau," the presence of the berimbau in Brazilian popular music was not a groundbreaking event. An important aspect of this composition is the manner in which Gil utilized the berimbau to draw upon familiar elements of Brazilian culture to help integrate distinctive non-Brazilian elements into Brazilian popular music.

Gilberto Gil was born in Salvador, Bahia, in 1942. In the late 1960s, he pioneered the tropicalista movement with Caetano Veloso, which incorporated the use of electric instruments and non-Brazilian elements into popular Brazilian music. As a result of the politically charged ideas conveyed in their music, Veloso and Gil lived in exile in London from 1969 to 1972, although during that time their compositions were recorded in Brazil by other Brazilian singers.

In 1968 Gil submitted "Domingo no Parque" for competition in the III Festival de MPB (Third Festival of Brazilian Popular Music), sponsored by *TV Record* in São Paulo. This festival marked the beginning of a new internationalization phase in Brazilian popular music, as the first Brazilian music festival that included electric instruments. At that time, electric instruments and rock arrangements were often regarded as a capitulation to U.S. cultural imperialism.[72] Also at this festival, Veloso and Gil introduced their concept of *Som Universal* (Universal Sound), a synthesis of popular Brazilian song and the latest developments in international pop.

The III Festival de MPB featured an extremely large number of entries based on northeastern Brazilian themes. This was a result of the success of "Disparada," the winning selection from the previous festival, which featured a mix of musical styles from northeastern Brazil and the interior of São Paulo.[73] "Domingo no Parque" is principally composed as a fusion of two northeastern rhythmic structures: the *baião* and a skeletal fragment of the motif from the capoeira Angola *toque*. *Baião* is a northeastern Brazilian popular music style that features a repeated ostinato as a rhythmic base (see T 2.9 and first measure of T 2.11).

Transcription 2.9: Baião rhythm

For the melodic portion of this piece, Gil borrows a motif from a popular call-and-response capoeira song, "O lê lê," in which the leader sings "O lê lê," and the group responds "La la e la" (see T 2.10 "O Lê Lê"). He borrows the leader's second statement (third measure "O lê lê") to construct a choral response ("É Jo sé") to each of his brief statements (see T 2.10).

Transcription 2.10: Comparison of "O Lê Lê" capoeira song (Grupo de Capoeira Angola 1996-disc) and "Domingo no Parque" (Gil 1968-disc)

"Domingo no Parque" tells a story, set in an amusement park, of three people who form a love triangle. This triangle can be seen as a dramatic representation of the diverse musical influences that Gil combines within this composition. This song was based on Bahian musician Dorival Caymmi's music, whose style features a strong connection to northeastern Brazilian music comprised of guitar and solo voice. Charles Perrone believes "Domingo no Parque" to be one of the earliest works from the "tropicalista cultural phenomenon."[74]

Gil envisioned a mixture of electric and acoustic instruments accompanied by a string orchestra and bound by a Brazilian rhythmic structure. He was influenced by the concept of a rock band/string orchestra arrangement from the Beatles' album *Sergeant Pepper's Lonely Hearts Club Band*.[75] Gil presented the song to the prestigious Quarteto Novo ensemble, featuring musicians Hermeto Pascoal and (percussionist) Airto Moreira, with the hopes that they would perform the song at the festival. Once Gil suggested the addition of the electric guitar, the members of the Quarteto refused to hear any more.

> Airto, the most shocked member of the group, did not permit the explanation to continue. As if he had heard a great blasphemy against the musical beliefs of his group, the percussionist rejected the invitation without giving Gil the smallest chance to argue (ironically, two years later, the purist Airto was in the United States, participating in the fusion experiences with jazz and rock commanded by the trumpet player Miles Davis; and later as a member of the group Weather Report, generally playing in the company of keyboards and electric guitars).[76]

At the suggestion of arranger Rogério Duprat, Gil invited the Beatles-style group Os Mutantes to perform the composition. At first the young musicians were not interested in playing a piece that featured a melodic-rhythmic motif that drew from capoeira, which they felt was "missing something."[77] Although the group was not inspired by the content of the piece, they were attracted to the potential controversy that could occur during the performance. University-age nationalist audience members comprised a portion of the audience at the festival, and they bonded together to support or reject certain compositions. In anticipation of a potential conflict, Gil devised a strategic plan to counteract the negative reaction to the presence of the electric instruments: a prominently featured *"brasileríssimo* [very Brazilian] berimbau, played by the percussionist Dirceu."[78] Gil was correct in his assumptions, as he received strong jeers from the university students in response to the "electric guitar and bass of the Mutantes."[79]

Gil consciously used the deeply rooted significance of the berim-bau to balance his attempts to incorporate non-Brazilian instruments and aesthetics into the fabric of Brazilian popular music. This process drew heavily on notions from Brazil's modernist phase, most notably represented through the writings of Oswald de Andrade in the early 1920s.[80] Andrade's "Manifesto da Poesia Pau Brasil" (Brazilwood Poetry Manifesto) emphasized Brazil as an underdeveloped or primitive culture that consumed refined or civilized products from countries such as the United States.[81] Gil was inherently aware of the implied connection be-tween electric instruments representing North American imperialistic culture. He was so concerned about the staunch nationalistic platform of the hard-line university students that he mocked their ideology by com-menting "Daqui a pouco vão dizer que o berimbau é um instrumento importado" (Before long they're going to say that the berimbau is an imported instrument).[82]

In a more recent version of "Domingo no Parque" released in 1986, Gil incorporated Baden Powell's berimbau trope in the introduction.[83] The berimbau begins by performing the phrase as a solo, then accompa-nies the guitar (see T 2.11).

Transcription 2.11: Introduction of "Domingo no Parque" (Gil 2000-disc)

Although this phrase is not repeated elsewhere in the composition, I am struck by the manner in which the introduction of this song has been reinterpreted to incorporate Baden Powell's trope for a younger genera-tion, who may well believe it originated in Gil's 1968 festival appearance.

"Meia-Lua Inteira"

The berimbau's presence in Brazilian popular music has continued to ex-pand in recent decades. On *Estrangeiro* (1989), Caetano Veloso recorded

"Meia-Lua Inteira" ("Full Half-Moon"), composed by Bahian percussionist Carlinhos Brown. This song follows the popular trend of samba-reggae music pioneered by the blocos afros in Bahia.[84] Veloso mixes the samba-reggae style with a base of traditional capoeira rhythm, reinforced with a pandeiro performing its capoeira-related rhythmic role. A "meia-lua" is a capoeira movement consisting of a sweeping leg kick that begins on one side of the opponent and arcs over his or her head. Continuing the move in the same direction, a second spin turns into a corresponding defense, by sweeping the leg under the opponent's feet. This song has multilayered references to capoeira as a Brazilian commodity that attracts the attention of foreign tourists, but in this instance, it inverts the power base of the "mocking foreigner" by "blowing in a weak man's face." Although there is no physical berimbau in the instrumentation of this musical arrangement, its melodic rhythms are reflected in the lyrics. "São dim don dão, São Bento" makes clear the berimbau's overarching role as an organizational element within the song. Capoeira has two "São Bento" berimbau motifs (São Bento Grande [large] and São Bento Pequeno [small]), each signifying distinct dance movements. Extending this concept, Brown's lyrics suggest that the berimbau's Saint Bento rhythm represents the courthouse judge as well as the marginalized Afro-Brazilian (or fugitive slave).

Saint dim dom dão Saint Bento
Great man of movement
Courthouse gavel
Disappeared deep in the forest
Was caught without any documents
In the "regional" temple [85]

The image of a berimbau simultaneously representing the judge, jury, and accused invokes the notion that the berimbau's power extends to the supernatural realm, and suggests that within the capoeira circle, essences of truth will prevail. (See related examples in chapter 6.) If a person enters the capoeira ring and is not properly prepared for the potential dangers, he or she will be metaphorically "caught" without their "documents." Later in the song, several connections are made between mestre Bimba and the berimbau. The allusion to a "regional" temple foreshadows a connection with mestre Bimba, who developed capoeira regional. The berimbau's music "São dim dom dão São Bento" merges the concept of actual capoeira rhythms with the spiritual essence of mestre Bimba:

> *Bimba berimba, who tells me*
> *A piece of wire, gourd, belly*
> *Saint dim dom dão Saint Bento*
> *Great man of movement*
> *Never was a marginalized vagrant*
> *Disappeared from the plaza in time*
> *Walking against the wind*
> *Over the silver capital.*[86]

The spirit of Bimba becomes the voice of the berimbau, and is recreated every time the rhythms of São Bento are performed within the ritual. Now, in Bimba's afterlife, he watches down upon the city of Salvador and protects those whose hearts follow the true ideals of capoeira regional— Bimba's capoeira descendants.

Olodum and "Berimbau"

In the early 1990s the Bahian *bloco afro* Olodum enlisted the berimbau's service as an active agent in a musical revolution against marginalization, to create connections between the local Bahian context and the broader African diaspora. Originally founded as an annual carnival parading organization, Olodum was reincorporated in the early 1980s to serve as a year-round cultural organization that promoted a socially active agenda. The success of this business enterprise now provides employment to hundreds of full- and part-time workers.[87]

Although the blocos afro have developed from the models of the Rio de Janeiro–based *escolas de samba* (samba schools), some musical instruments have been selectively omitted from these newer ensembles. For example, the pandeiro, a symbol of samba, has been removed from the instrumentation, and the *surdos* (large, cylindrical low-pitched drums) have been afforded a much more prominent position.

This example of localizing national traditions, part of a process that strives to differentiate Bahia from the rest of Brazil, perhaps extends back to 1763, when the capital of Brazil was moved from Salvador to Rio de Janeiro. One distinctive aspect of Bahian culture can be seen in its celebration of Independence Day. Bahian independence is celebrated only in Bahia on July 2nd, in commemoration of the evacuation of Portuguese troops. In contrast, the remainder of Brazil celebrates September 7th as the official day of independence, when Dom Pedro stood on the banks of the Ipiranga river near São Paulo and declared Brazil's independence from Portugal in 1822.[88] This perhaps explains why Bahians incorporated the term *afro* into their samba: to directly connect Bahia to the African diaspora while simultaneously disconnecting itself from culturally dominant parts of the Brazilian nation.[89]

Since Olodum and other carnival-based organizations must keep pace with changing popular culture, three elements are crucial to their continued success: knowledgeable directors; poignant songwriters; and a supportive public. Each year, directors must determine annual themes, select songs, and incorporate aspects of local and global symbolism that support the group's ideologies through artistic expression. These songwriters must succinctly "synthesize these discursive threads into a limited set of symbols," which must relate simultaneously to a broader African diaspora and to a local Bahian culture.[90]

In 1985 Olodum began to produce a yearly composition festival contest called FEMADUM (Festival de Música e Arte do Olodum) as a means to build their repertoire of pan-African-oriented material as well as to provide ideas for the group's annual carnival parade theme. This festival supplements informal rehearsals where new songs are presented to the community on a weekly basis. Each festival edition features a different research theme; winning entries receive the honor of having their music appear on subsequent Olodum recordings. Some songwriters became professionals through this process, as an array of commercial Bahian pop music groups have recorded material developed by the blocos.

The winning song of the 1992 contest was entitled "Berimbau,"[91] composed by Pierre Onassis, Germano Menguel, and Marquinhos. The chorus of this piece begins by naming the individual structural components of the berimbau—wire, wood, and gourd—which are then joined to transform into the berimbau. This is followed by a musical citation of the trope from Baden Powell's "Berimbau." Powell's phrase is modified in two ways: first, the berimbau performs this motif as a call-and-response with the drumming ensemble; and second, the trope is modified with superimposed lyrics derived from a popular capoeira song, "Oi sim, sim, sim, oi não não não" (Oh yes, yes, yes, oh no, no, no). This fusion from various sources thus becomes "Berimbau sim, berimbau não, berimba, berimba berimbau" (Berimbau yes, berimbau no, berimba, berimba, berimbau) (see T 2.12).

Transcription 2.12: Introduction of "Berimbau" (Olodum 1992-disc)

The berimbau is thus used as a springboard into a song that compels listeners to actively engage in issues of black consciousness and pan–African American musical cultures. In this context, "Berimbau" draws upon imagery of the berimbau to evoke associations with a hunter's bow, and then promotes a nonviolent strategy of resistance through the process of making music.

Oh berimbau
Piece of wire, piece of wood
These joined with the gourd and turned into a berimbau

Berimbau yes, berimbau no
Berimba, berimba, berimbau yes,
Berimbau yes,
Berimbau no, berimba, berimba,
berimbau

Oh berimbau
Shake off the dust, Madalena
Scare away the sadness and sing
I am Olodum, who are you?

Come, my love, with Olodum in
this melody [song]
Come, my love, let this
happiness flow
Sharpen your awareness,
color black color black

Leave the evil that surrounds us [alone]
If you defend yourself, the weapon is musical

Singing reggae, singing jazz,
singing blues
I exalt Jah, I say
"Olodum has just arrived"[92]

This song invites the listener to create a sense of self-awareness and fight negative forces through musical interaction. Contrasting symbolism can be seen in lyrics, for example, in the use of the term *negro*, which simultaneously represents positive aspects of black pride and beauty, and negative aspects in relation to racist stigmas. Professor Piers Armstrong explains that these stigmas and valorization "are products of the New World experience—slavery, and biracial or multiracial societies where blacks were disenfranchised by whites—the term *negro* relates to the experience of the diaspora despite its poetic recourse to the Mother Africa figure."[93] He believes that Olodum's use of the terms *negro* and *afro* suggests a unified connection throughout the African diaspora that symbolically relates to the continent of Africa. More specifically, the use of *negro* has replaced the local term *baianidade* (the essence of a uniquely Bahian feeling or cultural construct) that now represents a connection to global urban black cultures, as opposed to a regional distinction. Olodum was initially comprised of individuals with non-mainstream alternative lifestyles, and others who were interested in furthering debates about racist processes in Brazil, resulting in a constituency that was "conceived as an axis of dissident solidarity."[94]

The symbolism of the berimbau's components refers to miscegenation processes in Brazil, where the individual disparate elements join to create a comprehensive Brazilian entity. Moreover, the reference to a musical weapon as self-defense simultaneously suggests primitive associations with the hunter's bow being transformed into a musical bow. This "musical weapon" extends beyond the berimbau and invokes a unified African diaspora by singing reggae, jazz, and blues.

Use of these linguistic codes "suggests a cultural mobility that ranges from African legacy, to Afro-Brazilian experience, and to the global, represented by English, not so much as a language but rather as a stylistic marker of modernity itself, as an alterity in relation to local tradition."[95] In this case, there is a rejection of a national Brazilian identity toward a diasporic ethnic identity.[96] Olodum's use of these symbolic messages in conjunction with the berimbau allows the group to promote their ideological concepts through a myriad of potent images that resonate with the public. By positioning their debate as a celebratory protest against racism and marginalization, Olodum is drawing upon the Bahian imagery of the berimbau to promote a local product in a globalized marketplace, thus taking its place alongside reggae, jazz, and blues.

Chapter 3

Afrocentric Themes of Resistance

Following the transformation of the berimbau's role in Brazilian popular music from the mid-1990s to the present, new musical ensembles have emerged that are based on ideas of resistance. The musical examples in this chapter demonstrate a shift in emphasis from a Brazilian national identity toward an articulation of an empowered Afrocentric identity that has not been able to generate a sustained national political base. This discussion builds upon material presented in chapter 2 that shows a transformative concept of the berimbau's function within Brazilian society. Incorporated into this changing notion of identity, the berimbau continues to portray notions of tradition and history via capoeira, while simultaneously signifying aspects of modernity by its participation in cutting-edge musical trends.[1]

Another distinction of the musical examples in this chapter is that 1960s-era composers like Baden Powell and Gilberto Gil were selective in their use of non-Brazilian musical elements (such as North American jazz and rock) in their compositions. In contrast, contemporary musicians and composers borrow freely from North American music cultures without this type of scrutiny, including the incorporation of English-language titles for their compositions, albums, and names of musical ensembles.

Public dance gatherings that emerged in Rio de Janeiro and later in Salvador in the mid-1970s, offer insight into new ways that North American popular musical styles were incorporated into Brazilian music and culture. These dances were a prominent influence on contemporary black musical expression in Brazil. In recent years, Brazilian funk music has been revitalized, and is now one of the most popular forms of urban musical expression.[2]

The berimbau has served a variety of important roles related to identity in the construction of new musical genres: Brazilian rap and Brazilian electronic dance music. The range of symbolism and meaning that is assigned to the berimbau within these contexts depends largely upon the individual composer's background and experience. Nonetheless, it is clear that, in the following examples, the berimbau is invoked to distinguish several aspects of Brazilian identity within global popular musical genres. The 1960s struggle for civil rights in the United States was an inspiration for marginalized people of African descent throughout the Americas. North American musicians such as James Brown helped spark positive connections among Afro-Brazilians. Over the next few decades, Motown's soul music, and later Jamaican reggae, became incorporated into the social fabric of Brazilian musical resistance.

The Bailes da Pesada and Black Rio

Beginning in the early 1970s, a series of public dance gatherings began a process that led to a national expression of black cultural pride. These dances, initially known as the *bailes cariocas* (Rio de Janeiro–based dances)[3] and *bailes da pesada* (heavy dances), were popularized in Rio de Janeiro and later spread to São Paulo, Belo Horizonte, and Salvador. These dances were initially held at nightclubs in Rio's wealthier *zona sul* (southern zone) neighborhoods, and featured an eclectic mix of rock, pop, and North American soul music recordings, highlighting artists such as James Brown and Kool and the Gang. Following the success of these dances, other *equipes* (disk jockey/sound system groups) were formed and began to play in Rio's lower class *zona norte* (northern zone). Although some of these groups chose names like Revolução da Mente (Revolution of the Mind, inspired by James Brown), Black Power, and Soul Grand Prix, these dances were not exclusively directed at black consumers. By the mid-1970s, some of these groups began projecting images of North American black musical artists, sports figures, and record covers on the walls during the dances. In 1976 a newspaper article about these dances appeared in the *Jornal do Brasil*, entitled "Black Rio—The (Imported) Pride to be Black."[4] Following this publication, these soul dances became known as Black Rio. References to it soon began to appear in the lyrics of Gilberto Gil, and its imagery was co-opted by factions of the Brazilian black movement. In 1977 black activist Carlos Alberto Medeiros declared that the process of wearing stylized clothes and dancing to soul music did not address issues related to basic standards of living. Nonetheless, the dances began a process of cultural recuperation for people of African descent, who had been stripped of their identities as they were dispersed throughout the Americas. By expressing group unity through music, they were able to overcome previously insurmountable individual challenges.[5] Medeiros's observation suggests that the meanings associated with this movement transcended fashion styles and served to construct and reinforce ties to Afro-Brazilian or pan-African unity.

When Afro-Brazilians began to adopt related fashion styles such as large afro hairstyles, known as Black Power hairdos, and dashiki clothing, they were denounced as "un-Brazilian" and "implicitly antinationalist."[6] Anthropologist Peter Fry observed that these dances represented a "movement of great importance in the process of forming black identity in Brazil."[7]

Carlos Negreiros—an Afro-Brazilian musician from Rio de Janeiro who has performed with highly acclaimed musicians and ensembles including Milton Nascimento[8] and the Orquestra Afro Brasileira—actively participated in the *bailes da pesada* in the mid-1970s. He recalls that audiences listened to songs in English. Since the majority of participants spoke only Portuguese, they were under the impression that this music was "something revolutionary, [which] brought revolutionary attitudes and emotions with it."[9] In response to the energy from this music, audiences shouted aggressively, raised their fists above their heads and joined in the spirit of protest. They assumed the lyrics discussed heated topics related to the North American struggle for civil rights, but they later discovered that many of these were actually love songs, with content such as "my lover left me, and I'm going to go and get her in my car."[10] Negreiros recalls that the Brazilian recording industry observed this process, and began to issue new material with songs composed "in Portuguese that responded to the expectation that [Brazilians] had when [they] heard the music."[11]

The first Black Rio albums were produced in 1976 and featured popular artists such as União Black, Gerson King Combo, Robson Jorge, Rosa Maria, Tim Maia, and Tony Tornado.[12] With the exception of a

few artists like Tim Maia, the Black Rio movement was quickly surpassed by disco fever in the recording industry and nightclubs in the
late 1970s.

The Black Rio movement spread to other urban centers in Brazil, particularly Belo Horizonte, Minas Gerais, and Salvador. Symbols associated with North American soul music began to be utilized as a means
to create local expression, especially in the case of the blocos afro in Salvador.[13] In his study of the Bahian carnival, Antonio Risério most likely
provided the first documentation of the impact of Black Rio on the development of the first bloco afro, Ilê Aiyê, in 1974. Jorge Watusi, one of
Ilê Aiyê's founders, makes a comparison between the *bailes da pesada* in
Rio de Janeiro and the dances that transpired later in Salvador. He suggests that there was more commercialization in Rio, due to a lack of participants connected to the roots of black culture, whereas in Bahia, black
consciousness was expressed through fashion styles. With the passage
of time, fashion became less important and, following the creation of
Ilê Aiyê, a "more realistic Afro-Brazilian orientation" emerged.[14] Watusi
is suggesting that Salvador presents a more authentic portrayal of black
Brazilian culture (as opposed to Rio de Janeiro), thus emphasizing regional superiority over a cultural center that had traditionally dominated
cutting-edge Brazilian musical and cultural production. Successful results from Olodum's and Ilê Aiyê's visible grounding in Bahian popular
culture demonstrate how these groups have created a regional identity
that has distinguished itself from the established Brazilian national cultural models developed in Rio de Janeiro and São Paulo.

Since the mid-1980s various aspects of Afro-Brazilian culture have
undergone a rebuilding process, aided in part by new economic opportunities that offered upward social mobility for a broader spectrum of
the population.[15] Moreover, events such as the 1988 centennial commemoration of the abolition of slavery helped focus national media attention
on Afro-Brazilian cultural issues.

In 1995 the state of Rio de Janeiro declared an annual holiday known
as National Black Consciousness Day. This holiday pays homage to Zumbi, the last king of the Quilombo dos Palmares, Brazil's largest maroon
colony of escaped slaves in the late 1600s.[16] During the celebration of this
holiday in 2000, many middle-class Brazilians in Rio de Janeiro conveyed
to me their frustration with the needless abundance of holidays (such

as this particular day) that limited their access to financial and other legal transactions. They perceived that an excessive number of holidays was one of many reasons for Brazil's continued economic problems. Although I experienced many of these extended weekend holidays in Brazil, this particular holiday was frequently singled out as an unnecessary commemorative event.[17]

Samba Reggae and Reggae

The blocos afro promote themes of black consciousness, principally through the musical genre samba reggae, which has been influenced in part by concepts and aesthetics related to Jamaican reggae. Antonio J. V. dos Santos Godi suggests that "reggae is a cultural expression of a localized disorder . . . with its own temporal and territorial context" and is no longer confined to the borders of Jamaica.[18] Since reggae is now produced, disseminated, and consumed in many countries outside of Jamaica, it has come to represent newly defined local expressions as well. In Bahia, the term *reggae* is now used to signify "party," meaning both a musical genre and a pleasurable lifestyle.[19]

Reggae took hold in Bahian culture through the establishment of reggae bars in the working-class black neighborhoods of Maciel-Pelourhinho in the 1970s. This was where some groups held their rehearsals, as well as where alternative artists and black militants congregated. At this time, reggae was "regarded as a marginal cultural movement."[20] In 1979, the year of Olodum's founding, musician Gilberto Gil released "Não Chore Mais" (Don't Cry Anymore), a Portuguese-language version of Bob Marley's "No Woman, No Cry" that became associated with the struggle to end the rule of Brazil's military dictatorship. Following this song's success, Brazilian-produced reggae was sung "in clear Portuguese" and became popular on the airwaves.[21]

Reggae became strongly interlinked in Bahia with the *Movimento Negro Unificado* (Unified Black Movement) following the death of Bob Marley on May 11, 1981. Prior to this time, May 13 signified the commemoration of the abolition of slavery in 1888. Godi suggests that this new celebration (May 11) emerged as a result of a "mass-mediated and globalized cultural context" that was established through Afrocentric musical expression, as opposed to the older celebration (May 13) that "represented a historical-ideological construction based on the official decrees of the past."[22] In this Brazilian context, reggae music and Bob Marley, both of which were established global icons of musical resistance against dominant forces, became fused with the annual commemoration of when Afro-Brazilians officially gained their freedom from slavery. Therefore, the global symbolism of reggae music has incorporated a local meaning, which in turn serves to regionalize musical expression, and provides this new entity with a distinctive Brazilian label for its reintroduction into the international musical marketplace.

In the late 1970s and early 1980s, two blocos afro, Malê Debale and Muzenza, clearly identified themselves with Bob Marley and Jamaican cultural aesthetics. In the mid-1980s, Olodum created and popularized a drumming style that came to be known as the musical genre of samba reggae. This innovation derived from some of the percussion instruments from the Rio de Janeiro–based samba schools, and featured drumming techniques from Bahian candomblé. As a result of this process, "samba reggae would come to represent a determining example of the mix between the local roots of samba and an already global reggae."[23]

Although Jamaica and Bahia are geographically distant, the reggae and bloco afro cultural movements emerged in similar political, historical, and cultural environments. These groups developed similar concepts of a utopian Africa, which helped ideologically bring them together. This metaphor was mediated by new temporal and spatial concepts defined in large part by contemporary electronic music. Godi observes that this connection provided a dual focus, in which aspects that were "far away would appear close and points of reference of identity could be revisited by historic and geographic memory."[24] Young Brazilian musicians and consumers are using an extension of this concept in more recent genres of Brazilian funk and hip-hop, in new ways bringing into question notions of Brazilian nationality. Contemporary Afrocentric youth cultures are rejecting official nationalist cultural ideologies, and are in turn "articulating the specificity of their own social experience."[25] The resulting popular music promotes a diasporic ethnic identity, derived from internationally produced popular trends, that features a historical link to Africa. This vital component connects the separate developments of Jamaican and Brazilian identities.

Examples of this new identity as they relate to recent popular music genres are presented in the following sections. The berimbau has figured prominently in each of these examples, yet the extent of the musical bow's symbolism depends on the distinct background of the composer or musician. Beginning with the group Berimbrown, I consider aspects of Afro-Brazilian popular expression that were highlighted in the introduction to this chapter. I then present how the berimbau has been used in Brazilian electronic dance music, and how it is affected by sampling, filtering, and sequencing. In each of these musical examples, the berimbau functions as an indicator of Brazilian cultural identity within contemporary musical contexts.

New Genres
Berimbrown (Congopop)

The musical group Berimbrown presents an intriguing fusion of Brazilian and non-Brazilian musical styles and pan-American cultural identities. Berimbrown, from Belo Horizonte, Minas Gerais, was initially a neighborhood organization created in 1991, modeled after the Bahian blocos afro. After a period of transformation, it adapted formulas from the *mangue* movement, which incorporated eclectic themes and musical instruments from Brazilian folklore (such as three large African-derived drums, similar to *alfaias* used in Pernambucan *Maracatu*) into a standard rock band framework.[26] Berimbrown's music is described in their promotional material as a mixture of "*Afro-Mineiro* sound sources," which include the *congado* (processional dances that feature themes of royalty and coronation), capoeira, and the *folia de reis* (groups that play religious music in the streets in December and January), along with international pop rhythms such as "funk, soul music, rap and reggae." Berimbrown has titled this new composite sonority musical genre, *congopop*. This genre contains everything from "mineiro regionalism to African universalism," produced by musicians inspired by the *bailes do funk* (funk dances)[27] who have soul and funk music "impregnated in [their] DNA." The principal icon of Berimbrown's identity is the berimbau, which they believe is a "symbolic instrument with the capacity to make a lot from a little," thus enabling them to "mine art with [their] hands."[28]

Figure 3.1: Berimbrown CD cover (Berimbrown 2000-disc). Courtesy Berimbrown.

Berimbrown's group identity is summarized in its name, a fusion of the words berimbau with (James) Brown. The development of this identity can clearly be seen in the imagery on two subsequent album covers. *Berimbrown*,[29] the group's independently released debut, features a collage of multiple representations: National Brazilian culture, including images and icons of soccer, capoeira, and a homemade scooter; Regional Mineiro culture, including a banner from a congado Mineiro (processional dances that represent African royalty) carnival group; and icons of global urban black cultures, including a man in a James Brown–style dance pose, a long hair pick, and a pair of tennis shoes tied together as if they were hanging from a high-tension line (see Fig. 3.1). Their next album, *Obá Lá Vem Ela*,[30] contains multiple remixed tracks of Jorge Benjor's song of the same title. The cover artwork demonstrates how

Figure 3.2: Graphic that appears on *Obá lá Vem Ela* CD cover (Berimbrown 2002). Courtesy Berimbrown.

Berimbrown's identity has been condensed from a colorful collage of various cultural influences (on the first album) to a concise synthesis of James Brown and the berimbau presented in black and white (see Fig. 3.2). In this example, the berimbau has literally become James Brown with an Afro-laden gourd sporting sunglasses, and its open mouth is singing energetically. The font type used for the band's name is reminiscent of 1960s psychedelic culture.

Although James Brown serves as a central figure, the band's sound draws from a broad range of North American funk big bands including Earth, Wind and Fire, Sly and the Family Stone, and KC and the Sunshine Band.[31] Moreover, Berimbrown presents an eclectic mix of African American fashion styles from the 1960s to the present, including a broad range of hairstyles such as large afros, dreadlocks, high-top fades, and cleanly-shaven heads, as well as wide-collared plaid suits, bell-bottom jeans and Air [Michael] Jordan sports jerseys (see Fig. 3.3—mestre

Figure 3.3: Berimbrown (Berimbrown n.d.). Courtesy Berimbrown.

Negoativo is in the middle of the front row, wearing sunglasses and dreadlocks).

Growing up in Belo Horizonte, Berimbrown's cofounder and capoeira mestre Negoativo learned how to make a berimbau from a design that he saw in an introductory capoeira book.[32] He assembled various household materials, including a stick for the bow, clothesline for the string and a plastic margarine tub for the resonating chamber. He says, "This gave a sound. Really bad, but it gave a sound."[33] Later, when he was in school, he met a person who was selling painted berimbaus recently obtained from Bahia. He urged Negoativo to buy quickly, since the instruments were selling fast. As time passed, the person eventually disposed of his unsold berimbaus, and left them outside of his house for trash collection, which is where Negoativo picked one up and took it home. He states, "This is how I got a real berimbau. I learned how to play the berimbau by myself, and [this is how] I discovered the berimbau."[34]

Mestre Negoativo also comments on how Berimbrown represents a summary of his life's experiences and enables him to present multiple expressions of Afro-Brazilian identity in a single musical ensemble. "I'm proud to be someone who introduced the berimbau into a music that I could say is a summary of my own life: Berimbau from capoeira, soul music, James Brown . . . I wore an afro this big, [my] pants were so big, and the drums that we use in Berimbrown are from the *congado*, and from *maculelê* [Northeastern stick dance]. So for me, it's very big, to [promote] Berimbrown, principally, as a symbol of capoeira, which is my sign, which balances my equilibrium."[35]

Although the symbolism of the berimbau is still very strong within the context of capoeira, mestre Negoativo suggests that current technology is affecting the attitudes of younger capoeira practitioners. He remembers that when he was younger, individuals were associated with capoeira by carrying a berimbau with them as they traveled throughout the neighborhood. "You [had] to cross the streets with your berimbau in hand. . . . Today, you have those who put a capoeira CD in their bag, and [the earphones] in their ear. . . . For example, I give a capoeira class in an academy in the southern zone of Belo Horizonte, and all of the students arrive, everyone, with a cell phone. I had forty students in the room, putting forty cell phones on the ground. I didn't find anyone with a berimbau."[36] By recognizing these changing attitudes, mestre Negoativo has been inspired to update capoeira musical material within the synthesis of Berimbrown's musical ensemble. The recording *Berimbrown*[37] is packed full of multiple layers of quotes and citations from the capoeira tradition. Additional references to Afro-Brazilian and North American urban black culture are incorporated into this mixture, and the resulting fusion of these elements creates a multi-vocal musical and cultural expression that enables traditional Brazilian music to coexist with other forms of mass-produced popular musical expression.

Berimbrown's "Melô do Berimbau" demonstrates how traditional capoeira material has been utilized. The beginning of this song draws on a traditional capoeira ladainha (an introductory solo often sung by a master), the "Beabá do Berimbau" (The Alphabet/Primer of the Berimbau; see T 3.1).[38] The lyrics of these songs will be interspersed throughout the discussion as musical citations.

"Beabá do Berimbau" is a traditional capoeira song performed as a solo by the capoeira master at the beginning of a dance-game. Ladainhas serve to salute the spirits of previous masters and educate practitioners (and reinforce this education through repetition) about significant elements that pertain to the tradition. "Beabá do Berimbau" introduces physical components of the berimbau, including the names of the various parts and how it is played. Moreover, this song serves to instill the berimbau's spiritual and symbolic significance to practitioners, demonstrating that the berimbau itself possesses powers greater than its physical components.

Leader: *Eu vou ler o beabá*	Leader: I will read the alphabet[39]
Beabá do berimbau	The alphabet of berimbau
A cabaça e o caxixi	The gourd and rattle
Colega velho tem um	It has a piece of wood
pedaço de pau	old colleague
A moeda e o arame	The coin and wire
Colega velho aí está o berimbau	Here is the berimbau, old colleague
Berimbau é um instrumento	The berimbau is an instrument
Que você toca numa corda só	That you only play on one string
Vai tocar São Bento Grande	It will play *São Bento Grande*
Colega velho toca Angola	It plays *Angola* in a major key,
em tom Maior	old colleague
Agora eu acabei de crer	Now I've come to believe
Colega velho, o berimbau é o maior	Old colleague, the berimbau is the greatest
Viva meu deus	Long live my God
Chorus: *Iê Viva meu deus Camará*	**Chorus: Long live my God Comrade[40]**

Transcription 3.1: "Beabá do Berimbau" (E Silva 1997-int)

Presented as a story to an old colleague, the "Beabá do Berimbau" introduces the physical elements of the cabaça, caxixi, moeda, and arame. The berimbau always plays its music in a major key, so it will always bring happiness and positive energy to those who play it. The references to *pedaço de pau* (piece of wood), moeda, and arame suggest that when three unrelated lifeless objects are joined together in this context, a sophisticated musical instrument emerges. At the final moment of the ladainha, a call-and-response section begins, which highlights an extended salutation to past capoeira mestres, as well as spiritual and important symbolic references that pertain to the practice and history of capoeira.

In "Melô do Berimbau," Berimbrown's adaptation of this song, composed by Mestre Negoativo and Berico, the melody is set to a quick-paced rhythmic tempo, contrasting with the lyrical, free-flowing feel of the original. "Melô do Berimbau" (see T 3.2) also features a melodic range that is more condensed than its predecessor. The melodic range of "Beabá do Berimbau" moves from a fifth above to a fifth below the tonic, with a resolution on the tonic, whereas "Melô do Berimbau" is centered on the tonic in a pitched rhythmic, rap-style delivery. This song begins on the tonic, briefly jumps up a minor third, returns to the tonic, briefly moves down a major second (to the seventh tone), and concludes the phrase on the tonic.

Eu vou ler o beabá,	I will read the alphabet,
beabá do berimbau	alphabet of berimbau
A cabaça e o arame	The gourd and the string
e um bom pedaço de pau	and a good piece of wood
A moeda e o caxixi	The coin and the caxixi,
aí está o berimbau	there is the berimbau
Berimbau é um instrumento	Berimbau is an instrument
tocado em uma corda só	that is played only on one string
Pra tocar São Bento Grande,	To play *São Bento Grande,*
toca Angola em tom maior	it plays *Angola* in a major key
Agora acabei de crer,	Now I've come to believe,
berimbau é o maior	the berimbau is the greatest
Agora acabei de crer, ié - ié - ié - ié	Now I've come to believe, ié - ié - ié - ié
Dance, dance, dance samba-reggae	Dance, dance, dance samba reggae
Pastinha foi à África,	Pastinha went to Africa,
angoleiro do Brasil	angoleiro from Brazil
Pra mostrar a capoeira,	To show capoeira,
pelo mundo se expandiu	it expanded throughout the world
Água de beber, faca de furar,	Water to drink, knife to cut,

mandinga de pegar, camará	lowlife to take down, comrade
Zum-zum-zum	*Zum-zum-zum,*
capoeira matou mais um	capoeira killed another one
Matou mais um, diz aí pois é	Killed another one, they say, yeah.
Brown, Brown, Brown,	Brown, Brown, Brown,
Brown, Brown, Brown,	Brown, Brown, Brown,
Brown, Brown, Brown	Brown, Brown, Brown[41]

Transcription 3.2: "Melô do Berimbau" (Berimbrown 2000-disc). Lyrics courtesy Berimbrown.

The lyrics of these two songs are similar, yet a few distinctions can be made. Both songs begin with the same phrase, but in the second stanza, Berimbrown adds the word "bom" to "pedaço de pau," signifying a "good" piece of wood, rather than just a piece of wood.[42] Note that the reference to the old colleague has been omitted completely from this newer version. Perhaps this has been intentionally left out so that the song will have more appeal to younger audiences. This omission also enables a younger narrator to relate the events of this song, thus eliminating any potential conflict of a younger mestre overstepping his boundaries of being outspoken with an older (and more respected) mestre. The next discrepancy in the lyrics is that "Melô do Berimbau" refers to the berimbau as an instrument that is "tocado" (played) on one string, as opposed to an instrument "que você toca" (that you play). This alteration in the lyrics reinforces Berimbrown as the messenger, and de-emphasizes the listener as an apprentice who would learn how to convey these messages themselves through disciplined practice. Berimbrown retains "Agora eu acabei de crer / berimbau é o maior" (now I've come to believe / the berimbau is the greatest), but they omit the beginning of the call-and-response section, and the reference to "Long live my God." Instead, they highlight "Now I've come to believe," and place extra emphasis on the word "crer" (believe), and use this as a point of departure to move on to portray images and quotations from other sources. Although the omitted call-and-response section honors past masters and makes reference to spiritual aspects in relation to capoeira, elements of this function can be seen in the subsequent stanzas, which construct a brief homage to the respected mestre, Vicente Pastinha.

Through the process of blurring perceived traditional and popular musical boundaries, this reference to mestre Pastinha is borrowed from Caetano Veloso's "Triste Bahia" (Sad Bahia), a song described by Christopher Dunn as a historical collage in the form of a "sonic quilt composed of heterogeneous musical and poetic fragments," with temporal references from colonial Bahia to the present.[43] Veloso's lyrics state "Pastinha já foi à África / pra mostrar capoeira do Brasil" (Pastinha went to Africa / to show capoeira of Brazil), referring to Pastinha's exhibition of capoeira in 1966 at the International Black Arts Festival in Senegal.[44]

Berimbrown updates this reference to demonstrate that Pastinha was not only a capoeirista, or a Brazilian, but he was an "Angoleiro from Brazil," thus affirming his connection to what is commonly perceived as a continuation of the most traditional form of capoeira that exists today. Berimbrown also states that capoeira is no longer an object of exhibition, but has instead become a respected art form that is now practiced globally. Perhaps Berimbrown is consciously drawing upon the popularity of Veloso's song that directly quotes one of Pastinha's ladainhas expressing disenchantment with the world: "I'm already fed up / with life here on earth / oh mama, I'm going to the moon / together with my wife / we'll set up a little ranch / made of straw thatch."[45] Berimbrown's use of Veloso's material is another example of many musical citations that have been derived from traditional capoeira songs. This technique creates musical references that can simultaneously relate to more than one source.

For example, one musical citation includes Antonio Carlos Jobim's "Água de Beber" (Water to Drink), which features rhythmic interjections between the lyrics, a prominent berimbau Angola toque, and punctuated band chords responding to the phrases of "Água de beber" and "faca de furar." Another citation highlights a smoothly harmonized "Zum-zum-zum / capoeira matou mais um," a reference to the legendary war cry of Besouro that is discussed in chapter 2.

At the end of "Melô do Berimbau," a traditional capoeira ensemble supplants the popular music instrumentation, and the song concludes with the well-known capoeira song, "Paraná ê, Paraná ê Paraná."[46] This song is presented as if it were a supplemental field recording added to the material produced in the recording studio. Perhaps it is an attempt to add authenticity and demonstrate that members of Berimbrown know how to play traditional capoeira music. Moreover, in comparison to Baden Powell's "Lapinha," the process of borrowing musical passages within the capoeira and Brazilian popular musical genres now becomes explicitly clear—especially since this most recent example appears several decades later.

The process of referencing these songs raises questions as to which temporal space the band is citing: Are they drawing upon the resistance of bossa nova songs against the 1960s military government's censorship? Or are they referring back to colonial Brazil's era of slavery? One possibility is that they are referencing several zones and simultaneously invoking multiple sites of resistance, which makes their contemporary message even more powerful.

In recent years, Berimbrown has been revisiting well-known Brazilian popular music compositions by artists such as Gilberto Gil and Milton Nascimento. Nascimento is an internationally successful Brazilian composer and recording artist who began to flourish in the late 1960s. Initially born in Rio de Janeiro, Milton moved to Minas Gerais at a young age, and he incorporated many strands of music from the region into his works. His lyrics were often censored by the military dictatorship, and he often composed songs that featured abstract lyrics whose meaning could be interpreted by the people, and bypass censorship. One such song is his 1975 "Fé Cegá, Faca Amolada" (Blind Faith, Sharp Knife):

Now I don't ask anymore
where the road leads
Now I don't wait anymore
for that dawn
It will be . . . It's going to have to be
it will be a sharp knife
The blind glint of passion and faith,
sharp knife . . .

Plant the grain and remake
the daily bread

Drink the wine and be born again
in the light of every day
Faith, faith, passion and faith
The faith, sharp knife

The ground, the salt of the earth
the ground, sharp knife[47]

With metaphors related to religious and spiritual belief, including symbols of bread and wine, and being born again, Nascimento suggests a spiritual ascension through perseverance. By maintaining your faith, you will triumph. This message is tempered with the omnipresent sharp knife that accompanies the dangers of blind faith. It may also refer to the capoeira fight prior to the 1930s, which often featured combative techniques in which practitioners used straight-edge razors as a part of their deadly arsenal.

In November 2006, Berimbrown produced a video recording of this song with Nascimento as a guest. This collaboration demonstrates how renowned popular Brazilian music compositions are being reinterpreted to incorporate an emerging pan-Afro-Brazilian sound. Moreover, the lyrics can be reframed from the mid-1970s context of Brazilian governmental censorship to today's struggles within communities of African descent. Berimbrown connects this 1960s and 1970s resistance to colonial-era slave resistance by invoking the imagery of *maculelê*, an Afro-Brazilian stick/sugar cane martial dance developed on northeastern Brazilian sugar cane plantations. Contemporary maculelê features one wooden stick and a metal machete. By drawing upon maculelê, Berimbrown gives a new meaning to "sharp knife":

Maculelê, vai ter e ser faca amolada	Maculelê, will have to be sharp knife
Maculelê	Maculelê
Faca amolada maculelê	Sharp knife, maculelê[48]

This revised version of "Fé Cegá, Faca Amolada" begins with an uptempo 12/8 maculelê/Afrocentric-inspired dance groove, and then settles into a deliberately measured rhythm that implies a notion of slowly walking forward with attitude. This revised funk groove is peppered with recognizable James Brown–style musical references, such as a silent pause followed by a quick, repetitive high-pitched guitar motif. Although many of these sound sources are reminiscent of North American black musical styles, there are modifications to the model established by Chico Science's *mangue* movement from Recife and Olinda in northeastern Brazil, which served as a model for Berimbrown's musical framework. The three large drums from the *congado mineiro* have been replaced by three conical conga-style atabaques that are present in the maculelê dance. Through creative video editing, the percussionists move seamlessly between the large drums and the atabaques to create a musical notion of magical realism, compelling the viewer to question the present reality. Toward the end of the composition the entire song returns to the uptempo 12/8 maculelê stick and machete dance-fight, this time accompanied by imagery of dancers clashing machetes and a call-and-response chorus singing text based on the lyrics cited above.

As formidable popular Brazilian music composers from the 1960s and 1970s age, they are increasingly collaborating with younger artists to reach younger generations. Milton Nascimento, Caetano Veloso, and Gilberto Gil have either recorded with or sponsored groups such as Berimbrown, Grupo Afro-Reggae, and a host of other musical ensembles, in order to keep in touch with current musical trends, as well as promote groups that have emerged from economically impoverished communities.

The Berimbau and Electronic Dance Music

Today's popular Brazilian music is totally engaged in processes of cultural globalization in which musical influences from throughout the world continue to be incorporated and redesigned within the fabric of the country's popular musical expression. The use of non-Brazilian musical elements, including the use of English in musical ensemble names and song titles, is prevalent in Brazilian electronic dance music. In the following musical examples from São Paulo–based ensembles, the berimbau has been sampled, filtered, and remixed with contrasting results.

M4J:

"Capoeira" (Sample of "Clementina")

M4J is a São Paulo–based electronic music ensemble that promotes sampling of rhythms and sounds from Brazilian folklore by incorporating these elements into drum n' bass–influenced electronic music.[49] Their album *Electronic Experience*,[50] titled in English, features two works that contain samples of berimbau music. One track entitled "Intro 16 A" is very similar to the Pat Metheny and Lyle Mays recording *As Falls Wichita, So Falls Wichita Falls*,[51] a soundscape that prominently features the berimbau and percussion of Naná Vasconcelos.[52] M4J's track exhibits lush major seventh synthesized orchestral string chords and a high-pitched meandering melody, which are rhythmically supported by berimbau and percussion. The concept of mixing electronic music with Brazilian percussion was a strong component of the Metheny/Vasconcelos projects, which could have served as an inspiration for M4J's works as well.

M4J's "Capoeira" is based on a sampled loop of the Naná Vasconcelos composition "Clementina," an homage to the singer Clementina de Jesus. "Clementina" appears on *Storytelling*,[53] a collection of works that Vasconcelos envisioned as a journey through time and space. He constructed these soundscapes by drawing upon sounds found throughout northeastern Brazil as well as personal life experiences.

"Clementina" begins with Vasconcelos laughing, followed by a samba de roda–style rhythmic cell, comprised of berimbau, clay drum, handclaps, *cavaquinho* (small four-string guitar), voice, and a brief saxophone interjection (see T 3.3).

The first four measures of this piece demonstrate multiple levels of cyclical rhythmic phrases that combine to create a smooth, flowing, unified rhythmic groove. Although each voice in this rhythmic cell maintains its own identity, the base pattern is established over the course of four measures. For example, the berimbau establishes a motif in the first two-measure phrase, repeats it in the second, and the third and fourth phrases are subtle variations of the initial motif. This rhythmic base supports Vasconcelos's short melody that reinforces the samba de roda imagery.

Transcription 3.3: "Clementina" (Vasconcelos 1995-disc). Lyrics courtesy Naná Vasconcelos.

Clementina vem chegando	Clementina is coming
Clementina veio pro samba	Clementina came for the *samba*
Minha gente bate palma	My people clap their hands
Clementina vai cantar	Clementina will sing
Clementina vem chegando	Clementina is coming
Clementina veio pro samba	Clementina came for the *samba*
Minha gente abra a roda	My people open the circle
Clementina vai dançar	Clementina will dance[54]

This is followed with a wordless lilting melody and multiple vocal over-dubs that accentuate various kinds of rhythmic counterpoint, and the piece effortlessly weaves between the two. Although multiple overlapping melodic and rhythmic phrases occur in this composition, all are distinct phrases that occur in shorter and longer cycles. Since the length of each succession of events varies, the overall effect suggests a natural ebb and flow.

M4J's "Capoeira" begins with a sampled loop of "Clementina's" third and fourth measures. The tempo and pitch are increased, and the overall feeling of this groove becomes static. Rather than a relaxed organic samba de roda, the M4J work is mechanical, and creates quite a contrast to the original work. A brief look at the first few measures of "Clementina" demonstrates how each of the three voices—berimbau, handclaps, and drum—maintain its individual identity. No two measures feature a rhythm that is exactly the same, but these motifs create brief phrases that are repeated in larger fragments. In the M4J sample, a cross-section of this interactive rhythmic groove is extracted, and although this rhythmic cell is technically an exact replica, the new version becomes a static, one-dimensional mechanical entity. This is also due in part to an increased tempo, and homogenization of the independent voices. For example, in "Clementina" there are two distinct layers of handclapping, suggesting interactive participation among musicians. As a result of the sound processing in "Capoeira," the handclapping sounds more like a generic electronic handclapping preset sound (see T 3.4).

Transcription 3.4: "Capoeira" (M4J 1998-disc)

The following discussion among M4J band members suggests contrasting perceptions of the berimbau's significance in Brazilian society. Although they recognize the berimbau's unique sound, there is disagreement about how this sound is produced. This suggests that they perceive the berimbau as an exotic instrument that possesses mysterious qualities. They draw upon this mystique as a means to incorporate a distinct Brazilian identity in a globalized electronic music marketplace.

M4J band member Franco Júnior believes that Afro-Brazilian music is composed of rhythmic characteristics that are represented by the identities of particular musical instruments. Speaking of the berimbau within this context, he believes that it produces a specific rhythmic and sound environment that is only found with the berimbau. He notes: "no other thing in the world does it . . . so it's something unique."[55] Júnior expands this notion to the use of Afro-Brazilian musical instruments in Brazilian musical culture. "I don't think it's only berimbau, but everything that's folklore in Brazil has a very big cargo of rhythms, and swings that are from the black people, so everything that's done popularly in Brazil—the congadas, samba—all this type of thing, the instruments that are used are very rich in rhythm."[56]

Here Júnior associates the berimbau with a larger generic context of African-derived folkloric expression in Brazil as an exoticized other. He believes that an essential element of this otherness includes the actual musical instruments. Júnior sees the berimbau as a common household instrument in São Paulo: "It's difficult to find a house that doesn't have a berimbau, because [it's so common]. But to find someone who knows how to really play the berimbau is rare. There's all of the technique."[57] This comment demonstrates a perception of the berimbau as a ubiquitous musical instrument, but he suggests that there are precious few gifted musicians who have worked with the berimbau to bring it to a level of a culturally refined instrument.

M4J band member Manoel Vanni disputes Júnior's comments that berimbau technique is difficult. Vanni's exposure to the berimbau followed three general paths: as a tourist to Bahia, as a capoeira apprentice, and as a classically trained musician. As a young boy Vanni went to Bahia, purchased a berimbau, and received musical instruction from a Bahian musician. "I bought it as a tourist. And after that I was crazy about the berimbau."[58] The musical instrument that Vanni referenced was a small tourist berimbau that is specifically designed for children. Although he played with this instrument, he makes a distinction between his model and a full-size berimbau used within capoeira circles. "I was a young boy, picking up a small berimbau . . . , and I learned how to play [brincar] with it, play [tocar] it directly. . . . [Now,] if you take a berimbau of capoeira, for example in my case, I don't know how to pick up a berimbau of that size, with a huge cabaça there, with the hand, in a certain way, secure the berimbau, because it has a weight, it has a certain way to mess with the [coin/] stone there."[59]

While Vanni discounts Júnior's comments, he also affords a certain degree of respect toward berimbau musicians. Although Vanni has not practiced capoeira for at least twenty years, he believes that if he practiced for two hours, he would be able to play the berimbau again. Speaking of berimbau technique, he says "it's not so mysterious. It's more of a question of instinct, of feeling that you have, and the musical sound that you would like to take out [resides] within the instrument."[60] Vanni's experience with capoeira has led him to believe that the berimbau functions musically as a base that bridges the rhythmic motifs of the atabaque and the pandeiro.

As a musician, Vanni saw additional possibilities for music that could accompany capoeira. He laments that he "never had the opportunity to participate in a capoeira roda" accompanied by a band.[61] As a result of his exposure to Afro-Brazilian music and culture, he began to explore possibilities of folkloric sounds in new contexts. He describes this as an exploration of "Africana roots" of Brazilian popular music, but more specifically, "Brazilianized Africana, and . . . these types of Brazilian sounds inspired us to [launch the idea] of M4J."[62] This approach enabled the band to explore a broad perspective of sounds that would reflect a notion of Brazilian identity without restricting the group to the confines of specific musical genres that might be encountered in an "authentically Brazilian band."[63]

Vanni and M4J have been inspired and influenced by a broad range of music including late-1960s North American rock and roll, which they define as music that was created with artistic integrity, as opposed to a commodity constructed purely for commercial gain. Within the world of electronic music, musician Walter Carlos's album *Switched-on Bach* and projects by the German electronic music ensemble Kraftwerk influenced Vanni and M4J. This broad range of non-Brazilian musical influences demonstrates that there has been a clear shift away from charges of North American cultural imperialism such as those Baden Powell and Gilberto Gil experienced in the 1960s. Having incorporated a diverse combination of Brazilian and non-Brazilian musical influences into their music, M4J clearly attempts to synthesize and adapt global cultural expressions to create a homogenized sound environment that affords a priority to Brazilian sounds.

Another influence—Brazilian percussionist Naná Vasconcelos's collaboration with North American mainstream jazz musician Pat Metheny in the 1980s—may have served as M4J's model for integrating Brazilian musical timbres into non-Brazilian musical genres. When Vanni heard Vasconcelos's work with Metheny, he began to search for Vasconcelos's solo recordings, which led him to the song "Clementina." Vanni liked the diverse collection of sounds, and decided to incorporate them into one of M4J's projects. His initial compositional efforts of sampling and creating musical loops were intriguing, so he was inspired to continue with the objective of experimenting, "slicing," and imagining without a predetermined result.[64] Although M4J initially focused on Naná Vasconcelos, they were not interested in studying him as a musician. They began by focusing on the "musical sonority" of the berimbau's rhythm, and discovered that the best way to study the berimbau was to study Vasconcelos's musicianship. Júnior recalls, "we encountered the [road to] the berimbau through Naná."[65] This work also inspired M4J to explore new directions in dance music, thus enabling them to promote themselves as a distinctly Brazilian electronic music dance ensemble.

When M4J features the piece "Capoeira" during live performances, the group uses eight channels of sequenced music as basic tracks, and they improvise live music on top of those prerecorded tracks. The berimbau sample remains present and unaltered in all performances, since the work has been constructed upon the sample from Vasconcelos's recording. Due to the quick tempo and unaltered short melodic-rhythmic musical fragment of the berimbau passage in this work, Vanni believes that it is imperative to use a prerecorded looped berimbau sample rather than incorporate a live berimbau musician. He is convinced that for performance purposes in the electronic dance music context, the berimbau sample "is much better than if it was played live."[66] This comment likely refers to the static repetitiveness of this brisk tempo sampled loop, which would inevitably vary in either speed, intensity, or evenness if a musician were to play it over an extended period of time. Perhaps a live berimbau musician would be unable to re-create the pseudomechanical aesthetic obtained in the sample. By slicing a small piece of an extended series of repeated variations demonstrated by Vasconcelos in the original recording, the berimbau sample becomes a static mechanical entity that loses its humanistic quality.

Ram Science
"Berimbaus"

Ramilson Maia is a DJ and electronic music specialist from Bahia who now lives in São Paulo. In 1992 Maia began to develop his style constructed upon a base of Brazilian music, exploring concepts of techno and drum n' bass electronic dance musical styles from European musicians, and incorporating components of Brazilian music into his mix. He states: "I took a house beat of bass and snare drum, and [added] the sonorities of *cuíca* (friction drum) and berimbau, and with these things I told another story."[67] He believes that this was the basis of developing his individual style, as the press began to take notice of his work. "They said 'Wow! This guy is doing techno with *cuíca*. He does some house with berimbau. What crazy thing is this?'"[68]

Maia's experiments offer an alternative perspective of berimbau sound processing to that of M4J. The manner in which he manipulates the berimbau's sound production transforms the character of the instrument into multiple entities of berimbau personalities that do not primarily serve as a rhythmic base, but instead engage in a multi-tiered call-and-response conversation.

Maia suggests that São Paulo is a physical location in which many diverse cultural elements can be blended, and for him, electronic music is the ideal vehicle that can be used to incorporate these many perspectives. The uniqueness of São Paulo is somewhat similar to New York City in that it is a sprawling urban environment, one of the country's centers for the music recording industry, and a desirable location for musicians and artists from other regions.[69]

He believes that regional distinctions can reinforce a local ideal and serve as unique elements that can be mixed together in urban musical centers such as São Paulo. "I bought a lot of folklore recordings, from the northeast, I have collections of diverse things. Because in Brazil, each place has a unique rhythm that will drive you crazy."[70] Moreover, the mystique of regional elements can spur public interest in an artist's work, in which people ask where a particular musical element was obtained, or where its sound can be purchased. Maia explains: "The guys in the south don't know what the berimbau is, and if you go to Bahia, everything is berimbau. . . . It's a crazy story. If you go to the Amazon it's another story, if you go to Maranhão, it's another conversation."[71]

In addition to his use of regional Brazilian musical elements, Maia is also drawing from 1970s Brazilian-derived samba rock music for his current compositions. Through this process, he believes that he is translating the "concept of the seventies into the language of today for the youth."[72] Maia sees himself as a cultural interpreter, sifting and filtering information into contemporary sound environments that will appeal to young Brazilian consumers as well as international consumers interested in Brazilian-influenced electronic dance music.

The work "Berimbaus" is constructed from a variety of filtered berimbau samples and other sound sources that represent brief, isolated fragments evocative of a futuristic berimbau ensemble. This piece begins with an even eighth-note closed hi-hat rhythm and alternating low to high synthesized chords, interspersed with sporadic berimbau commentary (see T 3.5A). After a steady drum n' bass groove enters, the berimbau propels the groove with a driving rhythm based upon the initial motif (T 3.5B). The next section features a low bass line that accompanies the established rhythms for the other voices and could be interpreted as yet another berimbau (T 3.5C). The final section of new material appears as a four-measure phrase, approximating a skeletal fragment of the capoeira toque "*Iúna*" (T 3.5D). The remainder of the piece features various combinations of the preceding sections, including subtraction and addition of instrumental layers to provide contrast to the overall texture.

Music critic Marcelo Negromonte describes Maia's album *Electronic Experience*[73] as a work that explores more than the musical frontiers of Brazilian electronic music. He describes it as "music without stagnation, rich in textures that converge on the fringe." He portrays "Berimbaus" as a type of "berimbau antropofágico" (cannabilistic berimbau) in which the multiple layers of modified berimbau samples rapidly consume each other and mutate into new sonorous entities.[74]

Maia developed "Berimbaus" through an extended process, which began by listening to recordings of capoeira music from Bahia. "In that era, I had done a lot of research . . . and I received a recording of Brazilian music from one of my friends, and I began to listen to the recordings from Bahia with berimbaus, etc. . . . I began to sample things that I thought would make good samples [such as the berimbau]."[75] He believes that the rhythmic and melodic identity of each instrument will lead the direction in which it is adapted within the context of electronic music. He says: "the berimbau is very free, so it needs to be separated and worked with [to] make a groove. . . . [It is then] filtered to enter into the electronic context."[76]

Transcription 3.5: "Berimbaus" (Ram Science 1999-disc)

Initial reaction to Maia's experiments by Brazilian DJs was mixed, because adaptation of DJ aesthetics in Brazil was focused on the sounds that were emanating from European music cultures. Commenting on this, Maia states: "They hadn't heard the sounds with the berimbau, and they thought that it was kind of strange . . . and then [some person] in

Europe began to do things, and people thought that it was cool."[77] In this sense, Maia makes his musical experience "very personal," and visibly intercultural.

Although he is not attempting to create an exoticized product specifically designed for non-Brazilians to consume in the global marketplace, he is interested in introducing non-Brazilians to Brazilian sounds by drawing upon distinctly identifiable timbres that are representative of his Brazilian and Bahian heritage. "What I want to bring to these people is for them to listen to these timbres, and have them think 'wow, where is that from?' And there are people who don't understand what it is, and they come to know what it is."[78] Maia's use of these sounds is intended to get people to stop and think about the beauty of distinctly Brazilian musical sound sources. Through this process, he believes that they will gain an enhanced appreciation for Brazil's rich musical heritage.

Chapter 4

The "One Note Samba" Starts to Jam[1]

The berimbau emerged as a solo instrument in several genres of Brazilian popular music from the early 1970s to the present through the work of three berimbau artists: Naná Vasconcelos, Dinho Nascimento, and Ramiro Musotto. Each of these musicians relates to Brazilian national identity and the berimbau in a manner different from Baden Powell and Gilberto Gil. One principal point of distinction is that there were less cultural restrictions imposed on the berimbau by the capoeira tradition, and as a result they incorporated the berimbau into new musical contexts. Although many prominent Brazilian percussionists such as Airto Moreira, Papete, Dom um Romão, Guilherme Franco, Paulinho da Costa, Djalma Corêa and many others have recorded extensively with the berimbau, their recordings tend to remain framed within a narrowly defined vision of capoeira toques. In contrast, Vasconcelos, Nascimento and Musotto each present creative instrumental approaches that propel the berimbau's movement into featured, as opposed to supporting, performance roles.

Naná Vasconcelos is an internationally renowned berimbau musician from Recife, Pernambuco. His musical endeavors have been the source of documentary films by Toby Talbot and Didier Grosset.[2] While Vasconcelos has become internationally recognized as a berimbau musician, he has approached the berimbau as an outsider to the capoeira tradition, which is clearly visible through observation of his presentation of capoeira songs and berimbau toques in Talbot's documentary film. Had Vasconcelos been immersed in traditional capoeira performance practices, he might not have developed his unique styles of berimbau improvisations.

Dinho Nascimento is a musician and capoeira practitioner from Salvador, Bahia. He has developed alternative techniques for playing the berimbau, most notably the "blues berimbau," which is a combination of berimbau tradition and Nascimento's interpretation of North American blues music. In contrast to Vasconcelos's background, Nascimento developed his musical style as an individual who informally learned capoeira on the streets of Salvador, and has created innovative musical techniques and ideas that have challenged both capoeira practitioners and record producers.

Ramiro Musotto is a percussionist from Bahia Blanca, Argentina. Initially inspired by Vasconcelos's recordings, Musotto moved to Brazil in the early 1980s to formally study the berimbau. He has since become established as a formidable berimbau musician who is well known for creating multiple layered berimbau arrangements and experimenting with electronic sampling and sequencing in a broad range of Brazilian popular music contexts. During Musotto's berimbau apprenticeship, he moved to the heart of Salvador, Bahia, where he learned fundamental aspects of berimbau performance practices within the capoeira tradition. Therefore, his progressive multiple-berimbau popular music arrangements are steeped in fundamentals derived from musical aesthetics of capoeira.

Vasconcelos represents the pioneering generation of virtuoso berimbau soloists in popular music; while Nascimento and Musotto have both been influenced by Vasconcelos, they produce unique contributions derived from their own personal experiences and musicality. As the berimbau has moved farther into global popular musics, new performance techniques and organological development have affected the berimbau's physical presence as well as timbral and melodic characteristics. Vasconcelos and other Brazilian berimbau musicians traveled to various parts of the world in the 1970s, thus influencing a broad range of percussionists in Turkey, Japan, and Italy, who in turn have freely developed innovations in berimbau performance practice without knowledge of cultural aesthetics from capoeira's musical traditions.[3]

Naná Vasconcelos

Naná Vasconcelos (b. 1944) has earned respect throughout the world as an innovative musician. He is perhaps best known for his use of the berimbau, prominently featured in a contrasting variety of musical genres. One of Vasconcelos's main achievements was to gain popularity through his use of the berimbau as a solo instrument, in international jazz contexts—thus distancing it from the capoeira tradition. Vasconcelos's berimbau work has been acknowledged in numerous individual entries in popular music encyclopedias and interviews in newspapers and music publications.[4]

Vasconcelos began performing at age twelve, as a percussionist in the city of Recife's military band, in northeastern Brazil. He later became a regular participant of Sítio Novo, a neighborhood escola de samba, where he was able to compare and contrast snare drum technique and musicality with the military band. He was also a drumset musician for the band Bossanorte, in which he explored a vast array of metric and polyrhythmic combinations. He suggests that his knowledge of African-derived religious drumming traditions from his family's involvement in candomblé helped him interpret and perform odd-meter jazz songs such as Dave Brubeck's "Take Five."[5]

Vasconcelos later studied other Brazilian percussion instruments including the *tumbadora* (conga drum) and the berimbau. Although Baden Powell and Gilberto Gil had helped nationally popularize the berimbau since the mid- to late 1960s, a newspaper article from the early 1970s reinforced its strong continued connection to Bahian folklore, by describing it as "an instrument that is even today used only in the Bahian games of capoeira."[6] Vasconcelos often refers to the berimbau as a prominent source of his musical expression and development of his ideas: "the berimbau was very important for the way I developed . . . I discovered that everything was there in the berimbau."[7]

Vasconcelos learned how to play the berimbau for a capoeira section featured in a play called *Memória dos Cantadores* (Memory of the Singers), a project that was designed to demonstrate the richness of Brazilian culture. He later saw that the berimbau could move beyond the rhythmic and metric confines of capoeira, and began to incorporate ideas inspired from drumming rhythms, which led to his development of the berimbau's use outside of the capoeira context.

Vasconcelos was well aware of potential negative reaction from capoeira traditionalists regarding this type of experimentation. He admits that he was "very scared" to play his new berimbau style in public "because

I thought they were going to say I was damaging the tradition."[8] This is precisely the same type of anxiety that Gilberto Gil experienced when he composed "Domingo no Parque." Another example of the ramifications of this traditionalist rejection can be seen in conflicts related to Baden Powell's composition, "Lapinha."[9] As a resolution to this dilemma, Vasconcelos drew inspiration from eclectic avant-garde musician and composer Hermeto Pascoal's nontraditional uses of percussion and household objects to create new timbres and sounds.

Vasconcelos spent time exclusively practicing the berimbau because he was unable to practice the drumset in his apartment. As a result, he began to take musical ideas he had developed for use on the drumset and transpose them for the berimbau. "I realized that the hand position I had on the berimbau [corresponded to the] drumset. The left hand is the snare, and the right hand is the cymbal. I had the same situation here on berimbau. So I used to practice on the berimbau, and then transpose for the drumset, or for any instrument. . . . [The] berimbau was the main thing for that; it opened me to see sounds as music; to see noise as music."[10]

Vasconcelos's explorations of berimbau timbres utilize effects derived from nearly every inch of the bow, string, gourd, coin/stone, and combinations of the above.[11] He also began to derive additional pitched notes by simultaneously striking and pressing the stick against the string at different points. Brazilian music critic Marcus Vinícius noted that Vasconcelos could "even obtain a harmonic scale. This, for an instrument that only possessed two notes was a lot."[12] Observations in the Brazilian press suggested that Vasconcelos was a true innovator of tradition; perhaps this afforded him space to develop additional extended techniques and move the berimbau farther from its well-known folkloric context. "Now, with the entirely disfigured sound of capoeira the berimbau assumed more ample dimensions in Naná's hands: it stopped being a purely rhythmic instrument and began to be melodic, or better, melodic in the sense of 'klangfarbenmelodie' a melody of timbres in contemporary music."[13] His experiments with the berimbau were described as timbral melodies, suggesting that Vasconcelos was able to move from rhythms to rhythmic melodies.[14] Music critics who were unable to describe Vasconcelos's work with conventional music terminology resorted to new forms of description. One example draws connections to linguistic syntax, in which Vasconcelos's improvisations are perceived to construct "'sound ideograms . . .' Even the syllables are syntheses. There is an organicity, an organized onomatopoeic system, a syntax. It is political, it has spirituality (but not religion)."[15]

Perhaps one component of Vasconcelos's success is the exoticism that surrounds the berimbau beyond Brazilian borders. He is quite cognizant of non-Brazilian audience curiosity about the berimbau: "When they go to the theater and see me playing that piece of wood, a gourd and a string, they're impressed. Nobody knows what will come out of this, but it has a visual aspect, and it tells a story. This is gratifying because it demonstrates that music can say a lot with simple things."[16]

Vasconcelos realized that the berimbau would give him an immediate identity, since North Americans were extremely interested in its sounds as well as its shape. He recalls that, in the early 1970s, the only associations that North American musicians and audiences could make with the berimbau were primitive assumptions. "They used to call me Jungle man because they thought the berimbau was from the jungle, the Amazon. Also, for example, in the middle of concerts, I'd do a solo for berimbau and I realized it didn't look like anything they'd seen played before."[17]

Exotic aspects of the berimbau continued to fascinate North American music critics into the 1980s, with descriptions of the berimbau as "a Brazilian folk instrument that resembles an archer's bow stuck onto an Edam cheese."[18] Vasconcelos most likely capitalized on audience assumptions of primitiveness to dramatically enhance his musically and rhythmically dense performance approach. Notions of primitiveness quickly turned to curiosity when Vasconcelos began to construct and repeat fluid melodic rhythmic phrases, thus suggesting a sophisticated and developed musical instrument.[19]

Vasconcelos's adaptation of the capoeira tradition into a contemporary jazz context is demonstrated in the way he sings a popular capoeira song, "Ai ai aidê" in the documentary film *Berimbau*.[20] In the traditional version the choral response is clearly sung in a major key, with the final note being reinforced by the major third and fifth of the chord (see top two stanzas of T 4.1). In contrast, Vasconcelos substitutes a minor third for the traditional major third on the final note of "aidê" (see bottom stanza of T 4.1). Moreover, if one takes the pitch of Vasconcelos's berimbau into consideration, the berimbau could alter this harmonic perspective. Vasconcelos tunes his berimbau to an F, thus transposing his interpretation of "Ai ai aidê" from C minor to F major with a flatted seventh. Therefore the E flat changes in function from a minor third to a lowered seventh (E flat). Vasconcelos's harmonic adaptation suggests that he is transposing this melodic material toward the style of the northeastern *violeiro* (rural troubadour singing guitarist) tradition.

Transcription 4.1: "Ai Ai Aidê" capoeira song and Vasconcelos variation (Grupo de Capoeira Angola Pelourinho 1996-disc and Talbot 1971-vid)

An interesting aspect of Vasconcelos's presentation of traditional capoeira material is that he refrains from using the *repique* (indeterminate buzz sound effect), which D'Anunciação identifies as a fundamental aspect of berimbau musical aesthetics within the tradition.[21] Moreover, during this presentation he plays the motif with little or no variation on the berimbau, thus demonstrating a simplified version of capoeira berimbau toques. In the second part of the documentary video, Vasconcelos highlights how he has developed berimbau performance practice beyond the traditional context, which is much more rhythmically dense. In essence, he has reduced the musical density of the traditional context to accentuate the contrast with his innovations. However, had he developed the capoeira toques with the motif and subsequent variations, the contrast between these two styles would be less pronounced.[22]

Some of Vasconcelos's innovative performance techniques include a finger-controlled bounce stroke that enables him to consistently play quickly repeated stick strokes against the string, suggesting that he is playing at more than twice the speed of a typical capoeira berimbau context. He then alternates the stick strokes with quick stone or coin counterstrokes, which increase the musical density. This performance technique is markedly different from berimbau performance practice within capoeira, where most berimbau stick strokes are played with a large arm motion, perhaps as a means to produce the most volume in an acoustic setting.

Other techniques that Vasconcelos is credited with developing include plucking and muting the string with the fingers, scraping and playing the bow and gourd with the stick, and changing the angle of the stone contact point on the string, thus yielding more than one raised pitch above the fundamental. Vasconcelos also developed an enhanced role for the caxixi, which consisted of establishing a rhythmic ostinato while "the fingers of the same hand played different accents on the string with the stick."[23]

Vasconcelos develops his berimbau improvisations in two distinct ways. First, he begins with a single melodic-rhythmic motif, and with subtle variations he maintains the overall character of the rhythmic cell, while modifying the internal space with subtle changes.[24] Second, he develops his musical ideas by mixing and contrasting various timbres and several regional Brazilian rhythmic sound sources, such as the baião, samba, and *maracatu* (see T 4.2).

Transcription 4.2: Naná Vasconcelos rhythmic ideas with the berimbau (Vasconcelos 1980-disc)

Vasconcelos has repeatedly acknowledged North American guitarist Jimi Hendrix's innovative experiments with the electric guitar and Brazilian composer Heitor Villa-Lobos's symphonic treatment of northeastern Brazilian folk music as two influences that have dramatically shaped his style. He cites Hendrix as a musician who demonstrated that musical instruments do not need to be restricted to their original contexts, and Villa-Lobos as a composer who provided new contexts and soundscapes for popular folk melodies.[25]

In the mid-1970s Vasconcelos began a fruitful working relationship with classically trained guitarist and composer Egberto Gismonti. At that time, Vasconcelos was living in Paris. Gismonti traveled there to purchase a custom-made eight-string guitar on his way to record an ECM album in Oslo, Norway. When he learned that his band members had been detained in Brazil because they were unable to provide a financial deposit to the Brazilian government to guarantee their return, Gismonti invited Vasconcelos to record in order to preserve the session. The musical union between the two was an immediate success. Vasconcelos recalls the valuable contribution and diverse background that each musician provided to this collaboration: "When he started to play with me, because of my instrumentation and sounds, the Afro-Brazilian element was in his music for the first time. Egberto was coming from a schooled concept; he went to the conservatory in Vienna to be a classical musician. I come from the street so I brought those elements to his music. We both realized, how that was so different, but at the same time it was together, because of the way we think."[26] Vasconcelos's notion of the separation of European art music tradition from African-derived rhythmic concepts draws attention to frequent debates about musical competence between classically trained and popular musicians. There is similar friction between North American jazz and classical musicians.

Vasconcelos has headlined a series of solo albums that feature a broad spectrum of the percussionist's capabilities. Commenting about his albums, Vasconcelos states, "my records . . . have never gone out of print, because they are documents, they are not part of any movement or style."[27] One of Vasconcelos's most successful solo albums, *Saudades*, features Gismonti as a guest artist and provides additional documentation of the duo's collaborative efforts. The opening track on this album, "O Berimbau," was composed by Vasconcelos, arranged by Gismonti, and performed by members of the Radio Symphony Orchestra of Stuttgart, conducted by Mladen Gutesha. The eighteen-minute work features three extended berimbau solos and two string interludes that provide contrasting lush and agitated chromatic textures.[28]

Critical reception of this album has been mixed, and generally discusses expectations of Vasconcelos's percussive abilities as well as the integration of the orchestral passages. Vasconcelos believes that the recording process may have been rushed due to the orchestral musicians' "curiosity" in hearing the final results.[29] Descriptions by North American music critics echoed these sentiments, and questioned the most productive way to make "Vasconcelos's intensely rhythmic but rather specialized music accessible to a Western audience. *Saudades* is, alas, not the solution . . . the album places him in highly chromatic string-settings, which are utterly European in conception."[30]

These critiques raise questions about how North American journalists' impressions of Eurocentric orchestral string aesthetics should be incorporated with the African-derived berimbau. Are they suggesting that it would have been more appropriate for Gismonti to draw upon lush quotes from Wagnerian romanticism, or the rhythmic agitation in the style of Beethoven? Is it correct to assume that the African-derived berimbau is incompatible with European contemporary music?[31] If the string arrangement had accentuated "primitive" assumptions that accommodated audience expectations, might Western critics have come to different conclusions?[32]

Brazilian music critics, in contrast, suggest that Vasconcelos draws upon elements from diverse Brazilian and non-Brazilian musical traditions while maintaining his identity as a Brazilian percussionist. A description of one of his first solo albums, *Amazonas*, demonstrates how Vasconcelos synthesizes various musical influences into a unique autobiographical expression. Music critic Marcus Vinícius credits Vasconcelos with presenting folkloric-inspired music without attempting to claim any particular "authenticity, or to preserve a folkloric musical tradition from a particular region. Naná intends to solely re-create this same tradition, presenting in his points of contact and opposition, with universal folkloric elements."[33]

Within a Brazilian context, Vasconcelos presents his music as an organic synthesis of regional folkloric expression, which he believes enables the music to stand on its own terms. By drawing upon a broad spectrum of diverse musical traditions as a source of musical inspiration, Vasconcelos can present fundamental aspects of Brazilian folkloric music while simultaneously avoiding genre-specific categorization.

This approach has most likely enabled him to comfortably situate himself in a global musical context, where he most strongly presents his identity as a Brazilian and not as a "world" musician. Vasconcelos believes that his collaboration with musicians Don Cherry and Collin Wolcott in the group Codona, an avant-garde improvisation ensemble that consisted of many global musical influences, helped reinforce his philosophical approach of mixing elements of global music traditions. He recalls: "we all had ethnic instruments, but we didn't think 'ethnic,' we just thought 'music' . . . That made the music sound like just music, not Brazilian, Indian [or] Japanese.[34]

While aware of the berimbau within the capoeira musical tradition, Vasconcelos pursued innovations in performance technique that enabled him to develop a presence as a prominent Brazilian percussionist in internationally disseminated jazz music genres. Perhaps he developed an approach toward world music that is not based on a single cultural tradition that justifies his movement of the berimbau from a specific regional to a global fusion context. In contrast, the following section features a discussion of Dinho Nascimento, a Brazilian musician who has developed new berimbau techniques and performance practices, and has encountered resistance from capoeira practitioners regarding his musical innovations that reinforces some of the initial concerns expressed by Vasconcelos earlier in this chapter.

Dinho Nascimento

Dinho Nascimento is a Bahian-born composer, percussionist, and instrument designer who learned how to play capoeira informally in the streets of Salvador, Bahia. He earned a scholarship to study composition at the Universidade Federal da Bahia, and later moved to São Paulo to perform with popular music ensembles, where he began to explore alternative technical and musical possibilities of the berimbau. Nascimento's berimbau innovations include the development of a performance technique that enables him to play approximate melodic pitches, which he has incorporated into a musical context influenced by North American blues music. Nascimento's technical adaptations allow him to obtain a wider range of melodic intervals and glissandos than cannot be achieved through conventional berimbau techniques.

Nascimento has also made organological modifications to the berimbau, most notably with the development of the *berimbum*, a bass berimbau that consists of an enormous gourd resonator as well as a string and tuning apparatus from an electric bass guitar. He replaced the coin or stone with a very small glass bottle, since a sharp object would cut through the guitar string. The wooden stick used to play the string is covered with about three inches of cork to soften the timbre. These technological and organological innovations have inspired musical ensembles such as Berimbrown, discussed in chapter 3, to feature Nascimento as a special guest artist at their live performances and on their recordings.

Figure 4.1: Dinho Nascimento in performance (Pellegrini 2000). Courtesy Dinho Nascimento.

Nascimento often incorporates many different berimbaus into his percussion setup, since each instrument is tuned to a different chromatic pitch and affords him the option to accompany songs in various keys. He also switches berimbaus within songs to accommodate key changes. These berimbaus are arranged on a rack in ascending order and labeled by pitch (see fig. 4.1).

Although many of Nascimento's techniques are unique developments, some of his musical ideas are similar to elements featured in recordings of Naná Vasconcelos. Nascimento is aware of this and asserts that he independently explored these innovations, not through imitation of Vasconcelos's musical concepts. Since most of Vasconcelos's recordings have been released outside of Brazil (for example, on the European jazz label ECM), Nascimento has had limited access to Vasconcelos's material. These recordings were often difficult to obtain in Brazil, and when available, they arrived as expensive imports.[35]

Similar to Vasconcelos, Nascimento perceives a strong musical connection between the North American blues and the berimbau. Nascimento's experiences with blues music developed from various commercial North

American and Caribbean popular music recordings that he heard on the public airwaves in Bahia during his youth. He explains that loudspeakers were placed in a public square and connected to a record turntable that played a broad variety of North American, Cuban, Italian, French, and Brazilian music.

Nascimento is cognizant of the fact that he only has limited exposure to blues musical traditions, as he has not been able to travel and research regional American blues styles or listen to artists whose recordings he did not encounter, such as blues legend Muddy Waters. Commenting about the blues he adds: "I don't know the blues, because it has been sent to me from [the United States]. I've heard it and seen it. I've thought about it. It's from New Orleans, I have recordings from various regions that have the blues . . . [but] I only know the famous ones, and I don't know the others, because they haven't come here."[36]

Nascimento believes that artists such as Duke Ellington, B.B. King, and Harry Belafonte all present some aspect of blues aesthetics. He defines the blues as being representative of what he feels through music. As an extension of that definition, he feels the essence of the blues within the sound of the berimbau. Nascimento recalls that one of the blues recordings that he heard featured a banjo with a guitar. "When I heard a musician playing that way, through the tradition, when I heard the banjo, I heard a lot of blues."[37] He believes that the blues transcends a particular musical genre and signifies a "state of the spirit" and that the berimbau, of African origin, "has everything to do with the blues."[38]

Nascimento began to experiment with timbres he heard in blues recordings, and he combined those sounds with the berimbau. His technique for the "blues berimbau," performed with a conventional berimbau, involves a radically different performance approach. His inspiration for this modified technique has been drawn from the blues slide guitar technique, which features a hollow metal tube or bottle neck that produces a variety of glissando effects.[39]

In this modified berimbau technique, the instrument is placed on a stool with a small hole, which secures the bow, as opposed to the left hand supporting the weight. This enables both hands to play on the exterior side of the metal wire in various locations. The right hand continues to secure a stick and caxixi; the left hand holds a small drinking glass instead of a stone or coin.

As a result, the sonority of the berimbau is similar to the North American diddly bow (a metal string attached to a the exterior of a house, which functions as a resonator), popularized in Mississippi Delta–style blues. The first event in which Nascimento introduced his blues berimbau was a performance of a composition for a collaborative modern dance project. Nascimento received a very positive reaction from the public and was encouraged to record this idea professionally, leading to his 1996 solo recording, *Berimbau Blues.*[40]

The instrumentation of the title track consists of a berimbau and an acoustic double bass, with a second, lower-pitched berimbau added during the final section of the piece. Although this song references the blues, it contains some aspects that would not be featured in a typical country blues song. First, the bass is playing a walking quarter note line, which is often found in swing and other jazz styles. A typical blues thematic pattern consists of a twelve-measure progression, with an initial four-measure phrase that is repeated, and a secondary four-measure phrase that concludes the statement. Nascimento's melodic themes have generally been constructed following this model, but he alters this structure at times.

The piece begins with a four-measure introduction featuring a two-eighth-note caxixi motif on beats two and four. The principal melodic phrases that conform to the blues model are in sections A, C, D, and E, where B serves as a transition section. The A motif serves as both introduction and concluding statement (see T 4.3, Appendix 1).[41]

The introduction, A, and first B sections consist of a solo berimbau (see T 4.3A and B). The walking bass enters on the first note of the C section and plays throughout the remainder of the piece (see T 4.3C). The D section features a muted ascending motif that imitates the walking bass line (see T 4.3D). The E section incorporates an ascending sliding technique that sounds similar to blues slide guitar techniques (see T 4.3E). The only time the bass rests is in the E and E' sections, where it pauses for a brief moment on the fourth beat of the second measure in the E section, and then the two instruments play a joint motif of the second through fourth eighth notes in the third measure. When this break is repeated in the E' section, the space is filled by a short solo of Nascimento tapping on the small drinking glass that substitutes for the coin/stone, introducing a timbre not present in conventional berimbau practice.

Transcription 4.3: "Berimbau Blues" (D Nascimento 2001a-disc)

A second berimbau, pitched lower than the first, enters on the A section following E". This final A section functions as an extended improvisatory section. This second berimbau adds rhythmic commentary on the first berimbau's repeated A motif. The piece concludes with a ritard, and the principal berimbau plays a traditional blues tag line, followed by a sustained tremolo and descending glissando.

Reactions to *Berimbau Blues*

Nascimento encountered many levels of resistance to his innovations, from both capoeira practitioners and producers in the recording industry. For example, capoeiristas claimed that he was disfiguring capoeira principles and did not properly understand the berimbau's history and tradition. It is possible that there was additional resistance to Nascimento's attempts to simultaneously remain within both the capoeira and non-capoeira realms.

Nascimento believes that he received more attention than Naná Vasconcelos because most of Vasconcelos's recordings were produced outside of Brazil, and therefore did not receive the same scrutiny given to a Brazilian release. Vasconcelos's position as a musician who is clearly outside the capoeira realm has also afforded him some leeway with capoeira practitioners who saw Vasconcelos "as an experimental musician" as opposed to a capoeira practitioner.[42]

Nascimento encountered subtle challenges from producers and distributors during the process of recording *Berimbau Blues*. Principal complaints included the extensive presence of berimbau throughout the album, the album title, and cover artwork, a black-and-white picture of an Afro-Brazilian man in a fetal position with a painted berimbau in full-color (see Fig. 4.2). The title of the album appears in a rainbow cross-fade from orange to red to blue.

The company claimed that the name *berimbau* in the title, as well as a photo of the berimbau on the cover, would limit the selling potential of the recording and would most likely be placed in the often overlooked folkloric music section of record stores. They also shunned the use of the word *blues* in conjunction with berimbau, which suggested a non-Brazilian musical genre, and would therefore not be accepted by the public.

Figure 4.2: *Berimbau Blues* CD cover (D Nascimento 2001a-disc). Courtesy Dinho Nascimento.

Only after Nascimento received the Sharp prize for *Berimbau Blues* (a Brazilian Grammy-style award) did he gain respect from his peers within capoeira and the Brazilian music industry.

Once capoeira practitioners began to accept his work, they commented that, prior to Nascimento, berimbau examples in popular music recordings failed to evoke an appropriate aesthetic quality conforming to performance practice within the capoeira tradition. Listening to *Berimbau Blues* with a fresh perspective enabled them to hear how the berimbau was played, and according to Nascimento, they said "wow, this guy's from capoeira . . . This music made the connection for them so strongly that they [played it for] their capoeira classes. . . . So for them, they felt the bridge of capoeira and [popular] music. This is really funny, because

Figure 4.3: *Gongolô* CD cover (D Nascimento 2001b-disc). Courtesy Dinho Nascimento.

the berimbau had been used a lot in Brazilian music. [Gilberto] Gil had
used it, Caetano [Veloso], Baden Powell had played it on the guitar . . .
but for them, *Berimbau Blues* [made the connection]."[43]

In 2001 Nascimento released another recording, entitled *Gongolô*,[44]
which is derived from a Bantu word that Afro-Brazilian children use to
indicate the descending spinning motion when their *pipa* (kite) has become entangled with the line of another pipa. On the cover of *Gongolô*,
two pipas have become entangled in the wire of Nascimento's berimbau (see Fig. 4.3). Nascimento presents a version of the Powell/Moraes
song "Berimbau" on this album, replacing Powell's guitar imitation of
the berimbau's melodic rhythms with an actual berimbau. This brings
Powell's initial concept full circle but removes Powell's innovative guitar

adaptation of berimbau sounds. Nascimento met with Powell shortly before Powell's death and played this recording for him. He states that Powell liked the version, and gave permission to change the composition in this manner.

Dinho Nascimento's experiments with the berimbau demonstrate how influences of non-Brazilian musical genres can inspire innovative performance techniques to develop new ways of conveying musical expression. Although Nascimento has found it difficult to negotiate boundaries—maintaining an identity as a capoeira practitioner while introducing new contexts and techniques for the berimbau—he believes that his continued success is allaying fears that his modifications will disfigure the capoeira tradition. Moreover, groups such as Berimbrown, who are interested in promoting the berimbau in new contexts, have sought out Nascimento's organological and technological developments.

Ramiro Musotto

A third berimbau musician, whose work contrasts with that of Vasconcelos and Nascimento, is percussionist Ramiro Musotto, who records with multiple berimbaus ranging from 50 centimeters (20 inches) to 3 meters (9.8 feet) in height. Born (in 1965) and raised in Bahia Blanca, Argentina, Musotto studied classical percussion, drumset, and the percussion of Argentinean folkloric music. In September 2009, Musotto died of cancer at age forty-five. When he was young his mother traveled to Salvador, Bahia, and brought him a tourist berimbau as a souvenir. This instrument sparked his interest, and in the early 1980s he discovered Naná Vasconcelos's recordings, including *Saudades*[45] the one that made the strongest impression on him. Musotto also heard many of the albums featuring Vasconcelos and Egberto Gismonti, as well as a rare Vasconcelos album that was recorded and released only in Buenos Aires, featuring Argentinean guitarist Augustin Pereira Lucena.

Inspired and intrigued by the berimbau, Musotto moved to São Paulo in 1982, where he studied the berimbau and Brazilian percussion with Zé Eduardo Nazário, a prominent percussionist who has performed and recorded with Egberto Gismonti, Hermeto Pascoal, Milton Nascimento, Gato Barbieri, and John McLaughlin. According to Musotto, Nazário developed a berimbau notational scheme that closely followed that of Kay Shaffer.[46] Musotto notes that both Shaffer and Nazário incorrectly transcribed their capoeira-based berimbau material "backwards," by beginning their transcriptions on the second beat.[47]

Musotto moved to Salvador in 1984, where he played his first carnival as a musician for Carlinhos Brown. Musotto later became a recording session musician, and he lived in the Pelourinho neighborhood for four and a half years, where he spent most of his free time with local capoeira practitioners and berimbau musicians. As a session musician, he "accompanied the first *Axé* music recordings, like 'Elegibô' by Margareth Menezes."[48] Also during this time, there was considerable cultural movement in Pelourinho, as the bloco afro carnival groups were flourishing. Musotto recalls that regular rehearsals of Olodum, Ilê Aiyê, the Filhos de Ghandy, and the Comanches were all generating attention for the neighborhood.

Musotto began to experiment with multiple berimbaus of various sizes during recording sessions; the first song that he recorded in this style was "Hino das Águas" (Hymn of the Waters).[49] This arrangement features three berimbaus: a large (2.5 meter/eight-foot) berimbau that provides a fundamental bass note, and two normal-sized berimbaus (approximately 144cm/4.5 feet), all tuned to roughly the same note, with the larger instrument an octave lower than the smaller ones.[50] The large berimbau only features the open fundamental tone with no stone or coin to interrupt the string. The only modification of this fundamental is the gourd movement against and away from the body, which produces an exaggerated wah-wah effect. The two smaller berimbaus use the stone or coin to interrupt the string and create a repique (buzz) effect (see T 4.4).[51]

Transcription 4.4: "Hino das Águas" berimbau excerpt (Menezes 1989-disc)

Musotto considers his exaggerated gourd movement effects one of the distinctive points that differentiate him from other berimbau musicians. He uses a thinner material than conventional berimbau resonance gourds, providing a much longer sustain than its counterpart. Most are made from calabash, but Musotto uses a much thinner gourd from a plant called *cuité*. He notes that most capoeira practitioners prefer the thicker calabash gourd because it provides greater volume; he compensates for this by placing a saxophone microphone inside the gourd to electronically amplify his instrument. Musotto also prefers to use a metal wire from a steel-belted radial tire for the berimbau string, due to the broad range of harmonics that this particular material provides. "Piano wire is good, but it doesn't have many harmonics. It gives a very defined note, and the string from a car tire is almost if it plays a chord. Because the first harmonic, the fifth, is sometimes louder than the tonic. And that's something I like a lot. It's something that's less refined."[52]

Following his success with multiple berimbaus tuned to similar pitches, he began to develop arrangements for harmonized berimbaus. Each berimbau was tuned to a different pitch, and then further manipulated with a stone or coin interrupting the string. Musotto's first experiment in this manner was on another Menezes recording of "Chegar à Bahia" by Caetano Veloso that was released only in Brazil.[53] He expanded this concept on Virginia Rodrigues's recording of "Noite de Temporal" (Stormy Night),[54] using at least five berimbaus tuned to distinct pitches as the only accompaniment to Rodrigues's voice (see T 4.5). Musotto states that on this recording: "I did a harmonization of the berimbaus. I used chords to make the tonic, third, fifth, and the bass, and when the chord changes I either change the berimbau, or the position of the stone on the string, and the chords change. And this is what I'm doing with multiple berimbaus so that I can harmonize."[55]

These berimbau patterns are based on the concept of a Ghanaian bell timeline, with three of the berimbaus (tuned to the root, third, and fifth) establishing a minor triad and reinforcing the rhythmic pattern.[56] Musotto moves this triad up a minor third by drawing upon the raised fundamental (i.e., coin pressed firmly against the string) of some berimbaus, playing the open fundamental of others, and in some instances, overdubbing other berimbaus tuned to different pitches.

Transcription 4.5: "Noite de Temporal" excerpt (Rodrigues 1997-disc)

Musotto has also worked extensively with electronic sequencers, and he developed a very exciting berimbau solo during a two-year tour with Brazilian pop artist Lulu Santos. "La Danza del Tezcatlipoca Rojo" (The Dance of the Red Tezcatlipoca)[57] is a berimbau solo accompanied by sequenced drum, keyboard, and percussion that appears as a solo or musical interlude in the middle of a concert that regularly played to audiences of between ten and twenty thousand.[58] This work is an excellent example of how the berimbau can simultaneously represent tradition and modernity, and easily move back and forth between musical styles while remaining comfortably situated in each domain.

Drawing upon metric modulation and contrasting drum machine rhythms, this work weaves its way between traditional capoeira, a 12/8 rhythm, and funk-rock based rhythms of various tempos. Musotto believes that capoeira practitioners enjoy this work because it contains fragments of traditional capoeira toques. This piece begins with the toque "Angola" (see T 4.6A), and moves to a modified version of the toque "Apanha a Laranja no Chão Tico Tico" in a modified time meter of 12/8 (T 4.6B). The first transition features a metric modulation that moves from 12/8 to 3/4 time, in which the eighth note of the 12/8 time signature becomes the sixteenth note in 3/4 time (T 4.6 Transition 1).[59] This establishes the groundwork for a slow funk rock groove (T 4.6C), which is supplanted by a sextuplet-based transition (T 4.6 Transition 2.a—this motif is also frequently employed by Naná Vasconcelos). Musotto follows with yet another metric modulation in which the sextuplet sixteenth note becomes a standard sixteenth note, with the sequencer displacing the pulse established by the sextuplets (T 4.6 Transition 2b). The final section of this work features a dense electronic dance music

Transcription 4.6: Musotto berimbau solo with electronic sequencer (Santos n.d.–disc)

rhythmic groove (T 4.6D), in which Musotto creates a call-and-response dialogue with the audience. The work concludes with a return to the "Angola" motif, thus bringing this electronically sequenced journey back to the realm of capoeira.

Musotto has never experienced resistance from capoeira practitioners, probably because he is able to convey knowledge of the capoeira tradition in his contemporary works. Perhaps the most scrutiny that he has faced is from being an Argentinean-born percussionist who plays the berimbau. He notes that this scrutiny is in his past, since he has pursued a successful career in Brazilian music for more than two decades.

Chapter 5

Creation Myths

⊲ ⊲

An exploration of the berimbau's presence in Brazilian art music reveals connections that have affected elements of capoeira scholarship. For the purposes of this chapter, I define Brazilian art music as a genre in which music is produced specifically for performances in concert halls. An analysis of the berimbau's use in Brazilian art music highlights interpretations of Brazilian nationalism that reinforces nation-building ideologies promoted by the Vargas regime beginning in the 1930s. This chapter begins with an overview of Brazilian art music and discusses how African-derived thematic material has been used in the genre since the late 1800s. Two major trends of Brazilian art music from the 1920s to the present include various phases of Brazilian nationalism and recent contemporary *vanguarda* (avant garde) music. Central to this chapter is a discussion of *Ganguzama*, the first symphonic work that incorporated the berimbau. Issues surrounding the composition of *Ganguzama* began a process that eventually led to the development of a comprehensive musical notation scheme by percussionist and composer Luiz D'Anunciação.[1] By using D'Anunciação's concepts, capoeira scholars have been able to pursue detailed studies, graphically depicting comparative performance methods among capoeira practitioners.

Following a discussion of *Ganguzama* and its use of the berimbau, I focus on D'Anunciação's development of berimbau notation and the emergence of percussion-based art music in Brazil. I also discuss a contemporary vanguarda composition for berimbau and prerecorded tape by Luiz Augusto (Tim) Rescala. Vanguarda composers such as Rescala pioneered juxtapositions of the natural acoustic timbres of the berimbau against electronically produced sounds that were prepared and recorded on magnetic tape. This work was a collaborative effort by Rescala and D'Anunciação, and in some aspects, serves as a technological blueprint for some of the berimbau and electronic dance music compositional processes that were discussed in previous chapters.

Brazilian Art Music

Sacred music developed more slowly in Brazil than in New World colonies under Spanish control, partly because of the minimal organization of a formalized church structure in Brazil. The Jesuits had implemented formal musical instruction in Bahia by the 1550s, where they encountered indigenous musical traditions that employed flutes, rattles, and other musical instruments constructed from human bones. Through a process of cultural reorientation, indigenous people were instructed how to sing in Latin and Portuguese. They also learned how to play small organs, harpsichords, and European woodwind instruments.[2] Besides vocal and instrumental instruction, Jesuit schools featured musical instrument craftsmanship. Consequently, the influence of the *viola* (ten- or twelve-string guitar) and *rabeca* (string instrument between a violin and viola in size) continues to be strong in northeastern musical traditions and is a direct result of the important Bahian and Pernambucan cultural centers during this early phase.[3]

Art music began to flourish in Brazil with the arrival of the Portuguese monarchy that fled from Napoleon's army in 1808. They eventually established Rio de Janeiro as the head of the Portuguese empire. Rio instantly became the center of Brazil's musical activity and flourished until 1831, when Emperor Dom Pedro I abdicated his throne. Subsequent political instability resulted in reduced musical activities between 1831 and 1840, when an interim regency of political rulers served as the administration for the child emperor, Dom Pedro II.

Prior to the 1860s, Europeans composed almost all of the operas presented within Brazil's borders. One of the first Brazilian operas to obtain international success was Carlos Gomes's *Il Guarany*, which premiered in Milan, Italy, in 1870. Although this work was set in mid-1500s Brazil, its text was in Italian, and it followed the nineteenth-century operatic tradition.[4] Between the 1880s and the 1920s, Brazilian composers closely followed composers of European romanticism. Also during this period, they began incorporating aspects of Brazilian popular music including the *lundu* (central African song and dance form that is related to many urban Brazilian song styles), *modinha* (sentimental song style that incorporates the lundu and Portuguese influences), and *choro* (Rio de Janiero–based urban instrumental music) into their compositions.

Brazil has continually struggled to climb out of the shadow of European art music. Works of many Latin American composers have been dismissed as mere imitations of European styles. One of the defining moments in Brazilian cultural nationalism was launched in February 1922 at the São Paulo Semana de Arte Moderna (Modern Art Week). The broad-based *modernismo* (modernism) movement included expressions in literature, fine arts, and art music.[5] One of the primary objectives of this event was to displace established icons of Brazilian art by de-emphasizing their aspirations to solely emulate models provided by European masters. Some of these Brazilian icons included Carlos Gomes, discussed above, a figurehead of Brazilian art music.[6]

Music critics José Maria Neves and Vasco Mariz concur that Mário de Andrade, an extensively published multidisciplinary author, poet, musicologist, folklorist, and journalist, was able to adequately theorize general trends of a select group of young Brazilian composers in the early 1920s.[7] One of Mário de Andrade's principal points of distinction is that he questioned specific musicological certainties of his era, such as the assumption of an exclusive African origin of syncopation in the Americas.[8] In 1928 he published *Ensaio Sobre a Música Brasileira* (Analysis of Brazilian Music), which proposed a systematic approach toward Brazilian musicological studies. Andrade also called for the incorporation of European compositional techniques such as melodic structure, harmony, and orchestral treatment. Mário de Andrade believed that by using a modified European technique, an "authentic Brazilian music" could emerge that would be universal and transcend labels of inferiority that had been bestowed upon a developing colonized country.[9]

Neves's analysis of early nationalistic music revealed the use of short melodic and rhythmic cells based on Brazilian folkloric musical manifestations. The resulting music was associated "with composers like Stravinsky, Falla [and] Bartók, without losing contact with its national roots."[10] He defines this as a "new musical objectivity" in which nationalistic spirit is less defined by the formulas of European academies, and leans more toward the romantic influences of neoclassicism. Neves believes that if Brazilian artists obtained "aesthetic autonomy," nationalism and its associated literary projects would eventually superimpose a structure with associated limitations. Neves concludes that, rather than developing their own unique styles, Brazilian composers transferred their dependence from Mozart and Bach onto Dvorak, Tchaikovsky, Bartók, Prokofiev, Stravinsky, and others.[11]

The music of Heitor Villa-Lobos introduced nationalistic Brazilian music into an international arena.[12] He is still the most prominently known Brazilian art music composer outside of the country. Although Villa-Lobos journeyed four three years across Brazil observing a broad variety of music making, he did not scientifically collect folk tunes for the purposes of incorporating them into his compositions. Villa-Lobos drew on indigenous exoticism as one of his thematic cornerstones, often using the stereotype of the *caboclo* (*mestiço* of indigenous and European heritages).[13]

Villa-Lobos also used imagery from Brazil's broad spectrum of ethnic identities. One example of this can be seen in his *Prole de Bebê no. 1,* (1921) a suite of piano pieces inspired by characters that appear in Brazilian children's songs, dances, and legends.[14] Villa-Lobos transformed these characteristics into toy dolls constructed of various materials as the basis for each movement, including "branquinha" (porcelain doll), "moreninha" (papier maché doll), "caboclinha" (ceramic doll), "mulatinha" (rubber doll), and "negrinha" (wooden doll), among others.[15] Certain qualities of these materials can be associated with these racial categories, such as the fragility of porcelain used in conjunction with the "branquinha" (a white doll). In contrast, the "negrinha" (a black doll) "only knows how to walk monotonally, does not sing, does not dance, but involves us with the magic rhythm of her steps."[16] Moreover, the introduction of "negrinha" only features the black keys of the piano.[17] Villa-Lobos also incorporated local variants of urban popular music into his compositions, most notably, the choro from Rio de Janeiro.

African-derived thematic material was prominently used in Brazilian art music from the late 1800s to the mid-1900s. The first orchestral Brazilian work to use African-derived themes was "Samba," the fourth movement of *Suíte Brasileiro*[18] by Alexandre Levy (1864–1892). This work reflected national ideals that Levy had formed from a six-month visit to Europe in 1887, which related to political unrest surrounding the formation of a new republic and the impending abolition of slavery in Brazil. The first known work that is titled "samba" draws upon a description of a rural samba celebration in the 1888 novel *A Carne* (The Meat) by Julio Ribeiro. The second notable work was Alberto Nepomuceno's "Batuque" from the *Série Brasileira* for orchestra (1891), which incorporated diverse themes from Brazilian folklore, including the song "Sapo Jururu" from the northeastern *Bumba meu boi* (a dramatic processional dance that celebrates the death and resurrection of a bull) and the *batuque* (a central African dance of Bantu origin). Nepomuceno's use of the *reco-reco* (notched scraper) was especially shocking to critics, since this musical instrument "frequently appeared in Brazilian folk dances."[19] In other words, a musical instrument that was clearly associated with the lower classes had been incorporated into an elitist musical genre. Levy's *Suite Brasileiro* remained unpublished when Nepomuceno's *Série Brasileira* was composed and premiered, so "the Nepomuceno composition had the impact of a totally new expression of national elements."[20]

In general, African-derived thematic material used in art music focused on songs and dances of candomblé and other folkloric manifestations. These musical representations of Afro-Brazilians revealed "exterior aspects of the black soul," often featuring "never-ending" stereotypical dances.[21] Although Afro-Brazilian musical instruments and dances are well known throughout Brazil, Mariz suggests that the majority of instruments "do not possess sonorous qualities" that promote their inclusion in large orchestral ensembles.[22] The work *Ganguzama*, discussed later in this chapter, demonstrates an effective example of how the berimbau was incorporated into a large orchestral work, and refutes Mariz's overly simplistic assertion. Art music compositions that employ African-derived musical instruments have seen limited performances, because orchestras have encountered difficulties obtaining the actual instruments as well as musicians who know how to play them (and are able to read music), both within and outside Brazil.

By the middle of the twentieth century, the use of African-derived thematic material was in decline. This is due in part to the emergence of a group of contemporary music composers, known as "Música Viva," led by composer Hans Joachin Koellreutter in Rio de Janeiro in the 1940s.

Koellreutter studied with Arnold Schoenberg, and brought dodeca-phonic (twelve-tone compositional) music to Brazil. He later moved to Bahia and founded the Seminários Livres de Música (Free Seminars of Music) in 1954, which developed into the Bahian school of art music composition and the music department at the Universidade Federal da Bahia (Federal University of Bahia).

Bahian composer Wellington Gomes da Silva teaches composition at the Universidade Federal da Bahia, and has compiled a comprehensive catalog of all works by composers of the Bahian group between 1966 and 1973.[23] These composers include Lindenbergue Cardoso, Ernst Widmer, Jamary Oliveira, Fernando Cerqueira, Agnaldo Ribeiro, Milton Gomez, and Tom Zé.[24] Silva found a variety of Brazilian musical instruments uti-lized in these compositions including reco-reco, agogô, tantan, chocal-ho, pandeiro, and atabaque, but in the works of the Bahian compos-ers' group, "the berimbau did not appear [in scores] between 1966 and 1973."[25] Nonetheless, Silva recalls various performances that took place in the Salão Nobre (Noble Hall) of the Federal University of Bahia's school of music. On these occasions, the berimbau was utilized "within the per-cussion [section] as a block of improvisation. . . . At times they put the instrument like berimbau, tamborim and various instruments that the musician would play that did not have any notation. . . . Many times I played [in the orchestra] hearing the berimbau in this way, without any system appearing in the score."[26] Although the berimbau may not be rep-resented in the actual scores of many Bahian compositions, it has been a strong presence in the performances of these and other composers. Unfortunately, it is now recalled only in the memory of musicians and audiences who were present at these performances.

Mário Tavares
Ganguzama

Mário Tavares was born in Natal, Rio Grande do Norte, on 18 April, 1928, and died 5 February, 2003. He was the principal conductor for the Orquestra do Theatro Municipal (Municipal Theater Orchestra) in Rio de Janeiro, and directed international festivals of popular song at TV Globo from the mid-1960s to the mid-1970s. Tavares conducted

Brazilian premieres of works by Beethoven, Villa-Lobos, Ravel, Bartók, Radamés Gnattali, and Camargo Guarnieri, and conducted world premieres of works by Francisco Mignone and Villa-Lobos, among others.[27] Tavares's compositions have been performed internationally, and his compositional style is considered to be representative of Brazilian nationalism.[28]

Tavares's best-known work is *Ganguzama*, a symphonic-choral poem composed in 1959 for four soloists, mixed chorus, and orchestra, with text by Brazilian author Álvaro Neiva.[29] *Ganguzama* is based on the development of Brazil's national character, comprised of indigenous, European (Portuguese), and African heritages. This work was composed at a time when Brazilian nationalist ideology was arriving at a realistic vision of the future, which coincided with the construction of the world's most modern and progressive city, the new capital of Brasília.[30] *Ganguzama* is a simplified historical narrative that begins with the arrival of the Jesuits, who instruct a supposedly "happy indigenous" population how to pray. The population of Africans and their descendants is utilized as a symbol contributing to the "happiness and glory of [the] land."[31]

The plot of *Ganguzama* is set around the death of Zumbi dos Palmares, the last king of Brazil's Quilombo dos Palmares, the largest community of fugitive Africans and Afro-Brazilians in the seventeenth century.[32] The people of this autonomous nation successfully raided many northeastern plantations and resisted various colonial military assaults. The Quilombo dos Palmares was finally overthrown in 1694, and according to legend, Zumbi was cornered by military troops at the edge of a precipice and jumped to his death to avoid capture. The dramatic nature of this event is featured as a key aspect in Tavares's work.

Less than one month after the death of Villa-Lobos in November 1959, *Ganguzama* won the Prêmio Cinqüentenário do Theatro Municipal do Rio de Janeiro (Fiftieth Anniversary Prize of Rio de Janeiro's Theatro Municipal) and thrust Tavares into the inner circle of Brazilian art music. Composer Francisco Mignone hailed *Ganguzama* in an article published in the *Diário das Notícias* as an "excellent artistic conception, one of the most nationalistic that has been composed in Brazil to the present day, with touches of genius only encountered in Villa-Lobos of whom Tavares is a legitimate successor."[33]

In response to this salutation, Tavares elaborates: "Mignone, who was my teacher in school, liked provocation, and we later had some big laughs together because of this commentary. But the fact is that I appear to have been helped by fate. Mindinha [Villa-Lobos's widow] was very much my friend, and the result of the competition became known days after the death of Villa-Lobos. I wanted the position in the Theatro [Municipal] and this helped a lot."[34]

Vasco Mariz reports that the 1963 premiere of *Ganguzama* was well received by critics, and that the music has certain "African essences, with certain residues of solutions from Bach's cantatas. The orchestration is majestic, thanks to the ample experience of the composer, and at times reminds one of Carl Orff. This work certainly merits being [performed again]."[35]

Ganguzama demonstrates the use of nationalist ideals in the late 1950s. Neiva alludes to the musical interaction of multilayered choral singing as a metaphorical recreation of the process that created the contemporary Brazilian. "Today, I think that the mark of nobility of the Brazilian soul, that in its singularity in the chorus of souls, from all of the nationalities, is this generous miscegenation, where, after four centuries, the white, the Indian and principally, the black came to create a different man, [and bring] a new personage to the stage of history."[36]

Ganguzama is a musical portrait of Brazilian nationality, divided into three scenes and comprising a total of twelve musical numbers.[37] Steeped in nationalistic themes and ideals, this work presents a musical interpretation of the birth, growth, and utopian realization of Brazil. As a historical project, *Ganguzama* envisioned an indigenous population who "hoped," African populations who "helped," the Jesuits who taught prayer, and the *Bandeirantes* (expeditionary forces who explored Brazil's hinterlands), who taught their skill of victorious battle. The musical intervention featuring the berimbau occurs in the "Holocaust" section of scene two.

Scenario of *Ganguzama*
Scene One: Message
Offering
Hosana

Scene Two: Crazy Inquietude (Instrumental)
Manoá (Instrumental)
Integration (Instrumental)
Holocaust [Berimbau Section]
Return (Instrumental)

Scene Three: Panorama (Instrumental)
Song of the Small Hammock
Hallelujah
Apotheosis[38]

Scene One is based on the discovery of Brazil, centered on the encounter of the Jesuits with the indigenous population, featuring thematic material from the romanticized first mass held on Brazilian shores.
This encounter is metaphorically depicted as the descent of the Southern
Cross constellation to the earth. A good angel who guards the destiny of
the people blesses this new partnership, and the final number of the first
scene intertwines love and hope into its hymn.

Scene Two begins with the presentation of a singular form of miscegenation that occurs with the birth of the *mameluco*, a baby of indigenous
and Portuguese heritage, which is musically portrayed by an orchestral
interlude. The "Holocaust" section featuring the berimbau is an eyewit-
ness account of a *quilombola* (quilombo resident), represented by a bass
soloist. He tells of the dramatic final moments of Ganguzama's life, when
the leader and his warriors leap to their deaths to preclude capture from
government military troops. The musical depiction is a call and response
between the bass soloist and a berimbau, supported by pedal tones sung
by the chorus. Music critic A. Hernandez describes this as one of the cul-
minating moments of *Ganguzama*, in which maximum dramatic effect
is achieved "with a minimum of sounds."[39]

The character of the quilombola, who could also possibly represent
a *Preto Velho* (spirit that represents old enslaved Africans in Brazil), features text that is constructed of incomplete words and phrases, suggesting that he is a person whose primary language is not Portuguese, or
that he has not been "properly" educated. Through these phrases, the
quilombola relates the final moments in which the quilombo warriors
leap to their deaths rather than succumb once again to slavery. He sings:

Nêgo véio tava lá!...	The old black man was there!
Ganguzama era Zumbi	Ganguzama was Zumbi
e Zumbi pulô pra Morte!	And Zumbi jumped to his death!
Nêgo veio vai conta:	The old black man came and will tell:
Nêgo 'stava na mussumba,	I was at the African tree
cum Ganguzama.	With Ganguzama.
Bandêra apariceu!	The flags of the Bandeirantes appeared
Ganguzama levanto,	Ganguzama raised up,
Ganguzama reagiu	Ganguzama reacted
Ganguzama morreu!...	Ganguzama died!...[40]

The manner in which this text is constructed clearly suggests that the quilombola is channeling an older spirit in the Brazilian spiritist religious practice of *umbanda*. The spirit of the Preto Velho is a prominent figure in this realm. This text is presented in broken Portuguese, perhaps suggesting a style of speech that is present in Afro-Brazilian religious song texts.

Following each statement by the bass, there is an improvised musical response played by the berimbau. At the conclusion of this passage, his voice fades following his statement that Ganguzama has died. The chorus and orchestra immediately swell to an explosive response:

Ganguzama não morreu!!!	Ganguzama has not died!!!
Plantou marco de epopéia	He planted the seeds of history
o baobá semilendário!	The quasi-legendary baobab tree[41]
É o banzo da Nossa Lira!!!	It's the sadness of Our History!!!
É o bronze da Nossa História!!!	It's the bronze of Our History!!![42]

As a contrast to the quilombola's text, the choral response features a poetic response constructed of sophisticated language with complete sentence construction. Following the choral passage, there is a brief return to the bass solo melody, which reaffirms, "the old black man has just told you." A series of melodic fragments derived from Afro-Brazilian folkloric dances concludes this section.

Scene Three opens in the middle of a densely forested landscape, which covered the entire country. A *Tupi* (one of Brazil's indigenous groups) mother sings a lullaby to awaken her child, the "first little Brazilian,"[43] thus representing the first individual from indigenous, African, and European heritages. This suggests a rejection of a single ethnicity as a national identity. In other words, if one is to be truly Brazilian, it is imperative that an individual come from a mixture of multiple heritages.

The thematic material from the beginning of the first section reappears and all of the involved heritages become related through hope, happiness, and pain. The conclusion features a chorus of the Apotheosis, which enables one to hear "a thousand voices coming, from every element, singing the poem of the three races that are only one race of three voices that speak in only one voice! The echo of light from these three voices repercusses in infinity, where Ganguzama lives forever, in the glory of his sacrifice. From this, Brazil was born, and because of this, Ganguzama survives."[44] Neiva concludes that the stoic figure of the King of Palmares is the "affirmation of a race that paints its kindness, more than its color."[45]

Use of the Berimbau in *Ganguzama*

Ganguzama is probably the first large-scale symphonic work of Brazilian art music to utilize the berimbau.[46] Although Villa-Lobos utilized some Brazilian percussion instruments in his compositions, he never composed for the berimbau. Brazilian music critic Victor Giudice hypothesizes that Villa-Lobos may have incorporated melodic-rhythmic fragments into his compositions to simulate musical motifs produced by the berimbau.[47] D'Anunciação does not accept this argument. Villa-Lobos had access to a broad array of non-Western percussion instruments, and incorporated them into his compositions. He would therefore have had no reason to melodically suggest the berimbau's sound within a symphonic orchestration. The only instances in which Villa-Lobos utilized Brazilian percussion instruments, he specifically indicated "percussão típica brasileira" (typical Brazilian percussion) in the score.[48]

Mário Tavares's use of the berimbau is connected with the dramatic moment in which the quilombola conveys his firsthand account of the death of Ganguzama. The berimbau appeared as an interjection or response to one of the most dramatic portions of the work, that "established a dialogue between bass and berimbau."[49] D'Anunciação recalls that Tavares was inspired by the resemblance of the berimbau's tone-

Figure 5.1: Graphic reproduction of Tavares notation of *Ganguzama* berimbau passage (Hernandez 1959). Reproduced by Eric A. Galm.

color to that of the Hungarian cimbalom.[50] When Tavares was composing *Ganguzama*, he heard the sound of the cimbalom, and wanted to put the essence of that sound into his composition. He then made a connection between the timbre of the cimbalom and the timbre of the berimbau. Since he was composing a nationalist Brazilian work, the berimbau's strong connection to Afro-Brazilian music and culture represented an ideal aesthetic that could be incorporated into this type of composition. The berimbau was a more appropriate instrumental choice: it could aesthetically create a dialogue similar to that of the cimbalom. This is the principal reason Tavares composed for the berimbau in *Ganguzama*.

Composer and violinist Nelson Macêdo performed in the 1963 premiere of *Ganguzama*, and remembers the powerful dialogues between the bass soloist and the berimbau that occurred two or three times (see Fig. 5.1). He explains that this moment was established by creating "a fermata with a group of instruments, [dynamically] piano, and an unchanging harmony . . . and then there was the intervention of the berimbau . . . the climax of that moment. It was strong, and very well placed. I liked it a lot."[51]

D'Anunciação's description of the same passage equates it to call-and-response patterns featured in the Catholic mass. When the music came to a stop, "it was something that was kind of religious. More or less kind of like what happens in a mass, when the priest sings and the congregation responds."[52]

D'Anunciação performed the berimbau part in *Ganguzama* in 1979 and 1999, and provides an intriguing interpretation of how this dialogue functions within the context of the entire work. He states that Tavares's intent was to draw upon a "phrase of capoeira," which was realized through the use of the toque Angola. D'Anunciação believes that, although capoeira has many toques with subtle variations, the fundamental "point of departure is *Angola*."[53]

D'Anunciação suggests that since the berimbau notation is merely suggestive in the dialogue with the bass, the berimbau musician must play within the spirit of the indications provided by Tavares. These berimbau responses could be approached from either a rhythmic or melodic perspective. D'Anunciação explains that, if the berimbau musician were to pursue a melodic perspective, there would only be two notes, the fundamental and raised note, within this dialogue. But if the berimbau musician were to explore this from a timbre-based improvisation, the "notes" could serve as starting points, followed by exploration of rhythmic modifications.[54]

Transcription 5.1 presents a comparative analysis of the intervention in *Ganguzama* between the bass vocalist and the berimbau, derived from noncommercial recordings produced in 1979 and 1999. The intervention occurs in two cycles, each consisting of an exchange of four phrases between the bass and the berimbau. A woodwind melody repeats the entire bass melody; upon completion of the fourth phrase, the berimbau enters again. The entire cycle is then repeated. Luiz D'Anunciação played the berimbau during both of these performances, and in each performance he used his two-stick technique. On the later recording he displays pronounced development in his proficiency with this technique, as well as greater exploration of additional timbres and rhythmic variance (see T 5.1).

Although more than forty years have passed since the 1963 premiere of *Ganguzama*, this event continues to be discussed today among musicians in Rio de Janeiro. Prior to the premiere, Brazilian musician Carlos Negreiros learned of rumors that the berimbau was going to be featured in an orchestral work at the Theatro Municipal. He knew that it was a special event that he needed to witness. He recalls that the berimbau musician at this performance was a popular music specialist who did not know how to read music, but he "lived to play the berimbau."[55]

Transcription 5.1: Comparison of 1979 and 1999 *Ganguzama* berimbau passage (1979-disc and 1999-disc)

Due to frequent court appearances for disorderly conduct, this musician listed a false name in English, "Shepard Scandal,"[56] when he applied for an orchestral performance permit. The first name was an homage to the first North American in space, Alan Shepard, and the last was his nickname. He played the berimbau so frequently that people began to imitate the sound of the berimbau with the mnemonic "scan-dan-dal," which evolved into the nickname Scandal.[57] D'Anunciação confirms that there was a berimbau musician known as Scandal in Rio at that time, and he could have performed the piece. "This was one of the guys who was a berimbau *bamba* (expert popular musician) from Bahia in that era."[58]

The other prominent story that survives about the premiere of *Ganguzama* is how the berimbau was incorporated into the orchestra. Because the berimbau performer did not read music, a signal was arranged where the conductor (Tavares) cued one of the orchestral percussionists, who then pulled the back of the berimbau musician's formal jacket, thus signaling him to begin playing. This process was repeated when it was time for the berimbau to stop.[59] According to D'Anunciação, orchestral percussionist Bituca[60] was "the one who pulled the berimbau musician's *paletó* [formal jacket]."[61]

In subsequent performances, the physical placement of the berimbau was moved from the percussion section at the rear of the stage to a riser directly behind the second violins, thus placing the berimbau in the string section. D'Anunciação explains that "this piece was a dialogue, so I had to be on a plane to respond to the bass as a soloist."[62]

The incorporation of the berimbau in *Ganguzama* developed an extended conversation between Tavares and D'Anunciação, which directly led to the establishment of formal notation schemes for Brazilian percussion instruments.

Development of Berimbau Notation

Luiz D'Anunciação introduced his berimbau notational scheme in 1971, and dramatically revised it in 1990 (see Fig. 5.2a).[63] Constructed on a one-line staff, the stems in the upward direction indicate the right hand, and the stems in the downward direction indicate the left hand. Two functions of the right hand are distinguished: the stick playing on the string, and a caxixi solo resulting in no stick contact with the string. The coin movement is represented by a note (coin contact against the string) or a rest (no coin contact against the string). Two other indications are made for the left hand, which feature the placement of the gourd against or away from the musician's stomach. D'Anunciação also provides an

Mão direita
$\left\{\begin{array}{l}\end{array}\right.$
Fig 5.2a

♩ = batida da vareta na corda

⊘ = caxixi solo (a vareta não percute a corda).

Mão esquerda
$\left|\begin{array}{l}\end{array}\right.$

✕ = contato da moeda com a corda

< = abre (desencosta a cabaça do corpo)

> = fecha (encosta a cabaça ao corpo).

EXERCÍCIO 21 (Toque de Capoeira de Angola).   Fig 5.2b

Figures 5.2 a and b: D'Anunciação (1971b). Courtesy Centro Nacional de Folclore e Cultura Popular/Instituto do Patrimônio Histórico e Artístico Nacional.[64]

example of how these sounds would be represented in the capoeira toque Angola. (See Fig. 5.2b.)

D'Anunciação's initial notational scheme appears to have been adapted and modified by capoeira scholars. Kay Shaffer[65] adopted similar notation devices, which D'Anunciação also published in the *Revista Brasileira do Folclore*.[66] While Shaffer lists D'Anunciação's article[67] in the bibliography, she makes no reference to D'Anunciação in the text, and presents the musical notation as a result of anonymous capoeira scholarship. "Due to the various [sound] effects produced by the berimbau, we've had to develop a notation system to reproduce them" (see Fig. 5.3).[68]

ANGOLA

Mestre Canjiquinha:

♩ = 92-96

Figure 5.3: Shaffer berimbau notation (1982). Courtesy Centro Nacional de Folclore e Cultura Popular/ Instituto do Patrimônio Histórico e Artístico Nacional.

Shaffer moves all of the stems to an upward direction, thus eliminating the distinction in function between the hands. The symbol for the caxixi solo is replaced with a triangle (Δ). Shaffer makes a notational modification of an X notehead for the indeterminate repique (buzz sound). Shaffer also introduces three principal additions: an encircled X ($\otimes$) that represents the coin making contact with the string without a simultaneous stroke from the stick; she replaces D'Anunciação's gourd indications with an A (aberto, open) and an F (fechado, closed), and expands D'Anunciação's concept of a crescendo to demonstrate the speed at which the gourd moves away from the body.

Shaffer's system demonstrates the first step in an extended process of adapting and modifying symbol-based musical notation schemes, which led to some confusion for musicians, composers, and scholars who had difficulty with common symbols among these related schemes. For example, in D'Anunciação's notation, the encircled X ($\otimes$) represents a caxixi solo, whereas Shaffer uses that symbol to depict coin movement. D'Anunciação uses an X notehead to represent basic coin movement (without distinction regarding determined or indeterminate sound); Shaffer uses this symbol to depict the indeterminate repique effect.

Capoeira scholars Almeida[69] and Lewis[70] have incorrectly credited Shaffer for the development of berimbau notation. Almeida comments: "there are many notations for berimbau rhythms that have not worked well because of the variety of musical effects produced by this deceptively simple instrument. One of the best is . . . presented by Shaffer in [the] book *O Berimbau de Barriga e Seus Toques*."[71]

Lewis presents his own musical notation without discussion of how it developed, and only mentions Shaffer in conjunction with discussion of variations within particular berimbau toques.[72] Despite extensive use of D'Anunciação's original concepts, there is no reference to D'Anunciação in either of these works. The only capoeira practitioner who has credited D'Anunciação in print for his contribution to berimbau notation is Nestor Capoeira.[73]

D'Anunciação's development of berimbau notation was inspired in part by conversations with Mário Tavares during their commutes to work in the orchestra at the Globo television station in Rio de Janeiro. Tavares often complained that he did not have a way to compose for the berimbau. Although he did notate some sketches (see fig. 5.1), Tavares claimed that it was not notation, but rather a *bula* (basic formula) in his score.[74] As a result, D'Anunciação began to research and develop musical notation schemes for Brazilian percussion instruments, which he continues to revise to the present.

D'Anunciação's first formal notational scheme was introduced in a lecture about Brazilian percussion instruments at the University of Colorado at Boulder in 1971. Percussion professor John Galm[75] had written a magazine article about Brazilian samba percussion instruments, and he suggested that D'Anunciação prepare an article about the berimbau. D'Anunciação recalls: "I brought a berimbau with me to the airport. When I arrived with my berimbau in hand, [Galm] knew exactly who I was. Clearly the idea [for the notation] came from that workshop. . . . A week or two before the course, I sat down and thought about how I would write for the group there. First of all, the berimbau is a novelty for Americans. I needed to have an instrument to show people what it was . . . when I gave the lecture, I already had come up with the actual symbols that I used, and when I returned, I had more or less the form of the article."[76]

Soon after this workshop, he submitted the article for publication in *Percussive Notes*,[77] a research journal of the Percussive Arts Society in the United States. He later submitted a Portuguese version of the article to the *Revista Brasileira do Folclore* (D'Anunciação 1971b), a publication of the Ministerio de Educação e Cultura: Campanha de Defesa do Folclore Brasileiro (Ministry of Education and Culture: Campaign in Defense of Brazilian Folklore), which also operates the Museu do Folclore (Folklore Museum) in Rio de Janeiro.

After D'Anunciação published this work, he began to realize problems associated with developing a symbol-based notational scheme. Although the article was a successful introduction to berimbau performance technique, he states: "My intention wasn't to create something that was only practical, where it was easy to learn, but something that would put the instrument in conditions of equality with other musical instruments [in terms of] musical notation."[78]

Following the introduction of this musical notation, he saw modifications and revisions of his original ideas by other scholars and composers, including the use of contrasting symbols to depict similar sounds, and different symbols to represent the same sounds (as in the case of Shaffer, discussed above). He recalls that, with each new work that was composed for the berimbau, the musician was required to learn a new set of symbols and notational scheme. D'Anunciação re-evaluated symbol-based notational schemes, and he eventually saw them as counterproductive to his goals of establishing a notational system for Brazilian percussion instruments. Moreover, he began to realize that musicians in other cultures would not be able to properly interpret his notational scheme without the assistance of his personal instruction. D'Anunciação responded to this dilemma by returning to conventional (Western) notation, which he sees as a universal language that is accessible to many music cultures throughout the world (see Fig. 5.4).

Figure 5.4: Revised D'Anunciação notation (1990a). Courtesy Luiz D'Anunciação.

In this conventional notation-based revision of his scheme, two fundamental elements remain unchanged: the stems for the right hand point upward, and the stems for the left hand point downward. Rather than utilizing a one-line staff, D'Anunciação develops a grand staff, consisting of three principal lines. There is now a separate line for both the *moeda* (coin) and the *uou* (sound of the gourd movement away from the body). D'Anunciação now makes a distinction with the coin by indicating a repique as a tremolo (similar to notation for a roll on a snare drum). This is the first musical notation that clearly indicates the rhythmic possibilities of the gourd movements.[79] At the top of the staff, the corda (right hand stick on the string) and caxixi now have a separate space and line (respectively), thus eliminating the need for an alternate symbol. This notational system also allows for expansion of several lines above the corda, thus enabling composers, scholars, and performers flexibility for modification within certain parameters.

D'Anunciação believes this conventional-based system has been constructed from a universally founded musical language that has been successful for over three hundred years. He rebuffs implications that the use of conventional notation favors European-derived concepts and values, which may not adequately represent musical aesthetics from non-Western music cultures. D'Anunciação suggests that if a musical notation scheme is developed specifically to represent a particular music culture, it will be an expression confined to the limits of its assigned purpose. In a comparison of musical notation to other cognitive systems, he notes that Arabic and Roman numerals coexist because they both have value as logical systems. Regarding conventional notational schemes, he states: "The European system is a Western system, and it was created to explain, to systematize a writing that represented sounds that served the model for European sounds . . . the musical notation system is European because a European invented it. . . . [If] you [favor] using this [system], transmitting the sonorous idea of another country, it will be the end result. You use the alphabet—whether a German, English or Russian invented it. German, Portuguese, English, Italian are all served by the same letters, but each one has its own accent."[80]

He equates this process with linguistic tools that enable a person to learn how to pronounce a word. With extended study, alternate pronunciations and regional variations can be adequately developed and expressed. While he acknowledges that the dominance of European culture is potentially dangerous, he believes that if any individual is composing beyond his own capacity, "he would err without doubt. It wouldn't give the feeling of what is there."[81]

D'Anunciação views his revised berimbau notation scheme as being applicable in a global context. He also believes that with this type of technical understanding, combined with a musician's sensibility for music, the mystique that is traditionally reserved for cultural insiders will be greatly diminished. He continues: "When you compose for berimbau, you [cannot] say, 'berimbau, play however you like.' In Brazil, that's easy. You find people who play berimbau, and you can say, play this, etc. But you leave here, and arrive in the US, Japan or wherever, and musicians say, 'what's the berimbau? How do you play the berimbau?' They don't have the *mão* [the hand]."[82]

As a result, D'Anunciação believes his system will be beneficial primarily to musicians who read conventional music. He asserts that "if you understand music, you'll be able to pick up the instrument and go play, because it's not that difficult of an instrument. All you need to know is how to pick up the stick, hold the coin, and how to place it within a musical context."[83] D'Anunciação is well aware that a technical instruction manual without considering musical aesthetics would be of limited value to a non-Brazilian musician. In order for any musician to understand the berimbau within a Brazilian (or more specifically capoeira) musical context, it is important to learn the boundaries and limits of themes and related improvisations and develop their own sense of berimbau musicality. D'Anunciação developed his material based on extensive observation of berimbau performance practices within the context of capoeira, as well as ethnographic research and lessons with capoeira masters. Mestre Nestor Capoeira has celebrated D'Anunciação's work as a realistic, comprehensive introduction to berimbau technique and musicality.[84]

D'Anunciação believes that, through the creation of a codified methodology, Brazilian percussion instruments will begin to gain value within Brazilian musical educational systems. Through this process, he is interested in demonstrating the compositional potential for these instruments, which will in turn be an incentive for expanded study within Brazilian university percussion departments. He also believes that through the proper understanding of Brazilian percussion technique, Brazilian art music in general will benefit from this process. For example, if a Villa-Lobos score requires a percussionist to play the reco-reco, D'Anunciação questions how the musician will technically and musically accomplish this. He believes that the articulation of each stroke has a particular diction, whether legato or staccato. Through the mastering of these techniques and converting them into a musical diction, Brazilian and non-Brazilian percussionists will be able to accurately realize the compositions of composers such as Claudio Santoro and César Guerra-Peixe.[85]

D'Anunciação's Two-stick Technique

The second part of D'Anunciação's work presents new techniques that distance the berimbau from its traditional context. One of his principal objectives was to distinguish his vision of the berimbau as a multi-timbre percussion instrument and establish its presence in art music beyond stereotypical quotations of capoeira music. He achieved this objective in two principal ways: he removed the caxixi from the berimbau's collection of sounds, and in its place introduced a technique for two sticks held in the same hand. D'Anunciação believes that if he maintained the berimbau exactly the same as it is found within capoeira, he would constantly remain within the berimbau's capoeira performance practice capabilities. "If I stayed within the toques of capoeira, the most that I could do would be [to play] toques that [remain within] capoeira. . . . I began to work with the berimbau so that it wouldn't always remain within the capoeira [context]."[86]

D'Anunciação's two-stick technique is similar in concept to that of a two-stick (in one hand) vibraphone or marimba grip.[87] The two-stick technique can produce multiple stick-based sounds and also facilitate melodic timbral phrases, staccato and legato articulations, tremolos on the string, wood, or gourd, and simultaneous string/wood/gourd combinations. As a result, you have phrasing that is completely different from that found in capoeira, and you then project a structure within a more "industrialized concept."[88]

D'Anunciação's interest in the berimbau has led him to compose two works for the berimbau: "4 Motivos Nordestinos" (4 Northeastern Motives),[89] and "Divertimento para Berimbau e Violão."[90] These works will be discussed in the next section.

Percussion-based Art Music in Brazil

D'Anunciação faced resistance to his efforts to establish percussion music in Brazilian art music circles in the early 1970s. When he proposed a percussion music concert to inaugurate a college orchestral percussion course, one prominent figure told him "my son, percussion doesn't make music."[91] He recalls that when he joined the Orquestra Sinfônica Brasileira (Brazilian Symphonic Orchestra) in 1971, the stagehands had placed the xylophone with the oboes and English horns and the remaining components of the percussion section remained at the rear of the stage. When D'Anunciação requested that the xylophone be moved back to the percussion section, a stagehand replied that it was an *instrumentino* (woodwind) and refused to move it. The conductor finally intervened and directed the stagehand to comply, but for the stagehand, "the xylophone was not a percussion instrument. It belonged up with the oboes, as something that held a lot more [value] . . . Things were that way."[92]

In the 1970s, D'Anunciação founded the chamber percussion ensemble Quarteto Instrumental, a novelty since there were no chamber percussion ensembles in Brazil at that time. The group featured two percussionists (D'Anunciação and his brother), flute, and piano, and performed works commissioned by Radamés Gnatalli and Francisco Mignone. This group performed in state public school systems and gained notoriety demonstrating percussion-based art music.

D'Anunciação believes that as a result of a strong percussion presence in Brazilian popular and traditional music, prejudices were in place against percussion-based art music. "Here in Brazil, percussion is the escola de samba, or a folkloric group, playing whatever drum, and is called a percussion group. . . . [For example,] *cavalo marinho* is not a group of percussion, it's an important popular Brazilian *auto* [religious-themed medieval-style dramatic presentation], but it's not a percussion ensemble. It has percussion, but it has dance, theater, something you do on the street. It's something fantastic. But here [in the university music school] it's called a percussion group."[93] As a result of these circumstances, D'Anunciação knew that the quartet needed to expand its repertoire of Brazilian compositions, and so he wrote his own work, *4 Motivos Nordestinos*.[94]

The first movement is "Cantiga de Violeiro" (The Guitarist's Song), a piece based on a northeastern guitar style, presented as a marimba solo. The second movement functions as an interlude to the third, which is a *xaxado* (northeastern song and dance form), featuring piccolo, flute, vibraphone, and marimba. The final piece, "Capoeira," begins with a theme based on the toque Angola that is introduced by the flute, and responded to by the berimbau (see Fig. 5.5). The remainder of the movement features a flute melody, supported rhythmically and melodically by berimbau and vibraphone. This work was well received in Brazilian and North American concerts, and it was eventually published in Germany and London.

D'Anunciação's other major work for berimbau is "Divertimento para Berimbau e Violão,"[95] which he refers to as a didactic piece to demonstrate the compositional suggestions and extended techniques that he

Figure 5.5: Flute melody that is repeated by the berimbau from *4 Motivos Nordestinos*, transcribed by Eric A. Galm (D'Anunciação 1990b)

introduced in his performance manual. This work has been well received by prominent Brazilian composers, including Nelson Macêdo, who considers it his favorite D'Anunciação composition. He especially enjoys the combination of berimbau and guitar, and notes that D'Anunciação's sonorous combination of these two instruments evokes the same happiness as instrumental duets such as Mozart's compositions for violin and viola.[96] Macêdo also enjoys D'Anunciação's choice of a northeastern Brazilian guitar melody, but treated and set "in a more sophisticated form."[97] As this work draws upon many of the extended berimbau techniques presented in D'Anunciação's performance manual, a berimbau musician would need to master all of the technical and musical exercises prior to attempting to play this work (see Appendix 3).

"Divertimento para Berimbau e Violão" begins with a slow ascending guitar motif that sets up an introduction for the berimbau featuring a sustained tremolo with varying dynamics. This initial tremolo immediately demonstrates control and dynamic variance produced by D'Anunciação's two-stick technique that would not be possible with only one stick. The second figure played by the berimbau (0:48) is obtained by subtle movements of the coin, manipulating the harmonics of the string.[98] This introduces what I call the A motif played by the guitar (0:55), which is repeated slowly and explored in a berimbau cadenza (1:17). In this section D'Anunciação demonstrates how he uses exaggerated movement of the gourd against and away from the body to conclude some phrases. At the Più mosso (1:37) D'Anunciação introduces the B motif, which is explored in various facets throughout the composition. This motif sets up a cadence in the middle of the composition (3:30) and again at the conclusion (6:42). The Andante section (2:26) introduces the C motif, a rhythmic pattern that suggests the work will develop into a vibrant dance for the remainder of the composition. This pattern continues moving forward until it is interrupted by the B motif (3:30) followed by a grand pause. The next section features an extended guitar cadenza (3:38), beginning with a motif similar in spirit to the introduction. As the guitar cadenza develops, the style initially suggests a Bach invention, and quickly changes to a Northeastern descending guitar motif. The guitar cadenza concludes with an interruption by the berimbau (5:09), which is followed by a sparse call and response between the two instruments. This develops into a more active commentary between the voices, leading to an implication of a metric modulation by the berimbau. The A motif reappears with a brief reflective exploration (6:14) and a return to the introductory motif (6:26), and the piece concludes with the B motif (6:42).

D'Anunciação's system can expand to accommodate new timbres and sound combinations by adding a line or space at the top of the berimbau staff. While this could potentially become a staff that utilizes an extensive amount of space on the page, an allocated space is given to a specific sound that remains consistent throughout the piece. This work is clearly the most technically complex berimbau composition that has ever been conceived in a comprehensive notational scheme. It demonstrates significant potential for berimbau performance practice that could transcend cultural barriers by enabling composers and performers to conceive of and reproduce sophisticated berimbau compositions in solo or chamber music ensemble contexts. D'Anunciação's musical notation scheme and two-stick technique are used and studied by a broad range of Brazilian composers, professional percussionists, and capoeira practitioners, which suggests that his work will help shape future developments in berimbau composition, musicality, and performance practice.

Luiz Augusto (Tim) Rescala
"Peça para Berimbau e Fita Magnética"

In the late 1970s, when D'Anunciação was in the midst of revising his notational scheme and developing his two-stick technique, composer Luiz Augusto (Tim) Rescala asked D'Anunciação if he would be willing to collaborate on an electroacoustic berimbau piece. This developed into "Peça para Berimbau e Fita Magnética" (Piece for Berimbau and Magnetic Tape).[99] Rescala composes for a broad range of musical contexts, including musical theater, orchestra, and electroacoustic music. In 1997, he was commissioned by the Centro Cultural Banco do Brasil (Cultural Center of the Bank of Brazil) to compose the children's opera *A Orquestra dos Sonhos* (The Orchestra of Dreams). The work is based on Benjamin Britten's *A Young Person's Guide to the Orchestra*, and contains themes of Brazilian folklore, music, and musical instruments at its foundation.[100]

"Peça para Berimbau e Fita Magnética" is a methodical investigation into sonorities and timbres of the berimbau. All of the recorded sounds on the performance tape have originated from elements of the berimbau, and have been electronically manipulated by Rescala. The work moves from the unfamiliar to the familiar, beginning with an abstract discourse of sonorities and concluding with a traditional berimbau toque as it would appear in a game of capoeira. According to Rescala, most works of this nature begin with familiar sounds and move to the abstract.[101]

As preparation for this work, Rescala learned basic berimbau performance techniques, because he "didn't want to write anything absurd."[102] He then approached D'Anunciação and invited him to record some material that would be manipulated for the performance tape. At the recording session, D'Anunciação played various individual berimbau sounds and sound combinations. The separation between composition and performance is not absolute in this musical relationship. Rescala and D'Anunciação's collaboration demonstrates the flexible roles that each participant plays in this creative process. D'Anunciação observes: "that's normal for the composer, principally in the *vanguarda* (Brazilian avant-garde compositional style). The composer says, 'I'm thinking of this,' but it really depends on what the artist can do on the spot. Because it really isn't written down, so you have to do it. It was a [collaborative effort, but Rescala] had good ideas and good suggestions, very logical things, because he's very intelligent."[103]

On both the recorded tape examples and the live performance, D'Anunciação remembers playing the berimbau in a variety of different ways: a single wooden stick, two wooden sticks held in the right hand, or a round metal file used to scrape against the metal berimbau string, conceptually somewhat similar to an inverted reco-reco.[104]

Rescala sketched basic elements of the form of the work prior to his collaboration with D'Anunciação, such as featuring only caxixi and tape in one section, and live unaccompanied berimbau in another. As he worked with D'Anunciação in detail, Rescala altered elements of the form as new ideas were generated between the two. During the process of composing with "sound material, you discover things that illuminate what you're working with ... [and] you arrive at a place that you're not looking for. This is what you do when you alter something. So there exists this element of surprise in electroacoustic music that's essential. It's happening because the process is always changing."[105]

The next step was to manipulate the recorded samples by changing their velocity, passing them through sound filters, manually editing the recorded tape, and rerecording the new sounds, and then repeating the whole process with this new material. Rescala reflects upon techniques and labor involved in manually editing audio tape. "The angle that you cut the tape affected the attack of the note. And the manner in which you joined two sounds ... [if] you made two like this [straight cut] it would be more abrupt, and if you were cutting this way [diagonally] you'd get a cross-fade. This was used in that era. If you recorded, then changed the velocity, an octave above and below the original sound, you could do it over and over, and put sounds together, etc. It's the same as you do today, it's just that it took a lot longer. And it was a work that was essentially manual.... Today ... you would spend much less time ... doing the same work, with the help of computers."[106]

Rescala began the piece "with a more abstract discourse, working with pure music in a sonorous game between timbres and densities," and progressed toward a sound structure that represented the berimbau within a "somewhat conceivable and more characteristic" context.[107]

This point of arrival is when the berimbau begins to play a traditional capoeira toque. D'Anunciação recalls, "I didn't stipulate a fixed toque from capoeira, but the idea is from within the toque of Angola ... but it's not realistically Angola."[108] He does not consider this an actual interpretation of the traditional Angola toque, because the musician must follow the structure and spirit of Rescala's composition. This style is related to contemporary vanguarda performance practice. Rescala adds that "this toque begins live, and later enters distorted on the tape ... [later] there is more freedom, but not a lot of space."[109] The freedom Rescala refers to is a brief space for berimbau improvisation, but limited to a variation within the context of the capoeira toque.[110]

Rescala utilized conventional notation that was embraced by many vanguarda composers, and devised graphic notational symbols in order for the live musician to interpret the taped recording: "It was a notation that was proportional with the measures of conventional notation—and metrically made to correspond with the pauses, [and] the tape contained the pauses while the musician was playing alone."[111] Presently, Rescala uses the berimbau notational scheme developed by D'Anunciação in 1990.

"Peça para Berimbau e Fita Magnética" begins with prerecorded elements from completely deconstructed berimbau sounds, as if from a science fiction construction project (0:00). Following more than a minute of taped berimbau sounds that have been filtered through a series of pitch, velocity, and timbre modulations, the acoustic berimbau enters (1:10). The sound of the acoustic berimbau is a reassuringly familiar sound, but the pitch of the berimbau begins to destabilize due to a subtle change in the coin position on the string. The berimbau begins to search for more tones, and eventually the recorded tape joins along with low bass-register tones (2:08). The acoustic berimbau then explores various timbres, and the tape moves from clear tones to white noise timbral distortion (3:37), building in intensity until a silent pause. An acoustic caxixi enters (3:46), whose sound is almost shocking due to the clarity in the timbre following the distortion from the previous tape passage. When the tape returns to some of the science-fiction types of sounds (4:11), it sounds less out of context when accompanied with the indeterminate pitch of the caxixi. A recorded section then takes precedence, featuring many modified berimbau sounds (4:51), some of which simulate a whistling tea kettle. The acoustic berimbau re-enters (5:10) and exhibits a more agitated timbral exploration of microtones, pitch bending, and tapping on the gourd. This acoustic berimbau cadenza is accompanied by a recorded berimbau playing the essence of a capoeira toque, in a different tempo (6:54). This recorded passage is slowly faded into the mix, yet it never completely overtakes the acoustic berimbau. A recorded low-pitched note enters (7:25), which evokes a low-pitched bell tolling in the distance. These recorded notes serve as a base for a final acoustic berimbau cadenza. During this exchange, a brief passage features the tape playing a clear tone and the acoustic berimbau primarily timbral sounds (8:12). The final recorded sound is a pitch bend in an upward direction (8:33), possibly signaling the acoustic musician for the final exploration (8:47), and conclusion with a decisive closing motif.

Rescala remembers a positive reception of the piece by the public, an interest in both the berimbau and the manner in which he manipulated the sound elements. One of the strongest aspects of this work draws upon his understanding of audience expectations and assumptions regarding the berimbau, including perceptions of limited melodic potential. "There's a curiosity here in Brazil, as everyone here knows the instrument, and they're enchanted with the berimbau. And principally, in this piece as well, because in this piece there's a timbristic exploration of the part of the instrument that exists between these two notes, and I think the curiosity is that people don't know what's between the two notes, such as the timbres and rhythms, because they're not important to the people."[112]

In this regard, Rescala is implying that Brazilian audiences place primary importance on pitched as opposed to unpitched sounds, perhaps because pitched sounds are more familiar than a broad array of timbres. D'Anunciação expands on this concept by observing that the berimbau not only spans these pitched and unpitched domains, but lives between them, continually shifting from one to another, and producing both simultaneously. He views this important duality of berimbau sound production as a mixture of indeterminate and determined sound. "In capoeira, [the berimbau] is used as an indeterminate sound, but you can [also] tune the berimbau, since the fundamental tone [can] emit one from the musical scale—a do, or a re, or a sol, etc.—and this determined sound, mixed with the repique and the caxixi, indeterminate [sounds], proportions a richness of very interesting options, combined with a very strong rhythmic constancy, that creates an atmosphere beyond the ordinary."[113]

D'Anunciação believes that Rescala was able to explore a broad array of timbres precisely because he remained within the domain of four principal sounds that comprise the berimbau's sound structure within the context of capoeira: two fundamental pitched berimbau tones, the repique, and the caxixi. He notes that if a berimbau were called upon to perform melodic scales, it would cease to be what is commonly assumed to be the berimbau. He compares it to American composer John Cage's development of the prepared piano, which emits a broad array of timbres and thus "stops being the piano."[114]

Rescala realized that Brazilian audiences have expectations about the berimbau within the confines of a capoeira or folkloric context. Brazilians "know more or less about the berimbau. But I think the surprise is to see it in another context, which isn't a traditional context. And it exists in other cases, with the berimbau and concert [music], but not this type of work."[115] Although he does not remember the name of the specific capoeira toque used in his composition, he places emphasis on audience recognition of the berimbau's existence within a capoeira sound space, thus bringing his work to an exciting and discernible conclusion by fulfilling their expectations. Since this work begins with unknown and abstract timbres, the resolution is amplified by the arrival at the familiar sound of the berimbau playing a familiar toque from capoeira.

Present at the premiere of Rescala's work, Brazilian composer Ricardo Tacuchian[116] recalls that the piece had a "very advanced language . . . [it] amplified the berimbau . . . and [was] very interesting."[117] Over twenty years later, he does not remember the specifics of the actual work, but he has retained a strong positive impression from that occasion. "The good impression that I had about that piece was as a musical piece. Finished, well resolved, well structured, and [Rescala] explored the berimbau with propriety, with technological recourses. . . . I remember that the integration of the instrument with the tape that he prepared was really equilibrated."[118]

In 2001 Rescala attempted to locate the various tape recordings from this work. Unfortunately, all of his tapes had disintegrated or were not playable on a reel-to-reel tape deck. Rescala is certain he could reconstruct the entire performance tape through the use of computer sound editing programs, which would take much less time to create than the original. He is interested in composing additional pieces for the berimbau, and he has schematically conceived some ideas, but he has not been able to develop them due to demands from other compositional projects and commissions.

Chapter 6

Visual and Literary Images of the Berimbau

As an extension of its associations with capoeira, the berimbau has come to represent "Afro-Brazilianness" in recent decades, appearing on capoeira academy logos, jewelry, and tattoos.[1] Walls of academies become sacred altars that prominently display berimbaus and photographs of "ancestors" (capoeira masters), most of whom are playing or holding a berimbau. One logo shows the berimbau incorporated into the Brazilian national flag, reinforcing the Brazilianness of the berimbau and capoeira within both a national and international context. This becomes an international symbol for Brazilian capoeira groups based outside of Brazil, and for non-Brazilian capoeiristas who use both the berimbau and the Brazilian national flag as markers of a distinctive brotherhood with Brazilian roots.

In Brazilian popular music, the berimbau has also become a symbol of capoeira to non-capoeiristas, where it has been appropriated as an icon of authentic Brazilian folkloric music, with illustrations of berimbaus on record covers.[2] A chain of record stores named Berimbau Music extends this concept to general audiences, perhaps to capture the public's attention and draw them inside the store. The berimbau is also a Brazilian tourist symbol seen on numerous store signs, company logos, and T-shirts.[3] In 1994 Bahian sculptor Bel Borba was commissioned by the Bahian telephone company to create public telephone booths that resembled berimbaus, although these sculptures are bent in the opposite direction. These phone booths are found throughout Salvador, and similar phone booths have been sculpted in Recife, Pernambuco, in the shape of green coconuts and *sombrinhas* (small umbrellas) used in the Pernambucan *frevo* dance.

Salvador's newspaper *A Tarde* featured a full-page exhibition of four berimbau-related articles, which resembled an in-depth promotional travel advertisement. One article boldly proclaimed: "Berimbau: Tourist Symbol of Bahia,"[4] and another reinforced its exoticized appeal as a "grand attraction at the Mercado Modelo,"[5] Salvador's main tourist marketplace, which was the world's largest slave market in the eighteenth century. Antônio Ferrigno—an Italian artist who captured many aspects of Brazilian landscapes in his portraits of Afro-Brazilian culture—painted a striking image of the berimbau in the early 1900s. One of his most famous collections is an extensive series portraying the coffee production process on a plantation in the state of São Paulo. In an untitled painting (see Fig. 6.1), a berimbau musician plays at what was once the door of a church, now in ruins. A young boy gazes at the altar, a statue of the Virgin Mary. Many interpretations can be derived from this image, including dichotomies between African and European religious beliefs (Catholicism and candomblé), and the contrast between young and old.

In this picture the berimbau is being played at the door of the church, whereas in many capoeira songs a frequent request is for a berimbau to play at the door of the cemetery. Since this church is in ruins, it is plausible that this represents the remains of a mausoleum. The contrast between the old man and the young boy could represent the old man reflecting upon his life as a youth, or perhaps the young boy, seeing the church (i.e., immediate neighborhood, or life in general) in ruins, finding solace through fixation on the untarnished Virgin. The image of the Virgin Mary in an Afro-Brazilian setting could also symbolize a connection to the orixá *Yemanjá* (the goddess of the sea), who is often believed to be associated with this Catholic image.[6] Yemanjá is a popular orixá in the Americas, as her spirit was responsible for overseeing the journey of the Africans who survived the treacherous middle passage.

This scene also portrays musical transmission. Although the young boy's attention appears to be directed toward the altar of the church, his proximity to the musician suggests that he is simultaneously internalizing the musician's performance. Berimbau musicians have described the process in which they learned how to play the berimbau as one that featured informal observation in public and later imitation of these movements in private.[7]

Figure 6.1: Berimbau musician outside
of church (Ferrigno 2000)

In terms of performance technique, it is difficult to discern whether
the musician is using a stone/coin or a pinching technique to modify the
pitch. It is most likely a pinching technique, similar to the Angolan musical bow technique previously discussed. The musician is also holding
the stick in a manner that contrasts with the conventional performance
technique, and the musician does not appear to be holding a *caxixi* (basket rattle).

A large sculpture of a berimbau musician is located in the lobby of
the Hotel Nacional in Brasília. Bahian artist Mário Cravo Jr. created this
work, *Tocador de Berimbau*, in 1950 (see Fig. 6.2). Constructed of wood
with veneer, and measuring three meters high, this work evokes provoca-
tive images of berimbau, capoeira, and internal exploration.[8] Rego called
this sculpture "an erotic interpretation" of its subject matter.[9] A more

Figure 6.2: *Tocador de Berimbau* by
Mario Cravo, Jr. (Photo by Eric A. Galm)

recent newspaper article reports that this sculpture "made a great impact when it was exhibited in the 1950s at Belvedere da Sé."[10]

Tocador de Berimbau features a berimbau musician who is personally intertwined in an exaggerated manner. The musician's mouth is open, perhaps singing or shouting encouragement in a game of capoeira. Another interpretation suggests that the berimbau player has become wrapped up in the joyous melodic rhythmic variations. Perhaps this is an external portrayal of the musician's internal emotional response to the music.

Other visual images that have appeared recently include a variety of cartoons. Two political cartoons featuring the berimbau were recently published in the *Jornal do Brasil,* by the cartoonist Ique. Both of these cartoons represent a political scandal that led to the temporary downfall

Figure 6.3: Illustration from children's story *Berimbau* (Coelho 2000). Courtesy Raquel Coelho.

of Antônio Carlos Magalhães, a senior senator from Bahia, who had strongly influenced the Senate for many years through intimidation of political adversaries. In 2001 Magalhães was connected with illegally obtained computer files that led to the expulsion of another Brazilian senator. The first cartoon depicts a jogo (game) of capoeira, in which Magalhães (in the upper left-hand corner) is attempting to avoid a *rasteira* (sweeping movement with a leg), administered by one of his political adversaries, Jader Barbalho. President Fernando Henrique Cardoso is playing the berimbau. The person in the front, wearing shorts that depict a "bad boy" (suggesting that he is carrying out another person's dirty work), is José Roberto Arruda, a senator who was forced to resign after he obtained Senate voting records on Magalhães's behalf.[11]

Magalhães was forced to step down as head of the Brazilian Senate, and eventually resign from his duties as an elected official.[12] The second cartoon shows Magalhães and a berimbau thrown out with the trash on the steps of the Brazilian national congress building. This use of the

Figure 6.4: Luana and her Magic Berimbau (Macêdo 2000). Courtesy Aroldo Macêdo.

berimbau demonstrates the pervasiveness of the national perception of the berimbau's symbolic association with Bahia.

Spiritual associations in relation to the berimbau can be seen in a children's book, *Berimbau* (see Fig. 6.3).[13] This story is about a young boy who goes walking in the woods and comes across some ruins, where he encounters an Afro-Brazilian man with a berimbau. The man begins to play, and the boy (who is named Leo) opens his eyes so wide it seems as if he is listening through them. When the man stops playing, he tells Leo that the upper part of the bow points toward the sky. Leo looks up and sees himself growing into a man, and sees his sons, his grandchildren, and the future. The lower part of the bow points toward the ground, and Leo eventually sees all of his ancestors, including his grandmother, great-grandmother, and the past. When the image disappears, the man hands the berimbau to Leo and says: "the upper part is the future, the lower part is the past, and in the middle, there's a young boy, who is a little distracted and full of stories in his head . . . and that little boy is you. . . . The berimbau is my present to you. Every time you

Figure 6.5: Bahian health campaign (Photo by Charles J. Wortman 2006). Courtesy Charles J. Wortman.

play it, remember me and these things I have told you."[14] This description is a concise explanation of how the berimbau is comprehended in contemporary capoeira practice. These themes also echo similar concepts discussed by some capoeira masters who believe that the berimbau possesses the ability to bring positive energy from the spirits high above, and the ancestors below, together in the present.

The berimbau was also incorporated into the short-lived comic book character Luana, created by Bahian Aroldo Macêdo (2000) in an attempt to create the first Afro-Brazilian heroine in this format (see Fig. 6.4). Culturally disparate mixed metaphors and stylized characteristics contribute to Luana's composite character. For example, she combines dreadlocks from the Rastafarian movement, eyes from Japanese *manga* animated artwork, slacks from the capoeira discipline, a small halter top, perhaps modeled after the blond-haired, blue-eyed pop phenomenon Xuxa, and enlarged lips from stereotypical North American black characters such as the "sambo." Luana possesses a *berimbau mágico* (magic berimbau), which enables her to travel through time and combat forces that threaten ecological and environmental issues. Her special powers were not able to overcome the mixture of images that comprised her character, as this comic venture only lasted for three months.

Figure 6.6: Bahian health campaign (Photo by Charles J. Wortman 2006). Courtesy Charles J. Wortman.

A Bahian health campaign took advantage of the berimbau's gendered imagery during the 2006 carnival season, where they appropriated the image of the berimbau to promote condom awareness, with the tip of the condom emerging out of the berimbau's gourd (see Fig. 6.5). The image is supported with text that reads "When things heat up, wear a condom. Protect yourself!" A second (see Fig. 6.6) reads "Summer Love."

Another example can be seen in the video of the late-1990s hit song "Dança da Garrafa" (Bottle Dance), a racy dance where a dancer places a bottle on the ground between her legs and slowly descends to "kiss" the bottle. In the video production, a berimbau telephone booth in the background is advantageously framed above the bottle between the dancer's legs. A man is also featured dancing over the bottle, playing with notions of gender inversion, thereby creating an extended subtext to the dance's meaning.[15]

Images of the berimbau have also appeared in Brazilian poetry, providing yet another manner in which to view the impact and meaning of the musical bow in Brazilian literature. The poem "Negro," composed in 1917 and published in 1932 by Raul Bopp, demonstrates romanticized laments of Afro-Brazilian souls residing within the berimbau.

Pesa em teu sangue a voz de	It weighs in your blood the voice
ignoradas origens	of unknown origins
As florestas guardaram na sombra	The forests kept in the shade
o segredo da tua história.	the secret of your history.
A tua primeira inscrição em baixo-relevo	Your first inscription in bas-relief
foi uma chicotada no lombo.	was a lash on your back.
Um dia atiraram-te no	One day they threw you into the
bojo de um navio negreiro	hold of a slave ship
E durante noites longas e	And during long, long nights
longas vieste ouvindo	you came listening to
O barulho do mar	The noise of the sea
Como um soluço dentro	Like a sobbing within
do porão soturno.	the gloomy hold.
O mar era um irmão da tua raça.	The sea was a brother of your race.
Um dia, de madrugada, uma nesga	One day, at dawn, a strip of sand
de praia e um porto,	and a port,
Armazéns com depósitos de escravos	Warehouses with rooms filled with slaves
E o gemido dos teus irmãos	And the wailing of your brothers
amarrados numa coleira	bound by a collar
De ferro.	Of iron.
Principiou aí a tua história.	That was the beginning of your history.
O resto, o Congo longínquo, as	The rest, the distant Congo,
palmeiras e o mar,	the palm trees and the sea,
Ficou se queixando no bojo	Remains lamenting in the gourd
do urucungo.	of the *urucungo* [musical bow].[16]

In this context, the musical bow serves as both repository of history and a conduit through which these stories are recounted. Moreover, essences of pain and suffering, longings for a distant homeland, and undocumented stories are all contained and retold through the musical bow's gourd.

Themes connected to this concept can be found in a short animated film entitled *A Lenda da Árvore Sagrada* (The Legend of the Sacred Tree), by Eládio Garcia Teles.[17] This film relates the story of a mysterious African tree, which, when brought to Brazil, began to recall its life in Africa, and was then transformed into a berimbau. Once again, as has been demonstrated in the work by Raquel Coelho and my own ethnographic information, the berimbau is believed to bring the past and the future together in the present.[18]

Miguel Lucena Filho (Miguezim de Princesa) is a journalist, lawyer and communications director for the Civil Police of the Federal District of Brasília. Lucena Filho's poem "A Vingança do Berimbau" is an artistic response to the inflammatory comments made by Dr. Antônio Natalino Manta Dantas in April 2008 (discussed in the introduction), which directly connects many of the major themes explored throughout this book.

(Courtesy Miguel Lucena Filho)

I

Superado pelo tempo,
Ensinando muito mal,
Fabricando mil diplomas,
Para entupir hospital,
O doutor da faculdade,
Botou, com toda maldade,
A culpa no berimbau.

I

Surpassed by time,
Teaching very poorly,
Manufacturing a thousand diplomas,
To choke the hospitals,
The doctor from the university,
Said with all his malice,
That guilty is the berimbau.

II

Disse o doutor Natalino,
Que o baiano é um mocó,
Sem coragem e inteligência,
Preguiçoso de dar dó,
Só liga pra carnaval,
E só toca berimbau,
Porque tem uma corda só.

II

Dr. Natalino said,
That Bahians are dumb,
Without courage and intelligence,
So lazy to give pity
Only connected to carnival,
And only plays the berimbau,
Because it only has one string.

III

O sujeito ignorante,
Não conhece o berimbau,
Que atravessou o mundo,
Com toda a força ancestral.
Na fronteira da emoção,
Traz da África a percussão,
Da diáspora cultural.

IV

Nem Baden Powell resistiu,
À percussão milenar,
Uma corda a encantar seis,
Na tristeza camará,
De Salvador da Bahia,
Quem toca e canta poesia,
Na dança sabe lutar.

V

O doutor, se estudou,
Na certa não aprendeu nada:
Diz que o som do Olodum,
Não passa de uma zoada,
E a cultura baiana,
É uma penca de bananas,
Primitiva e atrasada.

VI

Jimmy Cliff, Michael Jackson,
Paul Simon e o escambau,
Se renderam ao Olodum,
Com seu toque genial,
Que nasceu no Pelourinho,
E hoje abre caminho,
No cenário mundial.

III

The ignorant subject,
Doesn't know the berimbau,
That has crossed the world,
With all of its ancestral force.
On the frontier of emotion,
Brings from Africa the percussion,
Of the cultural diaspora.

IV

Not even Baden Powell resisted,
The timeless percussion,
One string that enchanted six,
In sadness comrade,
Of Salvador da Bahia,
Who plays and sings poetry,
In dance that knows how to fight.

V

The doctor, even if he studied,
It's certain that he didn't learn anything:
He says that the sound of Olodum,
Is no more than noise,
And Bahian culture,
Is a bunch of bananas,
Primitive and retarded [culturally, in terms
of class or education].

VI

Jimmy Cliff, Michael Jackson,
Paul Simon and many others
Have been captured by Olodum
With its genial beat,
That was born in Pelourinho,
And today leads the way
In the world scene.

VII

O baiano é primitivo?
Veja só o resultado:
Ruy foi o Águia de Haia;
Castro Alves, verso-alado,
De poeta condoreiro,
E gente do mundo inteiro,
Se curvou a Jorge Amado.

VII

Is the Bahian primitive?
Just look at the result:
Ruy was the Eagle of Hague;
Castro Alves, winged verses,
The "condoreiro" poetic style,
And people throughout the world,
Paid homage to Jorge Amado.

VIII

Bethânea, Caetano e Gil,
Armandinho, Dodô e Osmar,
Gal Costa, Moraes Moreira,
Batatinha a encantar,
João Gilberto, Bossa Nova,
Novos Baianos são prova,
Da grandeza do lugar.

VIII

Bethânea, Caetano and Gil,
Armandinho, Dodô and Osmar,
Gal Costa, Moraes Moreira,
Batatinha to enchant,
João Gilberto, Bossa Nova,
Novos Baianos are the proof,
Of [Bahia's] grandeur.

IX

Glauber, no Cinema Novo;
Gregório, velha poesia;
Gordurinha, no rojão;

Milton, na Geografia;
Anísio, na Educação;
Dias Gomes, na encenação;
João Ubaldo e Adonias.

IX

Glauber, in Cinema Novo;
Gregório, old poetry;
Gordurinha, in Rojão [Northeastern Musical Style];
Milton, in Geography;
Anísio, in Education;
Dias Gomes, in staging;
João Ubaldo and Adonias.

X

Menestrel da cantoria,
Temos o mestre Elomar,
Xangai, Wilson Aragão,
Bule-Bule a improvisar,
Roberto Mendes viola,
A chula-semba de Angola,
Nosso samba de além-mar.

X

Minstrel of singing,
We have master Elomar,
Xangai, Wilson Aragão,
Bule-Bule to improvise,
Roberto Mendes viola guitar,
The chula-semba from Angola,
Our samba from across the sea.

XI

Se eu fosse citar todos,
Que merecem citação,
Faria um livro de nomes,
Tão grande é a relação.
Desculpe, Afrânio Peixoto,
Esse doutor é um roto,
Procurando promoção!

XI

If I were to cite all,
Who merit citation,
I would write a book of names,
So large is the list.
I'm sorry, Afrânio Peixoto,
This doctor is ragged,
Wanting to be noticed!

XII

Com vergonha do que fez:
Insultar toda a Nação,
O tal doutor Natalino,
Pediu exoneração,
E não encontra ninguém,
Nem um nazista do além,
Para tomar a lição.

XII

Ashamed about what he did:
To insult the entire Nation,
That doctor Natalino,
Submitted his resignation,
And doesn't encounter anyone,
Not even a Nazi from beyond,
To take a lesson.

XIII

O baiano é pirracento,
Mas paga com bem o mal:
Dá uma chance a Natalino,
Lá no Mercado Central,
De ganhar alguns trocados,
Segurando o pau dobrado,
Da corda do berimbau.

XIII

The Bahians are pranksters,
But pay the evil with good:
Give Natalino a chance,
In the Central Market,
To beg for some coins,
Holding the curved stick,
Of the berimbau's string.[19]

This work demonstrates the many ways in which the berimbau and
its relationship to Bahian and Afro-Brazilian culture is joined with the
united power of the African diaspora as manifested in Jamaican reggae,
and interconnected with multiple strands of Brazilian arts, music, literature, and history. The first two stanzas are a direct response to Natalino's
comments. Lucena Filho poignantly pinpoints a source of the berimbau's
cultural power as being an "ancestral force" that compelled Baden Powell to become enchanted by the mystique of Bahia, the berimbau, and
Olodum. He then refutes the notion of a "primitive" Bahian culture with
a litany of preeminent intellectuals, including literary artists Ruy Barbosa

de Oliveira, Antônio de Castro Alves, Jorge Amado de Faria, João Ubaldo Ribeiro, Adonias Aguiar Filho, Gregório de Matos e Guerra, and Afrânio Peixoto; musicans and composers Maria Bethânia, Caetano Veloso, Gilberto Gil, Armandinho (Armando Silveira), Dodô (Adolfo Nascimento) and Osmar (Osmar Alvares Macêdo), Gal Costa, Moraes Moreira, João Gilberto, the group Novos Baianos, Batatinha (Oscar da Penha), Xangai, Wilson Aragão, and Elomar Figueira de Mello; film director Glauber de Andrade Rocha; playwright Alfredo de Freitas Dias Gomes; geographer Milton Santos; and educator Anísio Spínola Teixeira. Lucena Filho completes the imagery of the esteemed Dr. Natalino's fall from grace, by affording him the opportunity to take his place as a beggar playing a berimbau in Bahia's Mercado Modelo marketplace.

Conclusions

The berimbau is representative of a tradition that has been continually modified and incorporated into many musical genres throughout Brazil and the rest of the world. Through many years as an observer and performing musician, I have been able to reconstruct the history of the berimbau by drawing upon a synthesis of historical and ethnographic information. The berimbau has experienced a trajectory across a broad range of Brazilian social, cultural and musical contexts, demonstrating how it has become a symbol of identity and resistance in Brazil while retaining its identity as an African-derived musical bow. At this point in the discussion, I can now address the breadth of the berimbau's presence in Brazilian music and culture through analysis from three principal perspectives: the berimbau's association with capoeira; how it functions in relation to a nationalist Brazilian identity; and the berimbau as a physical and emblematic commodity.

One of the critical dynamics in this book is the manner in which the African presence is engaged in Brazilian society. My observation and analysis of the berimbau's presence offers an innovative way to trace, through the form and function of musical instruments, the mediation of African heritages in cultures with a legacy of slavery. Contemporary and historical issues of technology and transmission add yet another dimension to this mode of inquiry.

During the colonial and imperial eras, the berimbau was a musical instrument used by enslaved Africans and their descendants during times of work and leisure. Slave owners encouraged the use of African-derived musical instruments to attract attention in the public markets. Nineteenth-century chroniclers frequently noted the berimbau's presence in public marketplaces and on slave plantations, providing illustrations and brief descriptions of the instrument itself and its use in conjunction with dance.

After the abolition of slavery in 1888, the berimbau became less visible in public marketplaces, due in part to dominant social pressures that strived to distance Brazil from its legacy of slavery by de-emphasizing African-derived forms of expression. The berimbau rebounded to obtain a prominent position in Brazilian music and culture, most likely due to its formal alignment with capoeira in the early twentieth century. Both berimbau and capoeira have survived to the present day, and have been reinterpreted by Afro-Brazilians as powerful symbols of resistance. The berimbau moved from a regional Bahian to a national musical instrument in the late 1950s and early 1960s, disseminated through popular Brazilian music. The berimbau then began moving into global musical contexts in the early 1970s. Similar migrations of capoeira practitioners followed each of these expansions, providing additional visibility for the berimbau.

In looking at the social function of the berimbau within the realm of capoeira, other clues emerge that demonstrate how the berimbau achieved its prominent status. As capoeira changed from a fight to a dance in the early twentieth century, the berimbau became an inseparable element of the martial art. The berimbau likely became a neutral third party among capoeiristas who encountered each other for informal exhibitions on the streets of Bahia. Instead of subordinating oneself to the individual who was in charge of the dance proceedings, the berimbau's music metaphorically became the game's referee. The berimbau has been used to control dance in Afro-Brazilian social contexts at least since the 1850s, so it is plausible that this feature may have played a prominent role when the berimbau was incorporated into capoeira as a means to bring order to a street fight that had no rules. From this perspective, the berimbau assumed the function as a third-party negotiator. In order to participate in informal capoeira dance encounters, dance practitioners may have entered into a mutual agreement of respect for this third-party object, as opposed to subordinating themselves to the authority of another individual. While spiritual associations in relation to the berimbau vary among individual capoeiristas, the fundamental rule that the melodic rhythms of the berimbau must be obeyed is a principle unanimously agreed upon by all participants.

The union of the berimbau and capoeira can be seen as a key to their survival and upward mobility. As independent elements, both the berimbau and capoeira were social outcasts: the berimbau a distinctly identifiable instrument of black Brazilian culture, capoeira a combative slave-based fight that threatened social order. Following their union, they emerged in tandem to become symbols of national identity. Through this cultural ascension, capoeira moved toward inclusion in the middle classes and in wealthier neighborhoods. As a result of this process, both capoeira and the berimbau have lost aspects of their cultural roots, most noticeably in the form of capoeira classes being offered in urban gymnasiums alongside aerobics and other gymnastic fitness activities, including water-based "hydro capoeira."[1]

Organological change in the berimbau may have also played a key part in the berimbau's ascent in Brazilian society. Richard Graham[2] suggests that the physical modifications in gourd-resonated musical bows that resulted in the modern-day berimbau assisted with its upward mobility. Through this process the berimbau became representative of a mixture of various musical bows, and re-emerged as a musical instrument with a uniquely Brazilian heritage. Although the berimbau successfully underwent this transformation, it continues to be associated with folkloric expression, black music, the lower classes, and primitivism in Brazilian society.

It is in capitalizing on notions of primitiveness where berimbau musicians have been most successful. By taking advantage of its audience's assumptions, berimbau composers and performers have surprised and surpassed audience expectations by demonstrating that the berimbau can present a rich palette of musical timbres. This notion extends to berimbau solos at folkloric shows that I have observed both within Brazil and on international tours to the United States. Nevertheless, these notions of primitiveness serve as an important link to reinforcing the berimbau's African-derived heritage that maintains its character as a Brazilian musical bow.

The berimbau has helped define concepts of national, collective, and individual identity in various eras. In this regard, the 1960s music of Baden Powell served to promote the berimbau in Brazilian popular music. This use of the berimbau was representative of national ideals that drew upon its presence as a folkloric instrument, which in turn added elements of Brazilian authenticity to the musical compositions. The music of Gilberto Gil drew upon this icon to integrate Brazilian and non-Brazilian musical and cultural elements within a contested musical arena. Whereas Powell saw himself as literally putting all of Bahia's history and culture into his musical compositions, Gil consciously incorporated the acoustic berimbau for the purpose of balancing his use of electric guitars, rock and roll, and other non-Brazilian musical elements at popular music festivals.

In contrast, while the groups Berimbrown and Olodum draw upon the berimbau to represent authenticity, they do so to construct an alternative identity. The berimbau and capoeira are components of an expansive symbol bank that is used for the construction of a pan-African identity among young black Brazilians. This strategy is enacted to deny traditional models presented to them through Brazilian nationalist ideologies. Berimbrown co-founder mestre Negoativo³ comments that the range of fashion styles exhibited in the musical ensemble represent distinct African American fashion trends from various eras. He believes that the complete group image represents a summary of his life experience. During his youth, Negoativo participated in the bailes da pesada that traveled to Minas Gerais, and he accompanied the musical spirit of protest that emerged from the Bahian blocos afro. The multiple identities that coexist in Berimbrown can also be extended to represent the diverse realm of individual perspectives that comprise contemporary Afro-Brazilian identity.

As the berimbau becomes adapted for use in diverse musical contexts, it is being modified technically and organologically to accommodate different needs. Within this process, the berimbau is becoming more distanced from the capoeira tradition. What emerges as a universal trait among innovative berimbau musicians and composers is active pursuit of expanding the berimbau's musical potential. Naná Vasconcelos's principal contribution is a unique approach to melodic-rhythmic improvisation inspired by rhythmic ideas derived from other multitimbral percussion instruments, such as the drumset. Luiz D'Anunciação has removed the caxixi and developed a two-stick technique in order to expand the technical capabilities of berimbau sound combinations. This technique greatly enhances the berimbau's use within the realm of art music compositions, since there is now a broader range of expression available without losing the distinctive timbres that identify the sound of the berimbau. Dinho Nascimento has incorporated innovative technical and physical changes in order to accommodate his musical inspirations that include using the berimbau in music that he defines as the blues. Ramiro Musotto uses a different material for the resonating gourd, which accentuates the sound of the movement of the gourd against and away from the body. In most of these recent cases, the berimbau's volume must be enhanced by electronic amplification, because these modifications tend to reduce the instrument's overall sound production.

As the berimbau becomes distanced from the realm of capoeira and appears in alternative performance contexts, it undergoes physical modifications that change its sonority. Through this movement across contexts, questions arise concerning when it ceases to be the berimbau and begins to emerge as something else. In other words, how far can tradition be transformed and still be representative of that initial referential? Since tradition is constantly changing, do these new meanings represent that tradition? In order to answer these questions, I return to the composer and performer who popularized the berimbau in Brazilian popular music in the early 1960s, Baden Powell. In his composition "Berimbau," Powell translated the melodic rhythms to his guitar, which helped propel him to national and international success. When he composed "Lapinha" in the late 1960s, he was accused of stealing from, and thus disrespecting the tradition. In the case of "Berimbau," it could be argued that Powell was transforming folkloric material from one inanimate object to another: from berimbau to guitar. For "Lapinha" he borrowed directly from a capoeira song for use as a refrain to frame his newly composed verse. In this case, Powell extracted melodic and textual material that contained respected historical references within the capoeira tradition.

Powell used the same compositional process of drawing upon folkloric material for incorporation into both compositions, but "Lapinha" touched a cultural nerve. On the surface, it could be said that Powell only failed to correctly attribute the folkloric source. An analysis of the particular capoeira song's roots reveals that music within the realm of anonymous capoeira material may have strong links to other Brazilian musical genres. "Lapinha" and another capoeira song, "E Besouro," are both related to Noel Rosa's 1932 nationally popular samba tune "Fita Amarela." Rosa claimed authorship for a samba that apparently had been informally circulating throughout Rio de Janeiro samba circles. This suggests the possibility that sometime between the early 1930s and the late 1950s, when mestre Traíra's version of "E Besouro" was recorded, that "Fita Amarela" was adapted for use in a capoeira song, and was most likely nationally disseminated through the airwaves of Rio's Rádio Nacional.

Nevertheless, this circuitous route demonstrates a similar process of music-making among urban *sambistas* of Rio de Janeiro and urban capoeiristas of Salvador, where similar songs circulated freely from session to session. It also demonstrates the tenuous nature of traditional music. Thus, when capoeira practitioners accused Baden Powell of stealing from the tradition, which tradition were they defending, samba or capoeira? If it is the capoeira tradition, does it represent the period from the 1900s to the present that is inseparable from the berimbau, or does it stem from an earlier era? Greg Downey[4] comments that "E Besouro" breaks many conventional rules of capoeira song structures but believes that, since it is a popular song among capoeira practitioners, exceptions to the rules have their place within the capoeira tradition and history. These exceptions are necessary because the roots of the song have been derived from different traditions. Returning to the question of when the berimbau stops being the berimbau, perhaps the question should be rephrased: when does capoeira stop being capoeira?

As the berimbau has transcended social classes and racial boundaries, its sociopolitical movement has constantly been questioned. For lower-class black Brazilians who have had limited access to social ladders in Brazilian society, the berimbau symbolically represents a possibility of cultural ascension. As Dinho Nascimento candidly discussed, his musical innovations were met with resistance from both within and beyond the capoeira community, and perceptions from these two camps turned positive only after Nascimento's recording received a national award.

Naná Vasconcelos, most visibly perceived in Brazil as the individual who moved the berimbau into a global music context, did not become nationally recognized until he achieved international success with Gato Barbieri, Pat Metheny, Egberto Gismonti, Don Cherry, Colin Wolcott, and many others. Although Vasconcelos has become internationally renowned, his non-mainstream artistic vision has resulted in the majority of his recordings being produced by non-Brazilian record companies.

Vasconcelos has also benefited from non-Brazilian audiences who were not familiar with the berimbau or capoeira, and he therefore was not obligated to conform to cultural norms as dictated by the capoeira tradition.

Since Ramiro Musotto is from Argentina, he was able to pursue innovations as a cultural outsider who showed respect for the tradition by immersing himself in Brazilian culture, and who developed less radical performance techniques than Nascimento. Musotto extends conventional berimbau performance practice by incorporating metric modulation and creating new arrangements of multilayered berimbau textures that follow principles established through the capoeira tradition.

In addition to observing the berimbau's movement across social boundaries, other aspects such as the commoditization of this musical bow must be considered. This commoditization can be seen in two principal forms: actual berimbaus and representational berimbaus. Actual berimbaus include mass-produced (by hand), low-quality tourist berimbaus of various sizes, medium-quality berimbaus that are available in music stores, and capoeira berimbaus, often handmade from capoeira academies and practitioners, which are very heavy. Representational berimbaus include jewelry, capoeira academy logos, tattoos, and numerous examples found in Brazilian fine arts (paintings, sculptures), public spaces (telephone booths), and literary arts. The berimbau also supports dramatic roles, such as the quilombola or Preto Velho presented in Mário Tavares's *Ganguzama*, who appears to tell of Zumbi dos Palmares's death. In this case, the berimbau is representative of an elderly, wise African-derived spirit.

Deeper connections can be seen regarding spiritual associations with musical bows in the African diaspora. In Cuba, the *burumbumba* is believed to speak with the dead in African-derived religious practice.[5] In Brazil, the berimbau is played at some Brazilian capoeiristas' funerals. Other examples, ranging from capoeira-derived ethnographic information to Brazilian children's books,[6] suggest that the berimbau metaphorically joins ancestors with the spirits to create the present. These concepts are supported by similar multidimensional concepts found in central African spiritual beliefs.[7] Raul Bopp's imagery in the poem "Negro" utilizes the berimbau as a history of emotions. By focusing on enslaved Africans who have been stripped of their history, Bopp depicts their only retained memories from their distant homeland as "lamenting in the gourd" of the berimbau.[8]

With the berimbau as focal point, one can also make connections between various types of music in Brazil. For example, comparisons can be made between electroacoustic music composed for the concert hall and electronic dance music composed for nightclubs. The setting for the former is designed to keep audience members in their seats, the latter to keep the audience on the dance floor. Although these settings are vastly different, parallels can be seen in the compositional processes of vanguarda composer Tim Rescala and the electronic dance music of M4J and Ram Science. In each case the berimbau has been recorded or sampled, electronically processed, and repackaged in a new sound environment. While electronic dance composers modify the berimbau material, they are somewhat confined by the limits of the dance genres that they work in. The case of M4J demonstrates how a lyrical, organic-sounding sample from Naná Vasconcelos can dramatically change through increased tempo and raised pitch. A comparison with the original Vasconcelos song highlights aspects of Vasconcelos's musicianship and how he subtly modifies a rhythmic cell over various repetitions as a means to generate excitement. The M4J cross-section of this small fragment of Vasconcelos's work reduces the sound to a mechanically repetitive component within the larger piece.

Ramilson Maia of Ram Science takes a different approach than M4J, by using short berimbau fragments, and through an additive process, building a multi-layered berimbau drum machine. In contrast, Tim Rescala's work demonstrates another universe of expressive possibilities, since the composer has absolute freedom to create, and is not obligated to produce his work on top of a repetitive bass drum beat. Rescala's composition is successful for two reasons. First, he combined the allure of technology with an acoustic berimbau performer to accompany the pre-recorded tape. Second, he completely deconstructed an extensive timbre spectrum from the berimbau, and reconstructed processed elements of this realm on the recorded tape. As an added component, his soundscape makes the listener question which sounds are being emitted from the berimbau, and which from the speakers.

The boundaries between art and popular music came into question in the 1960s with bossa nova and popular Brazilian music by Baden Powell and Gilberto Gil. Powell's *Afro Sambas* were orchestrated and conducted by César Guerra-Peixe, and Gilberto Gil's "Domingo no Parque" was orchestrated and conducted by Rogério Duprat, both prominent art music composers and arrangers. Although art music and popular music have different societal functions, these recordings demonstrate that the concert halls of Theatro Municipal and the airwaves of nationally televised popular song festivals were not as remotely disconnected as indicated by the separate genre labels. The berimbau can be seen as a point of connection within these realms. When Carlos Negreiros learned that the berimbau was going to be featured in an orchestral work in Rio de Janeiro's concert hall in the early 1960s, he was well aware of the historical and cultural significance of that moment in time, and, although he had never set foot in the theater prior to that occasion, he attended that performance to witness the event.[9]

The development of a comprehensive berimbau notational scheme has also helped establish a presence for the musical bow in recent years. As a result of these innovations, the berimbau can now equally participate in compositional terms with other developed art music instruments. Prior to these innovations beginning in the 1970s, the berimbau was relegated to the percussion section as an accessory instrument, which served to establish and maintain a rhythmic base for musical compositions. With the development of musical notation in the style of D'Anunciação's revised scheme,[10] every note and timbre can be graphically represented in a systematic manner and then be consistently reproduced by the musician. Moreover, through D'Anunciação's methodology, musicians and composers from around the world can approach a comprehensive understanding of the broad range of sounds produced by the berimbau, without setting foot in Brazil.

As scholars begin to trace the berimbau's movement throughout the world,[11] it will be imperative to collect ethnographic data from all berimbau specialists who are creating new techniques and developing organological modifications for use in new local contexts. Information from these specialists and practitioners can then be compared and contrasted with data presented in this study as a means to construct a comprehensive image of the berimbau's meaning and significance in a global perspective.

There are still many aspects to be pursued about the berimbau in Brazilian music and culture. During my research, I encountered many art music works that utilize berimbau, and a comparative study could demonstrate an understanding of how the berimbau has functioned in each of these contexts. Moreover, a survey of the berimbau in Brazilian popular music lyrics could lead to a deeper understanding of the berimbau's presence within the imagery of song texts. The berimbau is not just a musical instrument, but also a symbol and a highly charged metaphor. Its form and function make it an exceptionally fluid point of convergence, enabling it to extend its reach into new musical contexts, while visibly retaining its identity as a Brazilian cultural product. A comparative study of the berimbau in relation to other folk musical instruments that have been incorporated into art music contexts, such as the Hungarian cimbalom and the Spanish guitar, would highlight the berimbau's case as a unique instrument in world music cultures. In the case of the berimbau, it is an instrument that has assimilated into processes of musical globalization while simultaneously maintaining a distinct identity as a Brazilian musical bow.

Glossary

Afro samba Term applied to Baden Powell's and Vinícius de Moraes's bossa nova music that incorporated elements of Afro-Brazilian themes including *capoeira*, the *berimbau*, and *candomblé*.

Afro-Mineiro Regional application of the term Afro-Brazilian. Mineiro is in reference to the state of Minas Gerais.

Agogô Metal double-bell played with a stick.

Alfaia Double headed rope tensioned drum used in *Maracatu*, a *congado* from Pernambuco.

Antropofagia Term used by modernist poet Oswald de Andrade to signify cultural cannibalism. The principle of this concept is that for Brazil to create national works of art, Brazilian culture producers should consume or incorporate techniques from European masters while simultaneously focusing within Brazil's borders for thematic inspiration.

Baião Northeastern Brazilian music and dance form. Representative of the desert-like sertão region, often played with accordion, triangle, and *zabumba* (small bass drum).

Bailes da Pesada Term applied to popular music dances that emerged in Rio de Janeiro in the 1970s. These dances featured recordings of North American popular music artists such as James Brown and the Jackson Five. Recent manifestations derived from these initial dances include the "bailes do funk."

Bandeirantes Expeditionary forces who explored Brazil's hinterlands during the colonial era under a unified *bandeira* (flag).

Batuque Name of secular dance of central African origin. Generic name for Afro-Brazilian drumming and dance styles.

Berimbau Generic name used in Brazil to signify gourd-resonated musical bows. Term is also applied to Jew's harp and mouth bows. For description, see *Berimbau de barriga*.

Berimbau de barriga *"Berimbau* of the belly." Signifies gourd-resonated musical bow that developed in Brazil, descended from various African musical bows. Consists of an *arco* (wooden bow), *cabaça* (calabash gourd), *dobrão* (stone or coin), *corda* (steel string), *caxixi* (basket rattle), and *baqueta* (thin stick). The stone or coin is used to interrupt the vibrations of the string and alter the pitch and timbre.

Bloco afro Afro-Brazilian carnival parading group that emerged in Salvador in the mid-1970s. Some associations, such as Olodum, have become year-round institutions that provide economic and social opportunities for their community. The plural is *blocos afro*.

Bossa nova "New Way." Musical genre that developed and flourished in the late 1950s until the early 1960s. Incorporated elements of *samba* and North American jazz.

Candomblé Religious practice influenced by several African cultural groups (Bantú, Fon, Yorubá), Brazilian indigenous cultures, and popular Catholicism. *Candomblé* instrumentation includes a strict number of three *atabaques* (conical drums of various sizes).

Capoeira Dance of possible Central African origin that incorporates qualities of acrobatics and martial arts to varying degrees. *Capoeira* was used as a fight among Africans and Afro-Brazilians during slavery and in the early post-abolition years in Brazil. Since the 1930s, it has transformed from a fight into a non-contact exhibition, leading practitioners to characterize it as a "game." *Capoeira* incorporates musical accompaniment, which includes the use of one or more *berimbaus*.

Capoeira Angola Modern style of *capoeira* that symbolically represents a continuation of the *capoeira* tradition. Generally characterized as slow game with "closed" body movements, by maintaining the body closer to the ground. Today, a three-*berimbau* ensemble of various sizes is strictly observed.

Capoeira Regional Modern style of *capoeira* that has incorporated elements of the *batuque* and other aspects of martial art aesthetics. Generally characterized as a fast game with "open" body movements, featuring longer extensions, and thus farther from the ground. Musical ensembles may feature one or more *berimbaus*.

Capoeirista Individual whose activities exist almost exclusively within the realm of *capoeira*.

Carnival Pre-Lenten public celebration that precedes Ash Wednesday. Celebrated in Catholic countries, and to a lesser extent in New Orleans. In Portuguese, *carnaval*.

Caxixi Basket rattle that accompanies the *berimbau de barriga*.

Choro Urban instrumental music developed in late-nineteenth-century Rio de Janeiro. Subgenres and influences include tangos, waltzes, and polkas, among others. Rhythmic characteristics accentuate syncopation.

Congada (also **Congado**) Dance procession that evokes essences of African royalty. The procession is to signify the coronation ceremony of the *"Rei do Congo"* (King of the Congo). During slavery, this figure served as an intermediary between enslaved populations and the slave owner.

Congopop Term derived by Berimbrown to signify their unique synthesis of global and local popular music styles.

Cuíca Single-headed drum with bamboo stick attached to the center of the head. Sound is produced through friction by rubbing a damp cloth along the stick.

Escola de samba "Samba school." Neighborhood *carnaval* associations that emerged in underdeveloped Rio de Janeiro neighborhoods in the late 1920s. These associations exist to varying degrees throughout Brazil, and now provide many social services to their community throughout the year.

Folia de Reis Religious musical ensembles that perform in the streets in December and January. Also related to Three Kings Day celebrations.

Funk (Brazilian) Used in the 1970s to signify North American black pop music, notably artists like James Brown and the Jackson Five. Since the 1990s, this term has expanded to included Brazilian electronic musics that are somewhat related to North American hip-hop, house, techno, etc. Sansone (2001) provides extended definitions of local usages of funk in various regions throughout Brazil.

Jogo Game. Often used by *capoeira* practitioners to describe the dance.

Lundu Central African song and dance form that is related to many urban Brazilian song styles including the *samba*.

Mameluco Baby of indigenous and Portuguese heritage.

Marimba Ten- or twelve-key wooden xylophone with gourd resonators of central African origin. It is no longer used in Brazil.

Mestizaje/Mestiçagem Process of cultural mixing and whitening in Brazil. Ideology is based upon the concept that Brazil's population is comprised of a mixture of African, indigenous, and Portuguese heritages. Through mixing these elements over many generations, preferred aspects would be enhanced, and supposedly less desirable aspects would be eliminated.

Mestre Master. Used to demarcate advanced *capoeira* practitioner. The status of *mestre* is obtained following an extended apprenticeship.

Modinha Sentimental song style that is representative of a mixture between the *lundu* and Portuguese influences.

MPB (Música Popular Brasileira) Acronym for *Música Popular Brasileira* (Brazilian popular music). Emerged as popular musical genre that followed *bossa nova* and featured combinations of many Brazilian and non-Brazilian musical genres. Now signifies general Brazilian popular music.

Orixá Deity within *candomblé*. Each represents an element of nature, such *Xangô*, the god of thunder, *Yemanjá*, the goddess of the sea, etc. Balances between these forces are often maintained by *Exú*, the guardian of the crossroads.

Preto Velho "Old black man." Represents the purified spirits of ancient enslaved Africans in Brazil within the religious practice of *umbanda*.

Quilombo Encampments of enslaved people who escaped to freedom in Brazil.

Quilombola Resident of a *quilombo*.

Roda Circle. Demarcates dance space in many genres of Brazilian dance, particularly *samba* and *capoeira*. The circle is formed by musicians and dance participants.

Samba Most popular form of Brazilian song and dance of central African, Portuguese, and (to a lesser extent) North American influences. Features a two-beat rhythmic repetition alternating between light and heavy emphasis. Multiple rhythmic cells are built upon this framework, establishing an interlocking syncopation that creates distinct musical personalities for each of the separate percussion instruments.

Samba de Roda *Samba* danced within a circle. Often includes Brazilian percussion instruments such as the *pandeiro* (tambourine), *timbal* (long conical drum), handclapping, and singing.

Samba reggae Musical style synthesis of *samba* and Jamaican reggae, developed and popularized by the *bloco afro* Olodum. Drumming style incorporates percussion instruments from the *escola de samba* with techniques derived from *candomblé*.

Sambista Individual whose activities exist almost exclusively within the realm of *samba*.

Toque Short repetitive rhythmic cell, also can be translated as "beat."

Tumbadora Term for a conga (conical) drum.

Umbanda Religion that has syncretized Afro-Brazilian religious practice, spiritism, and Catholicism. Developed in the twentieth century.

Vanguarda Term used to signify avant-garde art music in Brazil in the 1960s and 1970s.

Appendix: Musical Examples

1. "Berimbau Blues"
Dinho Nascimento[1]

Transcribed by Eric A. Galm

Molto Ritard

Coda

2. "La Danza da Tezcatlipoca Roja"
Ramiro Musotto[2]

Transcribed by Eric A. Galm

3. *Divertimento para Berimbau e Violão* (First Page)
Luiz D'Anunciação[3]

Reproduction courtesy Luiz D'Anunciação

Notes

» »

A Note Regarding Musical Transcriptions

1. See figure x.1. Throughout the text, Figures and Transcriptions will be referred to as Fig and T, respectively (e.g., "see T 1.1" = see Transcription 1.1).
2. Seeger (1958).
3. D'Anunciação (1990a). See Figure 5.4 and Appendix 3. D'Anunciação's musical notation is discussed in chapter 5.
4. T. 4.2 contains an "x" notehead, which represents playing the side of the gourd with the wooden stick.

Introduction

1. This chain of events has been adapted from several sources. The capoeira/police encounter occurred in New York's Central Park in the late 1990s (see Galm 1997), although there are usually several capoeira exhibitions on a daily basis in the Mercado Modelo. I have not seen any conflicts regarding performance permits; the book in the Biblioteca Nacional is *Berimbau* (Coelho 2000); *Ganguzama* premiered at Rio's Theatro Municipal in 1963, and was performed again in 1979 and 1999; berimbau telephone booths are found in Bahia, and the sculpture *Tocador de Berimbau* is located in the lobby of the Hotel Nacional in Brasília, and was originally created in Bahia. While some of the elements described in this encounter occurred in different geographical and temporal contexts, this speculative instance highlights how the berimbau is represented in several artistic disciplines that appeal to audiences of different ages, generations and social classes.
2. Carneiro (1975:15).
3. Anonymous (2008).
4. Graham and Robinson (2003) have begun preliminary work on the spread of the berimbau in a global context.
5. For example, see development of the Frevo Dance in Pernambuco (Lewis 1992) and life among enslaved people in Rio de Janerio (Karasch 1987).
6. Oliveira (1958).
7. Rego (1968).
8. Shaffer (1982 [orig. pub. 1976]).
9. See, for example, Almeida (1986), Lewis (1992), Dawson (1994), Dossar (1992), Capoeira (1995, 1999, and 2000), and Downey (1998, 2002, and 2005). For studies specifically on the berimbau, see D'Anunciação (1971 and 1990), Shaffer (1982), Pinto (1988-disc, 1990-disc, and 1991), and Graham (1991). D'Anunciação (1990) provides an introduction to extended berimbau techniques beyond the

realm of capoeira in the second half of his work. Although Downey (1998:141) incorporates a broad interdisciplinary analysis of the berimbau within the context of capoeira, he does not recognize its pervasiveness in Brazilian society. He states that the berimbau is now "rarely used outside of capoeira practice ... a few jazz musicians, especially those experimenting with traditional Bahian sounds, are noteworthy exceptions."

10. I use "berimbau" for brevity. Exceptions will be noted.

11. Maximum resonance and harmonic range of the instrument can be obtained by placing the tuning loop at a few specific locations where discernible harmonics can be heard between the tuning loop and lower end of the bow. This is based on the harmonic nodes on the string, similar to a monochord.

12. The dobrão is a generic term similar to "doubloon," and no specific coin is indicated, although capoeira practitioners give preference to copper (Galm 1997).

13. Names associated with the berimbau in Brazil include *berimbau, berimbau-de-barriga, urucungo, rucumbo, uucungo* (Cascudo 1972:157–58); *orucungo, oricungo, uricungo, ricungo, marimbau, gobo, bucumbumba, gunga, macungo, matungo, mutungo, marimba* (Cascudo 1972:895); *humbo, rucumbo, violâm, hungo, m'bolumbumba, berimbau de barriga, marimba, rucumbo, urucungo, gobo, bucumbunga, bucumbumba, uricungo, viola de arame, lucungo* (Shaffer 1982:14); *viola, médio* (Lewis 1992:137); *beira boi, contra-gunga* (Lewis 1992:231); and *bubumbumba, rukungu, birimbau* (Schneider 1991:40).

14. See Williams (2001:27).

15. This was a trend throughout Latin America, as newly independent republics developed laws and philosophies that were advantageously adapted from European sources within the notion of developmental scientific progress. In Brazil, this process began with Augusto Conde, a nineteenth-century modernist sociologist who followed the trend to scientifically prove evolutionism (See Aguirre and Salvatore 2001).

16. Alencar (1968). Gomes's work is discussed again briefly in connection with *Ganguzama* in chapter 5.

17. Folklorist Silvio Romero later followed evolutionist ideology by pursuing folklore as a way to understand the identity and characteristics of the Brazilian people. Studies of African cultural expressions in Brazil were undertaken not as a way to celebrate and validate their presence, but rather to understand the supposed potential danger that they were believed to present to a broader "civilized" society. These ideologies dominated intellectual thought until the declaration of Brazilian modernism in the early 1920s (See Borges 1995).

18. Neves (1981:36).

19. De Andrade (1928). For a descriptive analysis, see Jackson (1979) and Perrone (1996). Another important advocate of Brazil's modernist movement was Mário de Andrade, who conducted broad-based studies of musical expression throughout the country. He presented some of the first musical studies that incorporated detailed musical notation with song texts in many genres including children's songs, drinking songs, and folkloric songs.

20. Freyre (1933). Literally translated as Big House (slave owner's house) and the Slave Quarters. Published in English translation as *The Masters and the Slaves* in 1946.

21. Freyre's principal themes identified and defined an ideal Brazilian culture as a carefully balanced combination of Portuguese, African, and indigenous traits. He believed that this process would yield a unique *mestiço* (mixed-race) population, and thus become a distinctive national characteristic. As a result, Brazil's national amalgamation would eventually emerge as a "racial democracy," thus highlighting the valued European traits, and enhancing them with desirable aspects of African and indigenous traits, while simultaneously eliminating aspects that were considered less desirable. For more on this process, see Skidmore (1974).

22. General Eurico Dutra led the government from 1946 to 1951. He "seemed to promise a continuation of the Vargas system without the authoritarian trappings" (Skidmore 1986:63).

23. Skidmore (1986:11) notes that coffee-producing states eventually joined the coalition in reaction to a failed political policy regarding coffee prices.

24. Vianna (1999:51). Of course, processes of miscegenation had been occurring in Brazilian society for four hundred years prior to the development of these national policies. One of the defining elements of this process is that Portuguese culture dominates and redirects the supposedly subordinate influences of indigenous and African elements.

25. Williams (2001). Drawing from theories that discuss autonomous "pure art," he locates cultural production and cultural management temporally within this specific context. Through "cultural authority," regulators seek to confine cultural activities through positions of dominance from legal or commercially driven positions. Tangible cultural products (such as actual items or concepts) are the result of a hierarchical hegemonic structure that attributes some type of meaning to the entire system, although this meaning varies among all individuals and organizations involved in this process.

26. The first large-scale state preservation project was to restore the crumbling Catholic churches in the remote mining town of Ouro Preto, Minas Gerais. Built in the late eighteenth century, these churches were symbolic of private patronage from families made wealthy from the region's gold rush. Williams notes that this process created a multilayered connection between the officials in Rio de Janeiro, their satellite agents, local elites, and craftspeople that retained knowledge of technical and material construction in their collective cultural memory. Recognizing the value of local knowledge (and also connected with the Modernist movement), Capanema invited Mário de Andrade to prepare a model that would create a governmental entity to preserve Brazil's heritage.

27. Andrade developed a detailed scheme for systematically documenting cultural production throughout Brazil, including the creation of four national registries to be housed in corresponding museums. The four thematic focus areas were archaeology and ethnography; historical art; national and international fine arts; and national and international applied arts. Through the process of creating these

four registries, a collective national aesthetic was created, and a system enacted to superimpose tangible objects onto a "national cultural imaginary as works of artistic beauty and genius" (Williams 2000:99–107). Andrade's cultural project was realized on a limited scale with the development of the Missão de Pesquisas Folclóricas, which documented several traditions of northeastern Brazilian popular culture, music and dance in the late 1930s.

28. Although the Vargas administration gave preference to Eurocentric cultural expression, Afrocentric forms of expression also improved their societal position between the 1930s and 1950s.

29. Neves (1981:15) notes that in Brazil, popular music is "a music of the people, which moves towards nationalization of its constitutive elements and forms."

30. According to Renato Ortiz, popular culture was initially defined in the 1920s and 1930s as an expression that evolved from folkloric roots of "the people" (Ortiz in Stroud 2000:92).

31. See McCann (2001).

32. Vianna (1999:49) specifically cites *caipira* ("country music") from São Paulo, and rural northeastern rhythms.

33. I also address concepts of Brazilian popular music in relation to North American culture in Galm (2008).

34. R Ferreira (2000:49). For a more comprehensive discussion on questions of race and class in Brazil, see, for example, Hanchard (1994) and Skidmore (1995).

35. Pinho (2002:196). For an analysis of black movements in Brazil along with a discussion of differences in racial classification between the United States and Brazil, see Burdick (1998a).

36. See Crook (1993 and 2005), for example.

37. Olodum's president, João Jorge dos Santos Rodrigues, who has been interviewed by many academics and journalists, has publicly voiced most of the group's ideology. For an overview of Olodum's ideological position, see Crook and Johnson (1999).

38. By focusing on dance movements of participants at a bloco afro rehearsal, dance ethnologist Anna Scott highlights the impact of North American soul music on contemporary youth culture in Afro-Brazilian musical genres. She observes that these movements are borrowed from the North American style of James Brown, and they have undergone a transformative process resulting in a transcultural form of expression that presents a Brazilian identity (Scott 1998).

39. See discussion of the marimba in chapter 1.

40. Neiva (1958; 1963a; 1963b).

Chapter 1

1. For historical surveys of the berimbau in Brazilian culture, see Carneiro (1981), Fryer (2000), Galm (1997), Graham (1991), and Shaffer (1982).

2. Denis [1816–1819] in Scheinowitz (1993:328).

3. Brandão (1988). This work by Brandão was originally presented at the 1º

Congresso Afro-Brasileiro (First Afro-Brazilian Congress) in 1935. Although this research was conducted in the early 1930s, Brandão clearly worked with historical documents, as can be seen in the title of his 1914 publication *Viçosa de Alagoas: O Município e a Cidade (Notas Históricas, Geográphicas e Archeólogicas* (Exuberance of Alagoas: The municipal district and the city [Historical, Geographical and Archeological Notes]).

4. Carneiro (1975).
5. Brandão (1988:48).
6. *Ibid.*
7. Verse collected by Brandão (1988:48). An adaptation of this verse is directed at Caboclos (mestiços of indigenous and European ancestry), which uses the berimbau to reinforce stereotypical indigenous imagery: *Caboclo dorme no chão / no oco do pé de pau / com seu arco e sua flecha / tocando seu berimbau* (The caboclo sleeps on the ground / in the hole at the foot of a tree / with his bow and his arrow / playing his berimbau) (Bola Sete 1997:106).
8. Lewis (1992:40).
9. See Kubik (1979), Almeida (1986), and Lewis (1992), for example.
10. Both the berimbau and capoeira are believed to have descended from Central African cultures, primarily Angola. There was a direct trade of enslaved Africans from the Angolan Portuguese colony to Brazil.
11. "This might be ... how the gourd bow, in Angola and Brazil of past centuries a solo instrument, became a group instrument in Brazilian capoeira" (Kubik 1979:31). Although Kubik's observations derived from his own fieldwork, a more comprehensive investigation into historical studies may deepen understanding of how the berimbau's musical function changed from a solo instrument in central Africa and colonial Brazil to a capoeira instrument in the late nineteenth century.
12. Denis [1816–1819], in Scheinowitz (1993:329). I thank capoeira scholar Frederico de Abreu for providing this reference.
13. Ribeyrolles in Fryer (2000).
14. The first specific date Campos provides is 1891, when he notes a series of official attempts to separate the church from the public celebration. This eventually resulted in the procession being limited to the space immediately in front of the church. Campos then speaks of earlier Senhor dos Navegantes celebrations (demonstrating that this was a well-established tradition by 1891), in which the statue "traditionally began its procession at 7:00pm" (Campos 1941:131). Pierre Verger (1981:7) bases his study on official documents from the mid-nineteenth century, and utilizes more recent documents, such as Campos, as a guide for the knowledge of religious and popular festivals from this era.
15. *Fervilhava a multidão fusca. Batuques. Sambas. Rodas de capoeiragem. Ouviam-se pandeiros, cavaquinhos, violas, harmônicas, berimbau e palmas cadenciadas. Um pandemônio* (Campos 1941:131).
16. The master who is directing the game may play any one of these three berimbaus, although they usually play the gunga or médio in this capacity (D Ferreira 1997-int:24 Jan, Grande 1997-int).

17. See Lewis (1992:42–43) and Rego (1968:21–24).

18. See Assunção (2005) and Lewis (1992).

19. See Dawson (1994) and Karasch (1987).

20. Almeida (1986:25).

21. See Dossar (1992) and Lewis (1992).

22. For a detailed analysis of the meaning of the term *regional*, see Assunção (2005). Lewis (1992:60) posits that the name was initially used to demarcate the region of Bahia, and later represented all of the students who have studied with mestre Bimba. A 1972 interview with mestre Bimba in the *Jornal do Brasil*, suggests that he adopted the name *capoeira regional* in response to a bureaucratic process that would not openly support its African heritage. When he went to the Education Secretary of Bahia to officially register the name *capoeira de Angola*, the term *Angola* was rejected. As a result, it was necessary for Bimba "to re-submit the term *luta regional* [regional fight] in order for it to be accepted" (Gropper 1972). This statement is contradictory to Bimba's philosophy of creating a type of capoeira that was distinct from capoeira Angola as promoted by Pastinha, and Assunção (2005) demonstrates that Bimba was continually forced to justify the validity and relevance of his regional style.

23. Reis (2000) presents a good discussion about differences between capoeira Angola and capoeira regional.

24. Capoeira scholar Ricardo de Souza (1997) suggests that capoeira Angola musical ensembles did not consistently employ a fixed number of three berimbaus until the 1970s. Capoeira academies in the northeastern United States generally exhibited an unspecified number of berimbaus in the 1980s and early 1990s. There was movement to a fixed number of three berimbaus following the release of the Smithsonian Folkways recording *Grupo de Capoeira Angola Pelourinho* (1996-disc), which promoted a strong presence of capoeira Angola in Brazil and throughout the United States (Galm 2001).

25. Mestres of capoeira Angola have acknowledged that they play capoeira regional berimbau toques in non-capoeira settings (such as informal celebrations). Within the ritual of the roda, they adhere to toques that correspond to the practice of capoeira Angola (D Ferreira 1997-int:24 Jan, Grande 1997-int).

26. E Travassos (2000:63).

27. Galm (2001), Travassos (2000).

28. Variations of the marimba are prominent in music cultures throughout Central America. See Scruggs (1998) and Kaptain (1992). The marimba has been revived by folkloric groups in the state of São Paulo.

29. E Travassos (2000).

30. Shaffer (1982:33).

31. D Nascimento (2001-int). This hypothesis is concurrent with conflicts between people that I have observed during my time spent in Brazil. When a problem arises, it is much more appropriate to channel your anger through an inanimate object, rather than accuse a person directly. The problem is then viewed as a common problem between the two parties, which they can attempt to resolve together.

32. Nenel (2001-int). Capoeira scholar and practitioner Nestor Capoeira reinforces this notion: "according to the old mestres, 'the berimbau teaches.'" Capoeira (1995:42).

33. For a description of how this is discussed by mestre João Grande, see E Galm (1997:57). Grande demonstrates this concept musically in a berimbau video documentary (Ornellas and Tourinho 1989-vid).

34. Pastinha in Capoeira (1995:41).

35. Reis (2000:198–99).

36. This view is extremely prevalent among capoeiristas. In contrast, Lewis (1992) questions the practicality of the use of capoeira as a weapon in the quilombos (encampments of escaped slaves), as he believes that a strong focus would be directed toward developing traditional weapons. However, historical evidence from the twentieth century confirms that capoeira has been utilized as a military strategy in Brazil's war against Paraguay and to quell isolated domestic conflicts in Rio de Janeiro (Almeida 1986:27–28). Perhaps capoeira was most effective as a psychological weapon, or as a symbol of resistance. When this resistance was given a physical form, it could, in certain circumstances, turn into true physical resistance.

37. Capoeira (1995:12). Vargas was closely aligned with Nazi Germany in the 1930s. His physical education aspirations were derived from Mussolini's and Hitler's emphasis on youth, body, and athleticism (C Nascimento 2004-int).

38. Lewis (1992:60).

39. See E Travassos (2000).

40. See Sansone (1999).

41. See Sansone and Santos (1999). Also, organizations such as the Fundação Pierre Verger in Salvador, Bahia, employ education literacy programs emerging from capoeira music and dance.

42. On the other hand, capoeira's African-descended heritage is a key component within practitioners, and this is a fundamental aspect within contemporary practice.

43. For this aspect relating to the berimbau, see Galm (1997); in Kongo Mythology, see Thompson (1983).

44. Capoeira (1995:41).

45. Ortiz (in Rego 1968:74–75). In this reference, Ortiz cites a song accompanied by the *burumbumba*, directed towards the *"mbumba:" Buru mbumba, mamá / Buru mbumba / Buru mbumba, mamá / Buru mbumba, é."* He notes that there are three voice ranges that correspond with each word: *"Buru"* is sung in a low register, *"mbumba"* is sung in a medium register, and *"mamá"* is the in the highest register.

46. Silva (1997-int).

47. Carneiro (1981:213).

48. Mestre Negoativo is a co-founder of the music ensemble Berimbrown (discussed in chapter 3).

49. Negoativo (2001-int).

50. Reis (2000:172).

51. Oxumaré's colors are green, yellow, blue, pink, and white, or the principal colors of the rainbow; Yemanjá's colors are blue and white; and the Preto Velho's color is white (Cacciatore 1988).

52. S. Tomás in Reis (2000:172). The Preto(s) Velho(s) represent the purified spirits of ancient enslaved Africans in Brazil within the religious practice of umbanda. "They are the example of humility, simple knowledge, kindness and forgiveness. . . . They do not represent *orixás*, but some are connected along these lines" (Cacciatore 1988:215). Lewis (1992) also suggests a connection between the components of the berimbau and corresponding deities as practiced in umbanda, although this particular scheme was not related to him directly by capoeira practitioners. Edison Carneiro (1981) discusses the use of the berimbau in the musical ensembles of various Afro-Brazilian religious manifestations, and D'Anunciação (2001-int:13 Jun) notes that the berimbau is often utilized in the *pajelança* (religious curing rituals) in the state of Maranhão, although the musical instrumentation is very flexible. For a description of berimbaus being used for religious purposes in Maranhão, see Eduardo (1966).

53. Burdick (1998:55).

54. Moreira in Anonymous (1997).

55. Gondim (1997).

56. S Nascimento (2001).

57. Oliveira (1958:7).

58. Nô in Lewis (1992:142–43).

59. Lewis (1992:228). Also see Almeida (1986), Bola Sete (1997), and Capoeira (1999).

60. Capoeira (1999:183–84).

61. Lewis (1992:73).

62. Almeida (1986:60). Almeida was one of the first capoeira masters who opened an academy in the United States.

63. Lewis (1992).

64. It could be argued that, although women enjoy a dramatically increased presence in capoeira within recent decades, they have encountered a glass ceiling in terms of advancement toward top-tiered status within the discipline.

65. Lewis (1992:175). He does not state whether this is in Brazil, the United States, or both.

66. D Nascimento (2001-int).

67. *Ibid.*

Chapter 2

1. Powell (1963-disc).

2. Various artists (1968-disc).

3. Although "Lapinha" was composed after "Domingo no Parque," I discuss "Lapinha" first, in order to continue with the discussion of Baden Powell.

4. Gil (1968-disc). See later in this chapter for more information about Gil.

5. Tinhorão (1966)
6. Tinhorão in Rego (1968:329).
7. I use the term *postcolonial* to represent Brazil's efforts to define itself as a nation. Brazil first declared its independence from Portugal in 1822, and was under the rule of a monarchy until 1889, when Brazil proclaimed itself a republic (Skidmore 1999).
8. Skidmore (1986:164).
9. Skidmore (1986).
10. Dunn (2001:39–42).
11. A branch of the conservative Unido Democráta Nacional political party was known as the "Bossa Nova" faction that supported Goulart's ambitious land reform and economic stabilization projects (Skidmore 1988:252). The opposing faction to this group had subsequently been branded *a banda de música* [the music group] because its members had the habit of sitting on the front rows in the Chamber of Deputies (near the musicians if it had been a dance floor) and "opening sessions with aggressive attacks on their enemies" (Skidmore 1988:390).
12. Skidmore (1999:177).
13. Treece (1997:4).
14. Stroud (2000:88).
15. Stroud (2000:89).
16. During a 1992 visit to the Anokyekrom museum in Kumasi, Ghana, ethnomusicologist John Galm viewed an exhibit about the history of the Ashanti people and their defeat of the British expeditionary force, which was led by Lord Robert Baden Powell. Powell was impressed by the manner in which Ashanti raised their young, so he modeled the Boy Scouts after Ashanti boys' training rituals (Galm 2003-int).
17. Choro is an urban instrumental musical genre developed in Rio de Janeiro in the late nineteenth century.
18. Souza (2000).
19. Powell in Sanches (1999:4). Powell, Baden, and Vinícius de Moraes. 1966. *Os Afro Sambas*.
20. In this instance, *Benção* refers to a capoeira movement.
21. Rego (1968:334).
22. Powell in Sanches (1999:4).
23. De Moraes in Rego (1968:330).
24. Rego (1968).
25. Duarte (1967). I assume that Powell's notion of "authenticity" is related to being able to engage in an in-depth conversation that would not be achievable in a public setting.
26. Dreyfus (1999:91–93).
27. Rego (1968:336).
28. Castro (1990).
29. Rego (1968:335).
30. Powell in ESPN Brasil (2001). I recorded an audio version of this quote on 17

May 2001, which aired on television. This information is from a Baden Powell interview contained within a capoeira video produced by ESPN Brasil. I have been unable to obtain a specific citation for this reference.

31. Powell in David (1998).
32. Marcondes (2000:355, 715–16).
33. Powell in Dreyfus (1999:151). The Lydian mode has a raised fourth (#4) scale tone in the Gregorian Chant Modal System.
34. De Moraes in Rego (1968:335).
35. D'Anunciação (1990) explains that the berimbau's music is comprised of a rhythm that features variable pitches, resulting in this modified description.
36. Perhaps this impression has also been derived from Powell's use of a single berimbau musician accompanying him on the stage during performances of this composition.
37. Additional transcriptions appear in the Appendix.
38. For examples of guitar adaptations of mbira motifs in Zimbabwe, see Brown (1994) and Turino (2000).
39. D'Anunciação (1990a:72-74). See Fig. 36 and related discussion for key to D'Anunciação's notation scheme in chapter 5. Corda represents the right-hand stick played on the string; caxixi is the basket rattle produced by right-hand arm movements; moeda is the left-hand coin movement on or off of the string; and uou is the sound produced by the gourd movement away from or against the musician's body.
40. Dreyfus (1999).
41. Powell in Anonymous (1968b).
42. Lewis (1992:168). He cites *nganga* as a Bantu word signifying a medicinal and spiritual practitioner from the Central African Kongo region. According to legend, when Besouro appeared to be surrounded by military forces, he would "fly over their heads like a winged black beetle."
43. "Zum-zum-zum" is also a reference to the sound of the berimbau (Lewis 1992:167).
44. Newspaper critic's citing of capoeira lyrics (Rebôlo 1968).
45. Powell in Anonymous (1968a).
46. *Ibid.*
47. *Ibid.*
48. "Baden consulted the Aurélio Buarque de Holanda dictionary and asked us to transcribe the passage in which the *mestre* explains the significance of the word folclore: *'conjunto de tradições, conhecimentos, ou crenças populares expressas em proverbios, contos ou canções: conjunto das canções populares de uma época ou região; estudo ou conhecimento das tradições de um povo, expressos em suas lendas, crenças, canções e costumes'"* (group of traditions, knowledge or popular beliefs expressed in proverbs, stories or songs: group of popular songs of an era or region; study or knowledge of traditions of a people, expressed in their legends, beliefs, songs and customs) (Powell citing Holanda in Anonymous 1968a). Citing Bernstein and the related bibliographic information (in Anonymous 1968a),

Powell states: *"Se estamos tentando explicar música, deveriamos explicar a música, não toda de uma série de noções extra-musicais, proprias de apreciadores, que tem crescido à sua volta como parasitas"* (If we are trying to explain music, we should explain music, not as a series of extra-musical notions, characteristic of critics, who have evolved as parasites) (*O Mundo da Leonard Bernstein*, ed. Livros do Brasil-Portugal, 17; cited in Anon. [1968a]).

49. Canjiquinha in Duarte (1967).

50. Santo Amaro is approximately 80 kilometers (50 miles) from Salvador.

51. Canjiquinha in Duarte (1967).

52. "When I die, bury me in Lapinha / *calçaculote*, soft fancy clothes. / Goodbye Bahia, zum zum zum golden belt / I'm going to leave, because they've killed my Besouro."

53. Pastinha (1969-disc). For other capoeira music recorded in the late 1960s, see Bimba (1968-disc).

54. Suassuna (1975-disc). Capoeira scholar Greg Downey (1998) also presents a version of the lyrics that are similar to Suassuna's. Although Downey heard many variations of this song, he cites this as representative of the most frequently performed version.

55. Song about Besouro sung by mestre Traíra (Traíra 1958(?)-disc).

56. "Quando eu Morrer, disse Besouro" (Suassuna and Dirceu 1975-disc)

57. Downey (1998).

58. For more on GCAP's influence in the northeastern United States, see Galm (2001).

59. Downey (1998:124).

60. Thanks to Claudia Tatinge Nascimento for suggesting this connection to me.

61. Severiano and Mello (1999:122).

62. This figure is according to information presented at www.hot100brasil.com/timemachine1933.html, an internet resource that has constructed a "top-100" song list for each year of the past century, through extensive national and regional archival research.

63. "Fita Amarela" by Rosa (Reis 1932-disc).

64. For a related discussion regarding claims to authorship of the samba "Pelo Telefone," see Almirante (1977:21–28).

65. Sandroni (2001). Musical challenge competitions can be seen throughout the Americas and the Caribbean, where several forms of vocal challenge duels are prominent.

66. "A Melhor Coisa do Mundo" (Bola Sete 1997:100).

67. The aspiration for folkloric commercial success is also documented in a capoeira song registered by Rego (1968:101–2): *Néga fia teve aí / Deu dinheiro pra mamãe / Deu dinheiro pra papai / Deu carne, deu farinha / Deu café, deu feijão / Eu porque era menino / Me dero um tostão / Eu comprei meu berimbau / Pra tocá no Rio de Janeiro* (The black daughter was there / she gave money to my mother / she gave money to my father / she gave meat, flour / she gave coffee and beans / And since I was a child / she gave me a [worthless] old Brazilian coin / I bought my berimbau / To play in Rio de Janeiro).

68. Dreyfus (1999:179).
69. Iemanjá is the goddess of the sea within candomblé. The name of this deity also can be spelled Yemanjá.
70. Sanches (1999).
71. Matheus (2000).
72. Dunn (2002).
73. Stroud (2000:89).
74. Perrone (1989:98–99).
75. Beatles (1967-disc).
76. Calado (2000:123).
77. Calado (2000:129).
78. Calado (2000:137).
79. Calado (2000:136).
80. Brazilian modernism and the Semana da Arte Moderna are discussed in the introduction.
81. Andrade (1924).
82. Gil in Stroud (2000:108).
83. Gil (2000-disc).
84. See next section.
85. Lyrics from "Meia-Lua Inteira" (Veloso 1989), translated by Eric A. Galm. Original Portuguese lyrics appear on Carlinhos Brown's website: http://www.carlinhosbrown.com.br/musicas/todas-as-letras/buscar-por/trecho/meia-lua-inteira/cd-estrangeiro/.
86. *Ibid.*
87. Armstrong (2002).
88. Williamson (1992).
89. Thanks to Claudia Tatinge Nascimento for pointing out this distinction.
90. Armstrong (2002:183).
91. There have been several compositions titled "Berimbau" in Brazilian popular music.
92. Lyrics of "Berimbau" (Olodum 1999-disc), translated by Eric A. Galm.
93. Armstrong (2002:186).
94. Armstrong (2002:185).
95. Armstrong (2002:189).
96. This shift is noticeably present in the term *bloco afro*, as opposed to *bloco afro-Brasileiro* (C Nascimento 2004-int).

Chapter 3

1. For more on the notion of resistance in relation to Afro-Brazilian musical genres, see Fryer (2000).
2. Sansone (2002:138–39) defines the term *funk* in the 1970s as a reference to United States–produced modern black pop music, including James Brown and the Jackson Five. This has been extended in the 1990s to represent various electronic musics that are tenuously associated with hip-hop, house, electronic funk,

and other North American black pop music. He later provides local definitions of funk in various regions throughout Brazil.

3. *Carioca* is indicative of a person from Rio de Janeiro.

4. Vianna (1988:27).

5. Medeiros in Vianna (1988:28).

6. Winant (1994:144). Hanchard (1994:111–19) also provides a brief overview of the "black soul" phenomenon.

7. Fry in Vianna (1988:28).

8. One of Milton Nascimento's compositions is discussed later in this chapter.

9. Negreiros (2001-int:30 Mar).

10. *Ibid.*

11. *Ibid.*

12. Vianna (1988:30).

13. As mentioned previously, the blocos afro are Bahian carnival parading groups that took to the streets as an attempt to reclaim carnival culture as a decisively Afro-Brazilian form of expression.

14. Watusi in Risério (1981:31–32).

15. Sansone (1999).

16. This is discussed in relation to the work *Ganguzama*, discussed in chapter 5.

17. It is also possible that this holiday is frequently cited because its creation is in response to a special interest group, as opposed to satisfying a deep need in the national psyche.

18. Godi (2002:207).

19. Godi (2002:218).

20. Godi (2002:215).

21. Peter Fry (1982-vid) presents a documentary of Olodum's preparations for the group's carnival parade. This example demonstrates that the organizational schemes of the blocos afro were based on models of the neighborhood escolas de sambas established in Rio de Janeiro.

22. Godi (2002:214).

23. Godi (2002:213).

24. Godi (2002:213–14).

25. Pinho (2002:202–3).

26. For comprehensive discussions on the *mangue* movement in Recife, Pernambuco, see Galinsky (1999) and Teles (2000).

27. Berimbrown (n.d.) This term has emerged in recent years. It is related to the dances that have emerged following the spread of the dances from the Black Rio movement. See Sansone (2002).

28. This reference relates to the state of Minas Gerais (general mines), one of the principal locations of Brazil's precious metal and gemstone deposits.

29. Berimbrown (2000-disc).

30. Obá La Vem Ela (2002-disc).

31. Thanks to Kenneth Yarbrough for helping pinpoint these specific representative groups.

32. Since 2001 mestre Negoativo changed his name from Negativo to Negoativo. Although *Negativo* refers to a capoeira movement, he did not like the literal connotation of the term (negative). Instead, he adopted *Negoativo*, which signifies a way to dance with an energetic attitude (Abreu 2007-int).

33. Negoativo (2001-int).

34. *Ibid.*

35. *Ibid.*

36. *Ibid.*

37. Berimbrown (2000).

38. The transcription and lyrics have been derived from my fieldwork and are slightly different from the recorded music example (Pastinha 1969-disc).

39. This word is possibly associated with the Portuguese word *cartilha* (primer or spelling book).

40. Capoeira Ladainha, "Beabá do Berimbau." Public domain, as sung by Efraim Silva (Silva 1997-int).

41. "Melô do Berimbau" (Berimbrown 2000-disc).

42. Cabaça and caxixi are interchanged between the two versions, but I see this as an incidental variation. Also, the discrepancy between *Vai tocar São Bento Grande* (it will play São Bento Grande) and *Pra tocar São Bento Grande* (in order to play São Bento Grande) is subtle, but both versions evoke similar meanings.

43. Dunn (2001:167).

44. *Ibid.*

45. Dunn (2001:168).

46. See Almeida (1986:88) for an example of improvised verses in this song.

47. Fé Cegá, Faca Amolada (Nascimento 1975-disc), translated by Eric A. Galm. Original Portuguese lyrics appear on Milton Nascimento's website: http://www2.uol.com.br/miltonnascimento/letras/fecegafaca.htm.

48. Fé Cegá, Faca Amolada (Berimbrown 2005-vid).

49. Drum 'n' bass is a style of electronic dance music that originated in England.

50. M4J (1998-disc).

51. Metheny (1980-disc).

52. Vasconcelos is discussed in chapter 4.

53. Vasconcelos (1995-disc).

54. "Clementina" lyrics (Vasconcelos 1995-disc). Courtesy of Naná Vasconcelos.

55. Júnior in Vanni (2001-int).

56. *Ibid.*

57. *Ibid.*

58. Vanni (2001-int).

59. *Ibid.*

60. *Ibid.*

61. *Ibid.*

62. *Ibid.*

63. *Ibid.*

64. *Ibid.*

65. Júnior in Vanni (2001-int).
66. Vanni (2001-int).
67. Maia (2001-int).
68. *Ibid.*
69. For example, Dinho Nascimento and Ramilson Maia are both Bahians who have moved to São Paulo. Although the group Berimbrown is based in Minas Gerais, it often travels to São Paulo for appearances on television shows and at large-venue concerts.
70. Maia (2001-int).
71. *Ibid.*
72. *Ibid.*
73. Maia (2000-disc).
74. Negromonte (2000). This is most likely derived from concepts associated with Brazilian modernist Oswald de Andrade's *Manifesto Antropófago* (Cannibal Manifesto) and the idea of Brazilian culture as a digestion of various cultural sources.
75. Maia (2001-int).
76. *Ibid.*
77. *Ibid.*
78. *Ibid.*

Chapter 4

1. This title is in reference to Antônio Carlos Jobim's song entitled "Samba de Uma Nota Só" (One-Note Samba). Since popular references abound throughout Brazil noting that the berimbau has only one string, it raises questions as to whether or not this might be a passing reference to the berimbau.
2. Talbot (1971-vid); Grosset (1990-vid).
3. See Graham and Robinson (2003). The berimbau is also currently being disseminated through a global expansion of capoeira.
4. See Cook and Morton (2000) and Hovan (2000).
5. Jeske (1982:52).
6. Vinicius (1973).
7. Vasconcelos in Robinson (2000).
8. *Ibid.*
9. Both "Lapinha" and "Domingo no Parque" are discussed in chapter 2.
10. Vasconcelos in Robinson (2000).
11. Vasconcelos also developed a manner of securing the gourd to the bow in order to avoid accidental movement of the tuning loop that would affect the desired pitch (Graham and Robinson 2003).
12. Vinicius (1973).
13. *Ibid.*
14. Perhaps another undertone to this statement is the superficial notion that African rhythm joined with European melodies in Brazil's cultural mixing process. In this

light, Vasconcelos would therefore be transforming the African-only musical bow into a culturally enhanced musical bow that could now play melodies.

15. Dias (2001).

16. Vasconcelos in Rocha (2000).

17. Vasconcelos in Diliberto and Haas (1990:41).

18. Jeske (1982:52).

19. Vasconcelos also incorporated elements of theatrical presentation into his performances. Ethnomusicologist John Galm recalls an early 1980s berimbau solo when Vasconcelos was on tour with Pat Metheny. During the solo, Vasconcelos leaped from the stage, across the orchestra pit and hopped along the backs of the audiences' seats, and returned to the stage, all without missing a beat (J Galm 2003-int).

20. Talbot (1971-vid).

21. D'Anunciação (1990a).

22. Vasconcelos is clearly a talented musician, and this point is merely an observation of how traditional and contemporary material is presented side by side.

23. Graham and Robinson (2003).

24. For an example of how Vasconcelos subtly modifies a single rhythmic example played on the berimbau, see T 3.3.

25. Dunn (1996).

26. Vasconcelos in Robinson (2000).

27. Vasconcelos in Rocha (2000). Some of Vasconcelos's recordings have remained in print, some have been reissued (e.g., *Africadeus*), and others remain out of print (e.g., *Amazonas*).

28. T 4.2 has been derived from the second extended solo section of this work.

29. Vasconcelos in Rocha (2000).

30. Cook and Morton (2000:1505).

31. This could possibly represent an example of resistance to the berimbau in non-capoeira contexts from a non-Brazilian perspective. I return to this discussion later in the chapter.

32. Other critiques focus on Vasconcelos's improvisational abilities, and highlight his overall musicianship. See Zipkin (1980:33–34).

33. Vinícius (1973).

34. Vasconcelos in Diliberto and Haas (1990:41).

35. During my fieldwork in Brazil in 2000–2001, many of Vasconcelos's imports were two to three times more expensive than domestic Brazilian releases.

36. D Nascimento (2001-int).

37. *Ibid.*

38. *Ibid.*

39. Nascimento's technique is conceptually similar to that employed on the *berimbau de lata* or *marimbau*, a monochord steel string that is attached to a board and wrapped around the sides of tin cans at each end, which functions as a double-ended bridge. The instrument is placed on the lap, and a metal slide is secured in one hand, similar to a lap steel technique. The right hand holds a small stick in a horizontal position and the stick is lightly bounced on the string.

40. D Nascimento (2001a-disc).

41. Note: This is only a partial transcription of the major themes. The entire transcription appears in Appendix 1.

42. D Nascimento (2001-int). Mestre Nenel (2001-int) clearly specifies that "Naná Vasconcelos . . . is not a capoeirista." Composer Nelson Macêdo (2000-int) states that Vasconcelos's work with the berimbau is the only innovative popular music example that he knows outside of the tradition of capoeira. Since Vasconcelos became successful in the United States, "he was the most visible."

43. D Nascimento (2001-int).

44. D Nascimento (2001b-disc). In St. Croix (US Virgin Islands), Gongolô is used to refer to a long millipede spiraling down the exterior of a drainpipe (Fredericksen 2004-int). This suggests another way in which linguistic and cultural connections can be pursued throughout the African diaspora.

45. Vasconcelos (1980-disc).

46. Shaffer (1982). See discussion that includes Shaffer's berimbau notation in chapter 5.

47. Musotto (2004-int).

48. *Ibid.* Menezes was promoted in the United States by David Byrne, whose opening act was often more popular on stage than Byrne's (see Menezes 1989-disc).

49. Menezes (1989-disc).

50. On this recording, the bass berimbau is tuned to A, whereas the two smaller berimbaus are tuned to A#.

51. Transcription 4.4 is based on a musical score devised by D'Anunciação (1990a) that arranges the three berimbaus from low to high pitch ranges. The lowest berimbau enters first, so this transcription begins on the bottom staff and moves upward.

52. Musotto (2004-int).

53. Menezes (1993-disc).

54. Rodrigues (1997-disc).

55. Musotto (2004-int).

56. For a detailed analysis of Ghanaian percussion music, see Locke (1987).

57. Santos (n.d.-disc). This recorded track also appears on Musotto (2003-disc).

58. This track also appears on Musotto's solo album *Sudaka* (Musotto 2003-disc).

59. Note: This is a partial transcription of the major themes. For a complete transcription, see Appendix 2.

Chapter 5

1. D'Anunciação is a Brazilian percussionist, composer, and author. He is the principal percussionist of the Orquestra Sinfónica Brasileira in Rio de Janeiro, and has also developed comprehensive notational schemes for several Brazilian percussion instruments.

2. Appleby (1983:4).

3. Neves (1981).

4. Appleby (1983:47). Verdi claimed Gomes as his immediate successor, a move that reinforced the importance of continued European dominance in Brazilian art music (Béhague 1976).

5. This event is also discussed in the introduction.

6. Neves (1981).

7. *Ibid.* Mariz (1997).

8. De Andrade (1944).

9. Andrade in Neves (1981:148).

10. Neves (1981:49).

11. *Ibid.*

12. Béhague (1994).

13. A Ferreira (1986:302).

14. See Carvalho (1994) for a discussion of stereotypical imagery in Brazilian children's songs.

15. Marcondes (2001:821).

16. Mariz (1997:37).

17. Béhague (1994:63).

18. Appleby (1983:85) lists this work as *Suite Brésilienne.*

19. Appleby (1983:89).

20. *Ibid.*

21. Mariz (1997:30).

22. *Ibid.*

23. W Silva (2001-int).

24. Zé composed one work and moved to the realm of popular music.

25. W Silva (2001-int).

26. *Ibid.* This topic merits future study, as some scores have formally incorporated berimbau (see Boudler 1983).

27. Marcondes (2000:766–67).

28. D'Anunciação (2001-int), Mariz (1997), Neves (1981), Tacuchian (2001-int).

29. This work has been performed four times: in Rio de Janeiro (1963, 1979, and 1999), and once in São Paulo (2000) (Tavares 2001-int).

30. See related discussion of late 1950s political and economic issues in chapter 2.

31. Neiva (1963a).

32. A similar title for Zumbi is "Ganga Zumba." For an archeological perspective on real and imagined histories regarding the Quilombo dos Palmares, see Allen (2001).

33. Mignone in Hernandez (1959).

34. Tavares in Marques (2001:37). Tavares is referring to the success of the composition in relation to his career. Villa-Lobos was an independent composer who held no formal orchestral position (D'Anunciação 2004-int).

35. Mariz (1997:36).

36. Neiva (1963a).

37. This summary is adapted from Neiva (1958, 1963a, b).

38. Scenario of *Ganguzama* (Neiva 1958, 1963a, b)

39. Hernandez (1959).

40. Quilombola lyrics during berimbau intervention (Neiva 1958).

41. This tree is found throughout Africa.

42. Choral response to quilombola passage (Neiva 1958).

43. Neiva (1963b).

44. *Ibid.*

45. *Ibid.*

46. Supported by ethnographic information from D'Anunciação (2001-int), N Macêdo (2000-int), and Tacuchian (2001-int). A second choral work featuring the berimbau, the *Missa de São Benedito* (St. Benedict Mass) by José Maria Neves, was composed in 1960 and premiered in 1966. A second performance in 1966 of this thirty-minute work featured singer Clementina de Jesus at a prominent theater in downtown Rio de Janeiro. This work was performed again in 1967 at a ceremony held at the newspaper *O Globo*, which honored sixteen non-Brazilians who expressed "their love and dedication to Rio and its people" (Anonymous 1967).

47. Giudice (1996).

48. For a detailed discussion of the use of Brazilian percussion instruments in Villa-Lobos's compositions, see D'Anunciação (2006).

49. D'Anunciação (2001-int:25 Apr).

50. A cimbalom is a large chromatic concert dulcimer with a damper pedal invented around 1870. It has been featured in symphonic works, most notably *Hary Janos* by Zoltan Kodaly (Anonymous 2003:855–56).

51. N Macêdo (2000-int).

52. D'Anunciação (2001-int:25 Apr).

53. *Ibid.*

54. *Ibid.*

55. Negreiros (2001-int:1 May).

56. *Ibid.*

57. *Ibid.* This most likely has been derived as an adaptation of the Portuguese word *escândalo* (scandal).

58. D'Anunciação (2001-int:2 May). D'Anunciação could not confirm this with absolute certainty, since all of the other percussionists who performed the premiere of this piece have passed away. Tavares remembers that the berimbau performer for the premiere was a popular musician brought in for the performance, but he did not remember any details about the individual musician.

59. Versions of this story were related to me by D'Anunciação (2001-int 2 May), N Macêdo (2000-int), and Tavares (2001-int).

60. Bituca (Edgard Nunes Rocca) was a famous drumset performer who played with many prominent bossa nova musicians; he authored *Bateria, Método e Prático* in 1962.

61. D'Anunciação (2001-int:2 May).

62. *Ibid.*

63. Published under the name Luiz Almeida da Anunciação. See D'Anunciação (1971a, b). For a review of other berimbau notation schemes, see Galm (1997).

64. Right hand: stick played on string; caxixi solo (stick does not play string). Left hand : x = coin contact with string; < = open (hold gourd away from body); > = closed (hold gourd against body).

65. Shaffer (1982:43).
66. D'Anunciação (1971b).
67. D'Anunciação (1971b).
68. Shaffer (1982:43).
69. Almeida (1986).
70. Lewis (1992).
71. Almeida (1986:81).
72. Lewis (1992:146–52).
73. Capoeira (1999, 2000).
74. Tavares (2001-int).
75. John K. Galm is Professor Emeritus at the University of Colorado, where he established both the percussion performance and the ethnomusicology programs. He is my father.
76. D'Anunciação (2001-int:2 May).
77. D'Anunciação (1971a).
78. D'Anunciação (2001-int:2 May).
79. While Pinto's (1988-disc) scheme specifically indicates gourd movement, the notation is limited to approximations within the boxes of the TUBS (Time Unit Box System)–based notation.
80. D'Anunciação (2001-int:25 Apr).
81. *Ibid.*
82. D'Anunciação (2001-int:2 May).
83. *Ibid.*
84. Capoeira (2000:114–16).
85. D'Anunciação (2001-int:2 May).
86. *Ibid.*
87. Galm (1997:62).
88. D'Anunciação (2001-int:9 May).
89. D'Anunciação (1990b).
90. D'Anunciação (1990a).
91. D'Anunciação (2001-int:2 May).
92. *Ibid.*
93. *Ibid.*
94. D'Anunciação (1990b).
95. D'Anunciação (1990a).
96. N Macêdo (2000-int).
97. *Ibid.*
98. This work features extended cadenzas with no barlines. I will use CD timing marks that correspond with the original recording (Escola Brasileira de Música 1996-disc) for points of reference.
99. Rescala (1981).
100. Marcondes (2000:673). This work features a brief berimbau passage when the "capoeira" section is introduced.
101. Rescala (2000-int).
102. *Ibid.*

103. D'Anunciação (2001-int:25 Apr).
104. D'Anunciação believes that this was the first public performance that utilized his two-stick technique for the berimbau (see D'Anunciação 1990a).
105. Rescala (2000-int).
106. *Ibid.*
107. *Ibid.*
108. D'Anunciação (2001-int:25 Apr).
109. Rescala (2000-int).
110. See Galm (1997) and D'Anunciação (1990a) for discussion of these rules.
111. Rescala (2000-int).
112. *Ibid.*
113. D'Anunciação in Capoeira (2000:116).
114. D'Anunciação (2001-int:23 May).
115. Rescala (2000-int).
116. Ricardo Tacuchian (11/18/39) studied composition with notable Brazilian composers, including Francisco Mignone and Cláudio Santoro. His compositional style pushes the boundaries of expectations found in the concert hall. In 1988 he composed the nonet *Rio/L.A.*, which is scored for "instruments that are infrequently used in concert music, including the electric bass, cuíca and the agogô, and elements of other musical styles, such as jazz, samba and pop" (Marcondes 2000:761). He has developed a musical-structure system called *Sistema-T*, which is the basis of his doctoral dissertation and a compositional tool he continues to draw upon in his present works.
117. Tacuchian (2001-int).
118. Tacuchian (2001-int).

Chapter 6

1. Almeida (1986).
2. *Viva A Bahia, No. 3* (Anonymous 1970-disc) is a folkloric recording of rural sambas, patron saint festival music, and marchas. The berimbau does not appear on any of the tracks on this recording.
3. Although the berimbau is principally associated with Bahia, berimbaus are sold at tourist markets in other urban areas such as Rio de Janeiro and São Paulo.
4. Machado (1993a:15).
5. *Ibid.*
6. For example, each is often represented by the primary colors blue and white (Cacciatore 1988).
7. D Ferreira (1997-int 24 Feb) and Negoativo (2001-int).
8. Cravo (2003-int).
9. Rego (1968:328).
10. Machado (1993c:15).
11. Araújo (2004-int).
12. Magalhães was re-elected to the Brazilian senate in 2003. For a summary of this scandal in English, see "Goodbye to Mean Tony" at www.brazzil.com/rpdjun01.htm.

13. Coelho (2000).
14. Adapted from Coelho (2000).
15. See "Na Boquinha da Garrafa" by Companhia do Pagode (Various artists 1997–vid).
16. "Urucungo" (Bopp n.d. in Carneiro 1981:23–24). A recent edition of Bopp's works (Bopp 1998:209) demonstrates how Bopp Experimented with different sounds and images of the berimbau in the final phrase "continuan a doer na corda do urucungo" (continued in pain within the metal string of the urucungo).
17. Teles (1999-vid). This video is in the archive at the Biblioteca Amadeu Amaral at the Museu do Folclore in Rio de Janeiro.
18. Coelho (2000), Negoativo (2001-int), and Grande (1997-int).
19. Thanks to Vincenzo Cambria for his assistance in translating this poem.

Conclusions

1. Rodrigues (2000).
2. Graham (1991).
3. Negoativo (2001-int).
4. Downy (1998).
5. Ortiz in Rego (1968).
6. E.g., Coelho (2000).
7. Thompson (1983).
8. Bopp in Carneiro (1981:23–24). Also see Bopp (1998:209).
9. Negreiros (2001-int). Brazilian musician Carlos Negreiros is discussed in chapter 3.
10. D'Anunciação (1990a).
11. E.g., Graham and Robinson (2003).

Appendix

1. Nascimento (2000a-disc).
2. Santos (n.d.-disc) and Musotto (2003-disc).
3. D'Anunciação (1990a:131). A recording of this work is on Escola Brasiliera de Música (1996-disc).

Bibliography

Aguirre, Carlos and Ricardo D. Salvatore. 2001. "Writing the History of Law, Crime, and Punishment in Latin America." In *Crime and Punishment in Latin America: Law and Society since Late Colonial Times*, Carlos Aguirre and Gilbert M. Joseph, eds. Durham and London: Duke University Press, 1–32.

Alencar, José de. 1968 (1857). *O Guarani*. São Paulo: Cultrix.

Allen, Scott Joseph. 2001. "'Zumbi Nunca Vai Morrer': History, the Practice of Archaeology, and Race Politics in Brazil." Ph.D. dissertation, Brown University.

Almeida, Bira. 1986. *Capoeira: A Brazilian Art Form*. Berkeley: North Atlantic Books.

Almirante. 1977. *No Tempo de Noel Rosa*. 2nd ed. Rio de Janeiro: Francisco Alves.

Andrade, Mário de. 1944. "Candido Ignácio da Silva e o Lundu." *Revista Brasileira de Música* 10:17–39.

———. 1972 (1928). *Ensaio Sobre a Música Brasileira*. 3rd ed. São Paulo: Martins.

Andrade, Oswald de. 1924. "Manifesto da Poesia Pau-Brasil" (Brazilwood Poetry Manifesto). Stella de Sá Rego, trans. "," *Latin American Literary Review* 14(27) [1986]:184–87.

———. 1928. "O Manifesto Antropófago." *Revista de Antropofagia* 1.

Anonymous. 1967. "A 'Missa de São Benedito' na Festa dos Cariocas Honorários." *O Globo*, Rio de Janeiro, March 21:2.

———. 1968a. "Baden defende seu samba e ataca os falsos criticos." *Folha de São Paulo*, São Paulo, June 13.

———. 1968b. "Baden: Um Violão em Repouso." *Jornal do Brasil*, Rio de Janeiro, February 4.

———. 1984. "Organology." In *The New Grove Dictionary of Music and Musicians*. Stanley Sadie, ed. London: Macmillan, 2:916.

———. 1997. "Cultura afro fará parte de atos católicos." *A Tarde*, Salvador, September 26.

———. 2008. "Polêmica do Enade UFBA: professor teve 'surto de imbecilidade', diz Wagner." *O Globo Online*, April 30.

Appleby, David P. 1983. *The Music of Brazil*. Austin: University of Texas Press.

Araújo, Samuel. 2000. "Brazilian Identities and Musical Performances." *Diogenes* 191(48/3):115–25.

Armstrong, Piers. 2002. "Songs of Olodum: Ethnicity, Activism and Art in a Globalized Carnival Community." In *Brazilian Popular Music and Globalization*. Charles A. Perrone and Christopher Dunn, eds. New York and London: Routledge, 177–91.

Assunção, Matthias Röhrig. 2005. *Capoeira: The History of an Afro Brazilian Martial Art*. London and New York: Routledge.

Bakan, Michael, Wanda Bryant, Guangming Li, David Martinelli, and Kathryn Vaughn. 1990. "Demystifying and Classifying Electronic Music Instruments." *Selected Reports in Ethnomusicology* 3(1): 37–66.

Béhague, Gerard. 1979. *Music in Latin America: An Introduction.* Englewood Cliffs, NJ: Prentice-Hall.

———. 1994. *Heitor Villa-Lobos: The Search for Brazil's Musical Soul.* Austin: University of Texas Press.

Berimbrown (Anonymous). n.d. Unpublished press release materials.

Berliner, Paul. 1981. *The Soul of Mbira.* Berkeley and Los Angeles: University of California Press.

Bola Sete, Mestre. 1997 (1989). *A Capoeira Angola na Bahia.* 2nd ed. Rio de Janeiro: Pallas.

Bopp, Raul. 1998. *Poesia Completa de Raul Bopp.* Edited by Augusto Massi. Rio de Janeiro: José Olympio; São Paolo: Edusp.

Borges, Dain. 1995. "The Recognition of Afro-Brazilian Symbols and Ideas, 1890–1940." *Luso-Brazilian Review* 32(2):59–78.

Boudler, John E. 1983. *Brazilian Compositions since 1953: An Annotated Catalogue.* DMA thesis, American Conservatory of Music.

Brandão, Alfredo. 1988 (1935). *Os Negros na História de Alagoas.* New ed. Maceió: Comissão Estadual do Centenário da Abolição.

Brown, Ernest D. 1990. "Something from Nothing and More from Something: The Making and Playing of Music Instruments in African-American Cultures." *Selected Reports in Ethnomusicology* 3(1):275–91.

———. 1994. "The guitar and the mbira: Resilience, assimilation, and pan-Africanism in Zimbabwean music." *World of Music* 36(2):73–117.

Burdick, John. 1998a. "The Lost Constituency of Brazil's Black Movements." In *Latin American Perspectives* 25(1):136–55.

———. 1998b. *Blessed Anastacia: Women, Race, and Popular Christianity in Brazil.* New York and London: Routledge.

Cacciatore, Olga Gudolle. 1988 (1977). *Dicionário de Cultos Afro-Brasileiros.* 3rd ed. Rio de Janeiro: Forense Universitária.

Calado, Carlos. 2000 (1997). *Tropicalia: História de uma Revolução Músical.* Reprint of 1st ed. São Paulo: Editora 34.

Campos, João da Silva. 1941. *Procissões Tradicionais da Bahia.* Salvador[?]: Publicações do Museu da Bahia; Secretaria de Educação e Saúde.

Capoeira, Nestor. 1995. *The Little Capoeira Book.* Alex Ladd, trans. Berkeley: North Atlantic Books.

———. 1999. *Capoeira: O Galo Já Cantou.* Rio de Janeiro: Editora Record.

———. 2000. *Capoeira: Os Fundamentos da Malícia.* Rio de Janeiro: Editora Record.

Carneiro, Edison. 1975. *Cadernos de Folclore: Capoeira, Vol. 1.* Rio de Janeiro: Ministério da Educação e Cultura/Campanha de Defesa do Folclore Brasileiro.

———. 1981 (1936). *Religões Negras: notas de etnografio religosa e de folclore.* 2nd ed. Rio de Janeiro: Civilização Brasileira.

Carvalho, José Jorge de. 1994. *The Multiplicity of Black Identities in Brazilian Popular Music.* Brasilia: University of Brasilia.

Cascudo, Luiz da Câmara. 1972 (1954). *Dicionário do Folclore Brasileiro*. 3rd ed. Rio de Janeiro: Editora Tecnoprint S.A.

Castro, Ruy. 1990. *Chega de Saudade: A História e as Histórias da Bossa Nova*. São Paulo: Companhia das Letras.

Coelho, Raquel. 2000 (1993). *Berimbau*. 4th ed. São Paulo: Editora Ática.

Cook, Richard, and Brian Morton. 2000. "Naná Vasconcelos." In *The Penguin Guide to Jazz on CD*. New York: Penguin Putnam, 1505.

Crook, Larry N. 1993. "Black Consciousness, Samba Reggae, and the Re-Africanization of Bahian Carnival Music in Brazil." *World of Music* 35(2):90–108.

———. 2005. *Brazilian music: Northeastern traditions and the heartbeat of a modern nation*. Santa Barbara: ABC-CLIO.

Crook, Larry, and Randall Johnson, eds. *Black Brazil: Culture, Identity, and Social Mobilization*. Los Angeles: UCLA Latin American Center Publications.

D'Anunciação, Luiz (Luiz Almeida da Anunciação). 1971a. "The Birimbau [*sic*] from Brazil: What is it and how to play it." *Percussive Arts Society* 3(3):72–77.

———. 1971b. "O Berimbau da Bahia." *Revista Brasileira de Folclore* 11(29):24–33.

———. 1990a. *A Percussão dos Ritmos Brasileiros: Sua Técnica e sua Escrita*. Vol. 1, *O Berimbau*. Rio de Janeiro: Editora Europa.

———. 1990b. *4 Motivos Nordestinos*. Hamburg and London: N. Simrock (composed 1972).

———. 2006. *Os Instrumentos Típicos Brasileiros na Obra de Villa-Lobos*. Rio de Janeiro: Academia Brasileira de Música.

David, Leni. 1998. "Encontro com Baden." *A Tarde*, Salvador, July 11.

Davies, Carol Boyce. 1999. "Re-/Presenting Black Female Identity in Brazil: 'Filhas d'Oxum' in Bahia Carnival." In *Representations of Blackness and the Performance of Identities*. Jean Muteba Rahier, ed. Westport: Bergin and Garvey, 49–68.

Dawson, C. Daniel. 1994. "Capoeira: An Exercise of the Soul." In *Celebration: Visions and Voices of the American Diaspora*. Roger Rosen and Patra McSharry Sevastiades, eds. New York: Rosen Publishing Group, 14–28.

DeVale, Sue C. 1988. "Musical Instruments and Ritual: A Systematic Approach." *Journal of the American Musical Instrument Society* 14:126–60.

———. 1990. "Organizing Organology." *Selected Reports in Ethnomusicology* 3(1): 1–36.

Dias, Mauro. 2001. "Os Documentos Sonoros de Naná Vasconcelos." *O Estado de São Paulo*, São Paulo, August 20.

Diliberto, John, and Kimberly Haas. 1990. "Naná Vasconcelos: The Jungle Man." *Rhythm: Total Percussion Magazine* 2(10):40–44.

Dossar, Kenneth. 1992. "Capoeira Angola: Dancing Between Two Worlds." *The Afro-Hispanic Review* 11(1-3):5–10.

Dournon, Genevieve. 1992. "Organology." In *Ethnomusicology: An Introduction*. Helen Myers, ed. New York: W. W. Norton, 245–300.

Downey, Greg. 1998. "Incorporating Capoeira: Phenomenology of a Movement Discipline." Ph.D. dissertation, University of Chicago.

———. 2002. "Listening to Capoeira: Phenomenology, Embodiment, and the Materiality of Music." *Ethnomusicology* 46(3)487–509.

————. 2005. *Learning Capoeira: Lessons in Cunning from an Afro-Brazilian Art*. Oxford and New York: Oxford University Press.

Dreyfus, Dominique. 1999. *O Violão Vadio de Baden Powell*. São Paulo: Editora 34.

Duarte, Isidro. 1967. "O Folclore É Nosso ou Quem Compôs a Lapinha?" *Jornal do Brasil*, September 28, Caderno B:1.

Dunn, Christopher J. 1996. "Naná Vasconcelos: Talking Pictures." *Rhythm Music Magazine* 5(1-2):14–17.

————. 2001. *Brutality Garden*. Chapel Hill and London: University of North Carolina Press.

————. 2002. "Tropicália, Counterculture, and the Diasporic Imagination in Brazil." In *Brazilian Popular Music and Globalization*. Charles A. Perrone and Christopher Dunn, eds. New York: Routledge, 72–95.

Eduardo, O. da Costa. 1966. *The Negro in Northern Brazil: A Study in Acculturation*. 2nd ed. Seattle and London: University of Washington Press.

Ellingson, Ter. 1992. "Transcription." In *Ethnomusicology: An Introduction*. Helen Meyers, ed. New York: W. W. Norton, 110–53.

Ferreira, Aurelio Buarque de Holanda. 1986 (1975). *Novo Dicionário da Língua Portuguesa*. 2nd ed. Rio de Janeiro: Ed. Nova Fronteira.

Ferreira, Ricardo Franklin. 2000. *Afro Descendente: Identidade em Construção*. São Paulo: EDUC and Rio de Janeiro: Pallas.

Ferrigno, Antônio. 2000. "Untitled Oil on Canvas." In *Mostra do Redoscobrimento: Negro de Corpo e Alma – Black in Body and Soul*. Nelson Aguilar, org. São Paulo: Associação Brasil 500 Anos Artes Visuais, 383.

Franco, Jean. 1994. *An Introduction to Spanish American Literature*. Oxford: Oxford University Press.

Freyre, Gilberto. 1933. *Casa Grande & Senzala: formação da família brasileira sob o regimen de economia patriarchal*. Rio de Janeiro: Maia & Schmidt.

Fryer, Peter. 2000. *Rhythms of Resistance: African Musical Heritage in Brazil*. Hanover: Wesleyan University Press.

Galinsky, Philip. 1999. "The 'Maracatu Atômico': Tradition, Modernity, and Post-Modernity in the Mangue Movement and 'New Music Scene' of Recife, Pernambuco, Brazil." Ph.D. dissertation, Wesleyan University.

Galm, Eric A. 1997. "The Berimbau de Barriga within the World of Capoeira." M.A. thesis, Tufts University.

————. 2001. "A Volta do Nosso Mundo: Capoeira in the Northeastern United States." Unpublished paper delivered at the international conference of the International Council for Traditional Music, Rio de Janeiro.

————. 2004. "Beyond the Roda: The Berimbau de Barriga in Brazilian Music and Culture." Ph.D. dissertation, Wesleyan University.

————. 2008. "Baianas, Malandros and Samba: Listening to Brazil Through Donald Duck's Ears." In *Global Soundtracks*. Mark Slobin, ed. Middletown: Wesleyan University Press, 258–80.

Giudice, Victor. 1996. "Berimbau em Roda Erudita: Popular até no cinema." *Jornal do Brasil*, Rio de Janeiro. September 6, Caderno B:1.

Godi, Antonio J.V. dos Santos. 2002. "Reggae and Samba-Reggae in Bahia: A Case of Long-Distance Belonging." In *Brazilian Popular Music and Globalization.* Charles A. Perrone and Christopher Dunn, eds. New York and London: Routledge, 207–19.

Goertzen, Chris. 1997. *Fiddling for Norway: Revival and Identity.* Chicago: University of Chicago Press.

Gondim, Abnor. 1997. "Presidente da CNBB comenta pesquisa Datafolha e anuncia a introdução de elementos afros nas missas." *Folha de São Paulo*, São Paulo, September 26, 1.

Graham, Richard. 1991. "Technology and Culture Change: The Development of the Berimbau in Colonial Brazil." *Latin American Music Review* 12(1):1–20.

Graham, Richard, and N. Scott Robinson. 2003. "Berimbau" and "The Berimbau in Popular Music." *Encyclopedia of Popular Music of the World, Volume II: Musical Practices.* John Shepherd, ed. London: Cassell, 343–45.

Gropper, Symona. 1972. *"A Capoeira Domada." Jornal do Brasil*, June 10.

Hanchard, Michael. 1994. *Orpheus and Power.* Princeton, NJ: Princeton University Press.

Hernandez, A. 1959. "Notícia de 'Ganguzama': o poema sinfônico coral de Mário Tavares com letra de Alvaro Neiva premiado no concurso do cinqüentenário do municipal." *Jornal do Comércio*, December 26–27.

Herskovits, Melville J. 1943. "The Negro in Bahia, Brazil: A Problem in Method." *American Sociological Review* 8(4):394–402.

Hood, Mantle. 1971. *The Ethnomusicologist.* New York: McGraw Hill.

Hornbostel, Erich Von, and Curt Sachs. 1992. "Classification of Musical Instruments." In *Ethnomusicology: An Introduction.* Helen Myers, ed. New York: W. W. Norton, 444–61.

Hovan, Chris. 2000. "Naná Vasconcelos." In *Music Hound World: The Essential Album Guide.* Adam McGovern, ed. Farmington Hills: Visible Ink Press, 791–92.

Ique. 2001a. Political cartoon. *Jornal do Brasil*, Rio de Janeiro, February 2, 8.

———. 2001b. Political cartoon. *Jornal do Brasil*, Rio de Janeiro, February 10, 18.

Jackson, K. David. 1979. "A View on Brazilian Literature: Eating the Revista de Antropofagia." *Latin American Literary Review* 7(13):1–9.

Jairazbhoy, Nazir Ali. 1990. "The Beginnings of Organology and Ethnomusicology in the West: V. Mahillon, A. Ellis, and S. M. Tagore." *Selected Reports in Ethnomusicology* 3(1): 67–80.

Jeske, Lee. 1982. "Profile: Naná Vasconcelos." *Down Beat* 49(February): 52–53.

Kaptain, Laurence. 1992. *The Wood That Sings: The Marimba in Chiapas, Mexico.* Everett: Honey Rock.

Karasch, Mary. 1987. *Slave Life in Rio de Janeiro 1808–1850.* Princeton: Princeton University Press.

Koetting, James. 1970. "Analysis and Notation of West African Drum Ensemble Music." *Selected Reports* I(3):115–46.

Kubik, Gerhard. 1975. "Musical Bows in South-Western Angola, 1965." *African Music* 4: 98–104.

———. 1979. *Angolan Traits in Black Music, Games and Dances of Brazil: A Study of*

African Cultural Extensions Overseas. Lisboa: Junta de Investigações Científicas do Ultramar.

Lewis, John Lowell. 1992. *Rings of Liberation*. Chicago: University of Chicago Press.

Locke, David. 1987. *Drum Gahu!: A Systematic Method for an African Percussion Piece*. Crown Point, IN: White Cliffs Media.

Macêdo, Aroldo. 2000. *Luana e sua turma, no.1*. São Paulo: Editora Toque de Mydas, 34.

Machado, Suza. 1993a. "Berimbau: Símbolo Turístico da Bahia." *A Tarde*, Salvador, May 29, Caderno 2: 15.

———. 1993b. "É a Grande Atração do Mercado Modelo." *A Tarde*, Salvador, May 29, Caderno 2: 15.

———. 1993c. "Eterna Fonte de Inspiração." *A Tarde*, Salvador, May 29, Caderno 2: 15.

Maggie, Yvonne, and Claudia Barcellos Rezende, eds. 2002. *Raça como retórica: A construção da diferença*. Rio de Janeiro: Civilização Brasileira.

Marcondes, Marcos Antônio, ed. 2000. *Enciclopédia da Música Brasileira: Popular, Erudita e Folclórica*. 3rd ed. São Paulo: Art Editora/Publifolha.

Mariz, Vasco. 1997. *Vida Musical*. Rio de Janeiro: Civilização Brasileira.

Marques, Clóvis. 2001. *Mário Tavares: Uma Vida para a Música*. Rio de Janeiro: Funarte.

Matheus, Letícia. 2000. "Baden é sepultado no São João Batista ao som de 2 dos sambas que compôs: Filho mais velho pega a violão do pai e toca 'Lapinha' e 'Samba Triste.'" *O Globo*, Rio de Janeiro, September 28, 23.

McCann, Bryan. 2004. *Hello, Hello Brazil: Popular Music in the Making of Brazil*. Durham, NC: Duke University Press.

Melo, Guilherme de. 1994 (1908). *A Música no Brasil*. 2nd ed. Rio de Janeiro: Instituto Nacional de Música.

Mitchell, B. R. 1993 (1983). *International Historical Statistics: The Americas 1750–1988*. 2nd ed. New York: Stockton Press.

Monates, K. K. 1999. *Iúna Mandingueira: A ave símbolo da capoeira*. Manaus: Fenix.

Moore, Robin. 1994. "Representations of Afrocuban Expressive Culture in the writings of Fernando Ortiz." *Latin American Music Review* 15(1): 32–54.

Mukuna, Kazadi wa. 1997. "Creative Practice in African Music: New Perspectives in the Scrutiny of Africanisms in Diaspora." *Black Music Research Journal* 17(2): 239–50.

———. 1998. "Resilience and Transformation in Varieties of African Musical Elements in Latin America." In *For Gerhard Kubik: Festschrift of the Occasion of His 60th Birthday*. A. Schmidhofer and D. Schüller, eds. Frankfurt am Main: Peter Lang, 405–12.

———. 2000 (1979). *Contribução Bantu na Música Popular Brasileira: perspectivas etnomúsicológicas*. São Paulo: Terceira Margem.

———. 2003. *An Interdisciplinary Study of the Ox and the Slave (Bumba-meu-Boi): A Satirical Music Drama in Brazil*. Lewiston, NY: E. Mellen Press.

Mukuna, Kazadi wa, and Tiago Olivera de Pinto, eds. 1990–91. "The Study of African Musical Contribution to Latin America and the Caribbean: A Methodological

Guideline." *Bulletin of the International Committee on Urgent Anthropological and Ethnological Research* 32/33: 47–48.

Myers, Helen, ed. 1992. *Ethnomusicology: An Introduction*. New York: W. W. Norton.

Nascimento, Silvia. 2001. "Dez mil vão ao santuário de Mãe Rainha." *A Tarde*, Salvador, March 26.

Negromonte, Marcelo. 2000. "Caipiríssima." *Fôlha de São Paulo*, May 8, Ilustrada, E7.

Neiva, Alvaro. 1958. *Ganguzama* libretto. From Tavares personal archive.

———. 1963a. "Justification of 'Ganguzama.'" From *Ganguzama* program notes.

———. 1963b. "Summary of 'Ganguzama.'" From *Ganguzama* program notes.

Nettl, Bruno. 1983. *The Study of Ethnomusicology: Twenty-Nine Issues and Concepts*. Urbana: University of Illinois Press.

Neves, José Maria. 1981. *Música Contemporânea Brasileira*. São Paulo: Ricordi Brasileira.

Niles, Christina. 1978. "The Revival of the Latvian Kokle in America." *Selected Reports in Ethnomusicology* 3(1): 211–35.

Officer, Lawrence H. 2002. "Exchange Rate Between the United States and 40 Other Countries 1913–1999." Economic History Services, EH Net. www.eh.net/hmit/exchangerates/.

Ohtake, Ricardo. 1988. *Instrumentos Musicais Brasileiros*. São Paulo: Rhodia.

Oliveira, Albano Marinho de. 1958. *Berimbau: O Arco Musical da Capoeira*. Salvador: Comissão Bahiana de Folclore.

Pareles, John. 1992. "Gilberto Gil on Pleasure, Fate and Other Things Worth Dancing About." *New York Times*, New York, November 16, C1.

Pellegrini, Cecília. 2000. "Dinho Nascimento: Gongolô." *Revista Capoeira: Arte e Luta Brasileira*. São Paulo: Editora Candeia 2(9): 28–29. Photo by Roger Spock.

Perrone, Charles. 1989. *Masters of Contemporary Brazilian Song: MPB 1965–1985*. Austin: University of Texas Press.

———. 1996. *Seven Faces: Brazilian Poetry Since Modernism*. Durham, NC: Duke University Press.

Pinho, Osmundo de Araújo. 2002. "'Fogo na Babilônia': Reggae, Black Counterculture, and Globalization in Brazil." In *Brazilian Popular Music and Globalization*. Charles A. Perrone and Christopher Dunn, eds. New York and London: Routledge, 192–206.

Pinto, Tiago de Oliveira. 1991. *Capoeira, Samba, Candomblé*. Berlin: Museum Für Völkerkunde.

———. 1994. "The Pernambuco Carnival and its Formal Organisations: Music as Expression of Hierarchies and Power in Brazil." *World of Music* 26: 20–38.

Rebôlo, Rui. 1968. "Aqui está o Besouro, Baden." *A Gazeta*, São Paulo, July 8.

Rego, Waldeloir. 1968. *Capoeira Angola. Ensaio Sócio-Etnográfico*. Rio de Janeiro: Editôra Itapuá.

Reily, Suzel Ana. 1994. "Macunaíma's Music: National Identity and Ethnomusicological Research in Brazil." In *Ethnicity and Identity: the Musical Construction of Place*. Martin Stokes, ed. Oxford: Oxford University Press, 71–96.

———. 2000. "Introduction: Brazilian Musics, Brazilian Identities." *British Journal of Ethnomusicology* 9(1): 1–10.

Reis, Letícia Vidor de Sousa. 2000. *O Mundo de Pernas para o Ar: A Capoeira no Brasil.* São Paulo: Publisher Brasil.

Richter, Felix Christian Steiger. n.d. *Salvador da Bahia: 100 Colorfotos.* Rio de Janeiro: Alpina—Céu Azul de Copacabana.

Risério, Antonio. 1981. *Carnaval Ijexá.* Salvador: Corrupio.

Robinson, N. Scott. 2000. "Naná Vasconcelos: The Nature of Naná." *Modern Drummer* 24(7): 98–102+.

Rocha, Janaina. 2000. "Naná vai levar vanguarda nordestina ao Percpan." *O Estado de São Paulo,* São Paulo. December 12.

Rodrigues, Rosana. 2000. "Alunos na Roda ão Som do Berimbau." *O Globo,* Rio de Janeiro, August 13.

Sanches, Pedro A. 1999. "Evangélico, músico não diz mais 'saravá.'" *Fôlha de São Paulo,* São Paulo, July 13, Ilustrada:4.

Sansone, Livio. 1999. *From Africa to Afro: Use and Abuse of Africa in Brazil.* Amsterdam and Dakar: Sephis—Codesria.

———. 2002. "The Localization of Global Funk in Bahia and in Rio." In *Brazilian Popular Music and Globalization.* Charles A. Perrone and Christopher Dunn, eds. New York and London: Routledge, 136–60.

Sansone, Livio, and Jocélio Teles dos Santos (Orgs.). 1999. *Ritmos em trânsito: Sócio-antropologia da música baiana.* São Paulo: Dynamis Editorial; Salvador: Programa a cor da Bahia e Projeto S.A.M.B.A., 1997.

Schechter, John M. 1992. *The Indispensable Harp: Historical Development, Modern Roles, Configurations, and Performance Practices in Ecuador and Latin America.* Kent, OH: Kent State University Press.

Scheinowitz, Celina de Araújo. 1993. "A Bahia e seus negros no olhar de um francês do século XIX." *Revista da Academia de Letras da Bahia* 39 (maio): 325–37.

Schneider, John T. 1991. *Dictionary of African Borrowings in Brazilian Portuguese.* Hamburg: Helmut Buske.

Scott, Anna. 1998. "It's All in the Timing: The Latest Moves, James Brown's Grooves, and the Seventies Race-Consciousness Movement in Salvador, Bahia–Brazil." In *Soul: Black Power, Politics, and Pleasure.* Monique Guillory and Richard C. Green, eds. New York: New York University Press, 9–22.

Scruggs, T. M. 1998. "Cultural Capital, Appropriate Transformations, and Transfer by Appropriation in Western Nicaragua: 'El Baile de la marimba.'" *Latin American Music Review* 19(1): 1–30.

Seeger, Anthony. 2002. "A Tropical Meditation on Comparison in Ethnomusicology: A Metaphoric Knife, A Real Banana and an Edible Demonstration." *Yearbook for Traditional Music* 34: 187–92.

Seeger, Charles. 1958. "Prescriptive and Descriptive Music-Writing." *Musical Quarterly* 44(2): 184–95.

Severiano, Jario, and Zuza Homem de Mello. 1999 (1997). *A Canção no Tempo: 85 Anos de Músicas Brasileiras.* 4th ed. São Paulo: Editora 34.

Shaffer, Kay. 1982 (1976). *O Berimbau-de-Barriga e Seus Toques.* Rio de Janeiro: Funarte.

Silva, Wellington Gomes da. 2001. "Correlações entre estratégias orquestrais e processos composicionais em obras do Grupo de Compositores da Bahia (1966–1973)"
[Correlations between Orchestral Strategies and Compositional Processes
in Works of the Bahian Composers Group (1966–1973)]. Ph.D. dissertation,
Universidade Federal da Bahia.

Skidmore, Thomas E. 1974. *Black into White: Race and Nationality in Brazilian
Thought*. New York: Oxford University Press.

———. 1986. *Politics in Brazil, 1930–1964: An Experiment in Democracy*. New York
and Oxford: Oxford University Press.

———. 1988. *The Politics of Military Rule in Brazil, 1964–1985*. New York and Oxford:
Oxford University Press.

———. 1999. *Brazil: Five Centuries of Change*. New York and Oxford: Oxford
University Press.

Slobin, Mark. 2000. *Fiddler on the Move: Exploring the Klezmer World*. New York:
Oxford University Press.

Souza, Ricardo Pamfilio de. 1997. "A Música na Capoeira: Um Estudo de Caso." M.A.
thesis, Universidade Federal da Bahia.

Souza, Tárik de. 2000. "O violão vadio do gênio errante." *Jornal do Brasil*, Rio de
Janeiro, September 26.

Stroud, Sean. 2000. "'Música é para o povo cantar': Culture, Politics, and the
Brazilian Song Festivals, 1965–1972." *Latin American Music Review* 21(2): 87–117.

Teles, José. 2000. *Do Frevo Ao Manguebeat*. São Paulo: Editora 34.

Thompson, Robert Farris. 1983. *Flash of the Spirit*. New York: Random House.

———. 1989. "Body and Voice: Kongo Figurative Musical Instruments." In *Sounding
Forms: African Musical Instruments*. New York: American Federation of Arts,
39–45.

Tinhorão, José Ramos. 1966. *Música Popular: Um tema em debate*. Rio de Janeiro:
Editora Saga.

———. 1986. *Pequena História da Música Popular—da Modinha ão Tropicalismo*. 5th
ed. São Paulo: Art Editora.

Travassos, Elizabeth. 2000. "Instrumentos Musicais Populares: o desaparacimento da
marimba." In *Cultura Material: Identidades e Processos Sociais*. Claudia Marcia
Ferreira, ed. Rio de Janeiro: Funarte/CNFCP, 57–65.

Travassos, Sonia Duarte. 2000. "Capoeira: Difusão & Metamorfose Culturais entre
Brasil e EUA." Doctoral thesis. Rio de Janeiro: Universidade Federal do Rio de
Janeiro.

Treece, David. 1997. "Guns and Roses: Bossa Nova and Brazil's Music of Popular
Protest, 1958–1968." *Popular Music* 16(1): 1–29.

Turino, Thomas. 2000. *Nationalists, Cosmopolitans, and Popular Music in Zimbabwe*.
Chicago: University of Chicago Press.

Verger, Pierre. 1981. *Notícias da Bahia 1850*. Salvador: Corrupio.

Vianna, Hermano. 1988. *O Mundo Funk Carioca*. Rio de Janeiro: Jorge Zahar.

———. 1999. *The Mystery of Samba: Popular Music and National Identity in Brazil*.

John Charles Chasteen, ed. and transl. Chapel Hill: University of North Carolina Press.

Vianna, Marissa. n.d. *"Terra da Felicidade' Orelhão em forma de berimbau, localizado no Pelourinho"* ("Land of happiness" Telephone booth in the shape of a berimbau located in the Pelourinho neighborhood). Photo of sculpture by Bel Borba. Salvador: Bahiatursa/Brascard.

Vinicius, Marcus. 1973. "Naná, o novo através do folclore." *Folha de São Paulo*, São Paulo, September 3.

Wachsmann, Klaus. 1984. "Classification." In *The New Grove Dictionary of Music and Musicians.* Stanley Sadie, ed. London: Macmillan.

Williams, Daryle. 2001. *Culture Wars in Brazil: The First Vargas Regime, 1930–1945.* Durham, NC: Duke University Press.

Williamson, Edwin. 1992. *The Penguin History of Latin America.* New York: Penguin.

Winant, Howard. 1994. "Rethinking Race in Brazil." In *Racial Conditions: Politics, Theory, Comparisons.* Minneapolis: University of Minnesota Press, 130–47.

Wright, John. 2001. "Jew's Harp." In *The New Grove Dictionary of Music and Musicians.* 2nd ed. Stanley Sadie, ed. New York: Grove, V.13: 112–14.

Zemp, Hugo. 1978. "Aré aré Classification of Musical Types and Instruments." *Ethnomusicology* 22(1): 37–67.

Zipkin, Michael. 1980. "Saudades" (Sound Recording Reviews). *Down Beat* 47 (August): 33–34.

Discography

(CD unless otherwise noted)

Anonymous. 1970. *Viva A Bahia No. 3.* Philips SCDP-PF-001/GB. LP.

Beatles. 1967. *Sgt. Pepper's Lonely Hearts Club Band.* Capitol SMAS-2653. LP.

Berimbrown. 2000. *BerimBrown.* Sonopress CRIBROWNCD01.

———. 2002. *Oba, Lá Vem Ela.* Trama single 641-2.

Bimba, Mestre. 1968. *Curso de Capoeira Regional.* JS Discos. LP.

Escola Brasileira de Música. 1996. *Mosaico.* EBM-2902.

Gil, Gilberto. 1968. *Gilberto Gil.* Philips R 765 024L. LP.

———. 2000. *Gilberto Gil: Enciclopédia Musical Brasileira.* Warner Music Brasil 857381557-2.

Grupo de Capoeira Angola Pelourinho. 1996. *Capoeira Angola from Salvador, Brazil.* Smithsonian/Folkways SF CD 40465.

M4J. 1998. *Brazil—Electronic Experience.* Trama 0004.

Menezes, Margareth. 1989. *Um Canto Pra Subir.* PolyGram 841 561-1. LP.

———. 1993. *Luz Dourada.* PolyGram 519 537-2.

Metheny, Pat. 1980. *As Falls Wichita, So Falls Wichita Falls.* PolyGram 26255.

Musotto, Ramiro. 2003. *Sudaka.* Fast Horse 81752-2.

Nascimento, Dinho. 2001a (1996). *Berimbau Blues.* Eldorado/Gente Boa 935106.

———. 2001b. *Gongolô.* Eldorado/Gente Boa GB002.

Nascimento, Milton. 1975. *Minas.* EMI-Odeon EMCB 7011. LP.

Olodum. 1992. *A Música do Olodum.* Continental 1.07.405.515. LP.

———. 1999. *A Música do Olodum 20 Anos.* Columbia 2-495526.

Pastinha, Mestre. 1969. *Capoeira Angola Mestre Pastinha e Sua Academia.* Philips SCDP-PF-001/GB. LP.

Pinto, Tiago de Oliveira. 1988. *Berimbau e Capoeira—BA.* Notes by Tiago de Olivera Pinto. FUNARTE INF-46. LP.

———. 1990. *Capoeira, Samba, Candomblé Bahia Brasil.* Berlin: Staatliche Museen Preussischer Kulturbesitz.

Powell, Baden. 1963. *Baden Powell: Á Vontade.* Elenco ME-11. LP.

Powell, Baden, and Vinícius de Moraes. 1966. *Os Afro Sambas.* Companhia Brasileira de Discos (Forma) FM16/FE1016. LP.

Ram Science. 1999. *Ram Science: É Música!* Trama T200 098-2.

Reis, Mário. 2000. "Fita Amarela" (originally recorded 1932). *Raízes do Samba: Mário Reis.* EMI Brasil 525279-2.

Rescala, Luiz Augusto (Tim). n.d. "Peça para Berimbau e Fita Magnética." Unpublished recording.

Rodrigues, Virginia. 1997. *Sol Negro.* Hannibal HNCD 1425.

Santos, Lulu. n.d. *Liga Lá*. Ariola 7432152339-2.

Suassuna, Mestre, and Dirceu. 1975. *Capoeira: Cordão de Ouro: Mestre Suassuna e Dirceu*. MusiColor 1-104-405-102. LP.

Tavares, Mário. 1979. *Ganguzama*. Recorded 7 December. Unpublished recording.

———. 1999. *Ganguzama*. Recorded [?] October. Unpublished recording.

Traíra, Mestre. 1958(?). "E Besouro." Audio recording deposited in the archive of the Biblioteca Amadeu Amaral, Rio de Janeiro.

Various artists. 1968. *A Bienal do Samba*. Phillips R 765 044 L. LP. "Lapinha" reissued in 1988 on *Fascinação: O Melhor de Elis Regina*. Philips 836-844-2.

———. 2001. *Destination Brazil: Sultry Rhythms of Corcovado Nights*. Sugo Music SR 0103.

Vasconcelos, Naná. 1980. *Saudades*. ECM Records ECM 1-147. LP.

———. 1995. *Storytelling*. Hemisphere 7243 8 334 442 0.

Videography

Berimbrown. 2005. Irmandade. Works/Screen Vision.

Fry, Peter. 1982. *Carnival Bahia*. Films Incorporated Video.

Grosset, Didier. 1990. *Goree, On the Other Side of the Water*. Unesco.

Ornellas, Eliana, and Marcos Tourinho. 1989. *O Som dos Instrumentos: O Berimbau*. IRDEB/TVE, Salvador.

Talbot, Toby. 1971. *Berimbau*. 16mm color, New Yorker Films.

Teles, Eládio Garcia. 1999. *A Lenda da Árvore Sagrada* (The Legend of the Sacred Tree). Rio de Janeiro: independent production.

Various artists. 1997. *Dance Bahia '97*. Polygram video.

Interviews

Abreu, Frederico de. 2007. 12 June, meeting, Salvador da Bahia. Handwritten notes.

Araújo, Samuel, Brazilian ethnomusicologist and musician. 2004. 12 April, telephone conversation, Rio de Janeiro. Handwritten notes.

Cravo Neto, Mário, Brazilian fine artist. 2003. Electronic mail correspondence, 13 November.

D'Anunciação, Luiz, Brazilian musician and composer. 2001. Lessons and interviews, 9 February to 27 June, Universidade Federal do Rio de Janeiro. Handwritten notes and MiniDisc recording.

———. 2004. Telephone conversation, 12 April, Rio de Janeiro. Handwritten notes.

Ferreira, Deraldo, capoeira master. 1996–97. Lessons and interviews, 23 September 1996 to 24 January 1997, Brazilian Cultural Center of New England, Cambridge. Handwritten notes and tape recording.

Frederiksen, Lynn E. 2004. Handwritten correspondence, 15 February.

Galm, John K. 2003. Handwritten correspondence, 11 November.

Grande, João, capoeira grand-master. 1997. 8 February, Capoeira Angola Center, New York. Handwritten notes and tape recording.

Macêdo, Nelson, Brazilian musician and composer. 2000. 22 December, informant's residence, Rio de Janeiro. Handwritten notes and MiniDisc recording.

Maia, Ramilson, Brazilian musician and composer. 2001. 19 May, informant's recording studio, São Paulo. Handwritten notes and MiniDisc recording.

Musotto, Ramiro, Brazilian musician and composer. 2004. 20 February, telephone interview, Buenos Aires, Argentina. Handwritten notes.

Nascimento, Claudia Tatinge. 2004. Handwritten notes, 10 March.

Nascimento, Dinho, Brazilian musician, composer, and capoeira practitioner. 2001. 17 May, informant's residence, São Paulo. Handwritten notes and MiniDisc recording.

Negoativo, Mestre (Ramon Lopes), Brazilian musician, composer, and capoeira master. 2001. 18 May, SESC Pompeia, São Paulo. Handwritten notes and MiniDisc recording.

Negreiros, Carlos, Brazilian musician. 2001. 16 March to 1 May, informant's residence, Rio de Janeiro. Handwritten notes and MiniDisc recording.

Nenel, capoeira master. 2001. 5 June, Academia da Filhos de Bimba, Salvador. Handwritten notes and MiniDisc recording.

Rescala, Luiz Augusto (Tim), Brazilian musician and composer. 2000. 6 December, informant's Electroacoustic production and recording studio, Rio de Janeiro. Handwritten notes and MiniDisc recording.

Silva, Efraim, capoeira master. 1997. 11 February, informant's capoeira academy, New Haven. Handwritten notes and tape recording.

Silva, Wellington Gomes da, Brazilian composer. 2001. 6 June 2001, Universidade Federal da Bahia, Salvador. Handwritten notes and MiniDisc recording.

Tacuchian, Ricardo, Brazilian composer. 2001. 19 June, informant's residence, Rio de Janeiro. Handwritten notes and MiniDisc recording.

Tavares, Mário, Brazilian composer. 2001. 27 June, Rio de Janeiro, informant's residence. Handwritten notes and MiniDisc recording.

Vanni, Manoel, Brazilian musician and composer. 2001. Also Present was Franco Júnior. 16 May, informant's residence, São Paulo. Handwritten notes and MiniDisc recording.

Vasconcelos, Naná. 2009. Personal communication with assistance from producer Anselmo Frugoli.

Index

Page numbers in *italics* refer to illustrations.